EMOTION AND THE PSYCHODYNAMICS OF THE CEREBELLUM

D1564420

EMOTION AND THE PSYCHODYNAMICS OF THE CEREBELLUM

A NEURO-PSYCHOANALYTIC ANALYSIS AND SYNTHESIS

edited by Fred M. Levin

KARNAC

First published in 2009 by
Karnac Books Ltd
118 Finchley Road
London NW3 5HT

British Library Cataloguing in Publication Data

A.C.I.P. for this book is available from the British Library

ISBN-13: 978-1-85575-577-2

Edited, designed, and produced by Sheffield Typesetting
www.sheffieldtypesetting.com
e-mail: admin@ sheffieldtypesetting.com

www.karnacbooks.com

CONTENTS

This book is dedicated to Professor Masao Ito of RIKEN Brain Science Institute, Wako, Japan, where he has been Director General since 1993. Formerly he worked with Sir John Eccles at the Australian National University, and later Chaired the Deptartment of Neurophysiology, Faculty of Medicine, Tokyo University, where he also had been Dean. Professor Ito, together with his team of outstanding scientists, has made major contributions to our understanding of the cerebellum (CB), and especially, has been cracking the code regarding how implicit memory works. Implicit memory is different from explicit memory, but just as important, or more so. Ito discovered the inhibitory action of CB circuits involving cerebellar Purkinje cells, and their unique characteristic plasticity, which he named long-term depression (LTD). Based upon his research, he has developed a theory and demonstrated experimentally that the CB is a general learning machine for acquiring not only motor skills, but for all of the activities of our minds and brains involving implicit memory, which is memory for how we do things. A book such as this would simply not have been possible without the discoveries of Professor Ito.

Fred Levin is board certified in psychiatry and in psychoanalysis. He is Associate Professor of Clinical Psychiatry in the Feinberg School of Medicine of Northwestern University, Chicago, Illinois, and on faculty of The Chicago Institute for Psychoanalysis, where he is also a training and supervising psychoanalyst. Since graduating with honors from Dartmouth College in anthropology, and Northwestern University Medical School, and being an exchange student in Japan studying Japanese culture and language (Waseda University/ The Stanford Center) he has been interested in bridging mind and brain, something he began in earnest during his residency training in psychiatry under Dr. Roy Grinker Sr. at Michael Reese Hospital in Chicago. By researching, teaching, and the clinical practice of psychotherapy and psychoanalysis, as reported in his approximately 110 publications (articles and 5 books) and many lectures around the world, he has gradually increased his understanding of how our brain seems to create its various functions, something he reports on in his current book, and hopes you find as interesting and helpful and he does.

PREFACE

In the preface to *Mapping the Mind* (1991), I explained that a number of books and articles had been written about the synthesis of psychoanalysis and neuroscience, but what distinguished my book was its effort to make *novel, specific,* and *detailed* correlations between psychological and psychoanalytic variables, on the one hand, and neuroanatomical, neurochemical, and neurophysiological variables on the other. Moreover, in *Psyche and Brain* (2003), I argued that integrating mind and brain is deeply relevant to both psychoanalysis and neuroscience, something I feel even stronger about today. Neuropsychoanalysis (NP) *requires* careful correlation of research findings across a multitude of disciplinary boundaries; this would then offer us the possibility of completing our major agendas for teaching, clinical practice, research, and theory building.

I believe that in *Emotion and the Psychodynamics of the Cerebellum* my colleagues and I are moving towards the very same agenda that motivated the two earlier volumes, particularly as regards our attempt now to carefully describe the critical importance of the cerebellum, including its many interlacing functions, especially its role in our emotional life. In doing so my collaborators and I are also keeping faith with Eric Kandel (2003).[1] For it was Kandel that encouraged us to take our precious insights in neuroscience and psychoanalysis and integrate them more fully; as he has done for explicit memory, so Ito is accomplishing for implicit memory.

Obviously, we still have much to learn in order to become optimally therapeutic with our patients, informative with our students, and collaborative with each other on scientific projects; however, there is no question that we are making very significant strides, and should be proud of the progress in NP. The journal NP has established itself through the dedicated and scholarly work of Mark Solms, Edward Nersessian, and a large number of others around the world, for example, Jaak Panksepp's monumental experimental work on mind/brain issues in animals. We also have the International Neuro-Psychoanalytic Society, with extremely high quality annual meetings. If this new book adds a bit to the larger opus, my collaborators and I will be truly delighted.

A Special Thank You

Along the way, it is very important to give a personal thanks to those who have contributed significantly to our learning. So I wish to mention the following people, and if I am leaving anyone out of this list, I apologize sincerely. In the meantime I thank all of the following people for what they have taught me: Mallika Akbar, Tzimon Barto, Jhuma Basak, Michael F. Basch, Linda Brakel, David Dean Brockman, Margaret Browning, Wilma Bucci, Alan Cadkin, Jean Carney, Bert Cohler, Titziano Colibazzi, Arnold Cooper, Tim Crow, Takeo Doi, Marta Duque, Gerry Edelman, David Edelstein, Dale and Christine Eickelman, Robert Embde, Mathew Hugh Erdelyi, Josefina Figueroa, David Forrest, Susan M. Fisher, Pierre Flor-Henry, Dan Hier, Paula and Gordon Fuqua, Glen Gabbard, Patrizia Giampieri-Deutsch, Eric Gillett, Hironmoy Ghosal, Marlene Goodfriend, Roy Grinker, Jr. and Sr., Meyer S. Gunther, June Hadley, Steve and Lenore Harris, Marty Harrow, Alexander Hippmann, Juhani Ihanus, Masao Ito, Tetsuya Iwasaki, Makoto Iwata, Charles Jaffe, Juan Pablo Jiménez, Eric Kandel, Otto Kernberg, Hans-Dieter Klein, Heinz Kohut, Waude Kracke, Ron Krasner, Bunsaku Kurata, Hiroyuki Kuramoto, Jim

Leider, Marianne Leuzinger-Bohleber, Fred Levy, (Harry and Pearl
Levin; Tobi, Larry, Debbie, and Paul Mattes; Sachiko, Daniel and
David Levin), Bonnie Litowitz, Lester Luborsky, Carlos Macedo,
Claudio Martinez, Raphael Moses, Itsuro Matsuo, Shohei Matsu-
zaki, Irene Matthis, Robert Michels, Ichiro Mizuta, Arnold Modell,
Rafael Moses, Michael Moskowitz, Masahiro Nishijima, Masahisa
Nishizono, Shin-Ichi Niwa, Malkah Notman, Ravi Nehru, John
C. Nemiah, Benny Oksenberg, David Olds, Rui A. Oliveira, Barry
Opatow, Myrna Orenstein, Stanley Palombo, Jaak Panksepp, Paolo
Pinto, Alfonso Pola, Michael J. Posner, Karl Pribram, Morton Reiser,
Arnold Richards, Steven P. Roose, Oliver Sacks, Dan Schacter, Jorge
Schneider, Nathan Schlessinger, Allan Schore, Andrew Schwartz,
Lorena Seeger, Henry Seidenberg, Sally Severino, Tim Shallice,
Howard Shevrin, David Silbersweig, Moisy Shopper, Joseph Slapp,
Elise Snyder, Henry F. Smith, Mark Solms and Karen Kaplan-Solms,
Brenda and David Solomon, Art Springer, Bhaskar Sripada, Larry
Squire, Fred (Yasuhiko) Taketomo, Vesa Talvitie, David Terman,
Colwyn Trevarthen, Katherine Uphoff, Antoinette Risdon, Paul
Stepansky, Paul and Marion Tolpin, Oliver Turnbull, Shigeto Tsuru,
Endel Tulving, Katsu S. Ushioda, Hiroshi Utena, Max Velmans, Vamik
Volkan, D. M. Vuckovich, Robert Wallerstein, Douglas Watt, Ralph
Wharton, Daniel Widlocher, Jerome Winer, Arnold Wilson, Harriet
Wolf, Ruth Yanagi, Ryuji Yanai, Jimmy Yao, Yoram Yovell, Lucy Zab-
arenko, and Charlie von Zedtwitz. Words cannot adequately convey
my debt of gratitude to these individuals.

Note

1.   Kandel, E. R. (1999). Biology and the future of psychoanalysis: a new
      intellectual framework for psychiatry, *Am J Psychiatry, 156*: 505–524.

This is a book about cognition, emotion, memory, and learning. Along the way it examines exactly how implicit memory ("knowing how") and explicit memory ("knowing that") are connected with each other via the cerebellum (CB). Since emotion is also related to memory, and likely, one of its critical organizing features, many fields of human endeavor have attempted to clarify its fundamental nature, including its relationship to metaphor, problem solving, learning, and many other variables. It has not been easy to pull together the various strands relating to emotion, so that clinicians and researchers alike could identify precisely and ultimately agree upon what emotion is and how it contributes to the other known activities of mind and brain. If I am correct, it will help our understanding of emotion psychoanalytically if we patiently delineate the complex picture of the human experience of emotion, but then integrate this with the efforts of brain scientists and psychoanalysts to understand how the mind view of emotion and the brain view of emotion connect. It is obvious from the title of this book that my colleagues and I believe the CB plays a decisive role in emotion (along with its other related activities, of course), and we have tried in this book to convey this newest part of the story of emotion and the CB with utmost clarity and accuracy.

Some of the core ideas presented in this book are significantly more detailed elaborations of conceptions first outlined in two chapters of *Psyche and Brain*[1] (coauthored with John Gedo, Ito Masao, and Colwyn Trevarthen) in which we presented how the CB uses error signals to make copies of other brain systems, such as the premotor system, and then operates various systems, such as the motor system, on is own. However, in this book we expand on the meaning of "makes copies", and consider in more detail the vast importance of the CB.

Part I of this book begins with Chapters One and Two on sleep and dreaming. My coauthors and I review the subject, and try our best to synthesize what we believe to be an updated perspective on explicit and implicit memory (i.e. the conscious and unconscious mind). The significant contribution of Part I. is a reexamination of the details of sleep and dreaming from the perspective of NP, with special regard to what we are calling "deferred action plans". The importance of such plans, and their relationship to what might be called "deferred actions", expressive of our unconscious drives, provides one early clue that the CB is an important contributor to the psychodynamic unconscious of Freudian theory (since the CB moves ideas and feelings as well as our limbs). Chapter One focuses primarily on what precisely is adaptive about dreaming; Chapter Two goes into more specific details regarding subsystems of the brain, particularly the periaqueductal gray (PAG), anterior cingulate cortex (ACC), and centromedian nucleus of the thalamus (CNT) that have an important relationship to the management of feelings and deferred action planning (see Chapter Two).

Part II examines some of the important early discussions of emotion within NP, specifically, those appearing in the inaugural (1999) issue of the journal NP, the main journal in the field. One of the critical areas of debate has concerned whether it would be possible at all to integrate neuroscience and psychoanalytic perspectives. Chapter Three presents what the difficulties might be as discussed in the target papers on emotion by Mark Solms and Edward Nersessian, and by Jaak Panksepp. Chapter Four analyzes learned commentaries on the target papers, by a distinguished group: Antonio Damasio, Andre Green, Joseph LeDoux, Allan Schore, Howard Shevrin, and Clifford Yorke. Although no quick consensus was reached in these discussions, nevertheless, some important points of agreement emerged, which serve as background for the explorations in the rest of this book. *It is interesting, moreover, that nowhere in any of these preliminary discussions is the CB mentioned. This indicates how easy it has been to overlook the CB when thinking about emotion, learning, and cognition.*

Part III introduces ideas on gene activation, spontaneity, and the priming of memory for learning within a clinical psychoanalysis. The subject of learning is important because it appears to be one of the key subjects connecting psychoanalysis and neuroscience to the CB (since we know, based upon Ito's work, that the CB makes important contributions to learning, for example, as regards the vestibulo-ocular reflex or VOR). Chapter Five introduces the subject of synapses, cytokines and the formation of new long-term memory. This represents an interdisciplinary look at how psychoanalysis activates learning via the impact of "emotional attention" (as noted in Chapter One). Chapter Six then takes an excursion into some recent neuroscience discoveries on the subject of cellular protein pathways that have possible deep significance for psychoanalysis. The analysis here may at times be difficult to follow, as the level of discourse shifts from higher levels of executive control systems to lower levels of neurochemistry, and back again. It should be obvious, however, that our idea is to integrate these various levels of observation: what is happening within cells and within extended networks of synchronized neurons will enable us to appreciate such variables as the construction of personal subjectivity and self experience. Chapter Seven then introduces some important contributions of NP to psychodynamic psychiatry and psychoanalysis, and builds on previous work in collaboration with Colwyn Trevarthen, John Gedo, Masao Ito, Howard Shevrin, Michael Posner, and the author. That is, we are heading towards a synthesis, while homing in more and more upon the CB, and the connectedness of implicit and explicit memory systems.

Part IV investigates the role of the CB in more detail, particularly its role in "recalibration" (error detection and correction) of the VOR within the visual system, and the significance of the CB's capacity for "modeling" other parts of the brain. Error correction involves the CB noting the difference between what is happening in the brain or body, and what the CB shows on its "monitoring screens" about the details of these same events. *This error detection and correction capacity is the critical variable that makes exact model building possible for the CB.* Chapter Eight enlarges on the novel idea that *the CB likely models systems other than the premotor system, including the entire limbic system and/or the SEEKING system.* It seems that this would provide some significant advantages, accruing from letting emotion be handled completely by the CB independently of either of these two systems! Chapter 9 then explores in more detail what may be the CB's contributions in the area of affect utilization and regulation, and related mind/brain systems for learning, memory, and adaptation in real time. The basic idea explored is to explain how the so-called "hyper-complex psychological functions" come into being; or, put differently, how the implicit memory system and explicit system come together in the CB's modeling activity, providing a unique synthesis of these two critical memory systems. Helpful here are the contributions of a number of critical others: Susanne Langer, who anticipated long ago, where we have just arrived regarding emotion; Rizzolatti, Fogassi, and Gallese (2006) who about a decade ago identified "mirror neurons"; and Ramachandran and Oberman (2006) who have made important suggestions about how mirror neurons fit into the picture of emotion and learning, ideas having impact on our understanding and treatment of illnesses such as Autism.

Part V reviews where we have been, providing a summary and conclusions in Chapter Ten. It is hoped that what emerges is a clearer picture of adaptive behavior and learning within the mind/brain from the perspective of NP, a perspective that now takes into account the special role of the CB in integrating within and across systems that deal with so-called cognitive and affective activities, implicit and explicit memory, unconscious and conscious mind/brain, past experience and future planning. It is our belief that the theorizing presented is credible, and could be most serviceable in furthering the study of the CB's contributions. Creating a "psychodynamics of the cerebellum" is also a specific way of further integrating mind and brain perspectives. Although we remain a long way from having a complete insight into every aspect of mind/brain, it certainly does appear that paying careful attention to the CB helps move us closer to many of our long-term goals of understanding mind and brain with detailed, specific, and novel correlations. This can only help our work with our patients, who deserve the best that we have to offer.

Note

1.   See David Forrest, *Amer J Psychiatry 161*: 1314.

PART I

THE UNCONSCIOUS REVISITED
AND RECONCEPTUALIZED

CHAPTER ONE

Sleep and dreaming, Part 1: Dreams are emotionally meaningful adaptive learning engines that help us identify and deal with unconscious (ucs) threats by means of deferred action plans; REM sleep consolidates memory for that which we learn and express in dreams

Fred M. Levin, Colwyn Trevarthen, Tiziano Colibazzi, Juhani Ihanus, Vesa Talvitie, Jean K. Carney, and Jaak Panksepp[1]

"Dreams provide an opportunity to learn more about the nature of the information that is processed during REM sleep."

Ramon Greenberg, 2003

Précis: Part 1 presents a neuro-psychoanalytic (NP) model of dreaming and its relationship to sleep, wakefulness, and the ucs. Psychoanalysts (M. Stern, 1988; Greenberg, 2003) hypothesize that when we sense ucs difficulties, an active dream life supports its resolution in real life. Specifically, dreams create "deferred action plans" that are later actualized in a manner that explores and reduces dangers. Such action plans are adaptive for both the individual dreamer and any dreaming species (Revonsuo, 2000; Revonsuo & Valli, 2000). What is learned during dreaming is consolidated by REM sleep activation (Bednar, 2003) and the new knowledge "fixed" by multiple consolidation and reconsolidation events, themselves activated by various transcription factors (Bornstein & Pittman, 1992). In Part 2, we speculate on which subsystems of the brain make what kinds of contributions to dreaming.

I. Introduction: A dreaming model as seen by neuro-psychoanalysis (NP)

The original pioneers on REM sleep memory fixation and consolidation in dreaming were psychoanalysts committed to neuroscience (Pearlman, 1971, 1973, 1979; Pearlman & Becker, 1973, 1974; Greenberg & Pearlman, 1974). The newest paradigm on dreaming we owe to Solms (1997, 1999, 2003a, 2003b, 2003c; Solms & Turnbull, 2002), Panksepp (1985, 1998a, 2003, 2005a), and many others;[2] it strongly supports the view of dreaming as an emotionally meaningful and psychologically adaptive phenomenon. Solms critically demonstrates that REM states and dreaming are not isomorphic but rather doubly dissociable phenomena (i.e. REM sleep can occur without dreaming, and dreaming without REM sleep). Solms' research supports the position that dreams facilitate emotional mastery over dangers and conflicts, and our learning how[3] to deal with them (see also Shevrin & Eiser, 2003). Critically, Solms demonstrates that without both an intact medial ventral frontal lobe (MVFL), and parietal-temporal-occipital cortical junction (PTOCJ) dreaming cannot occur (Solms, 2003b, p. 221). Since the MVFL is associated with self-related emotional and motivational functions, and since the PTOCJ is critical for mental imagery and object relations, dreams must be deeply psychologically meaningful mental events. Moreover, as both Solms and Panksepp point out, the main candidate for providing master control mechanisms for dreaming are clearly the meso-limbic meso-cortical dopaminergic (DA) pathways, which are the same pathways associated with the SEEKING system (Panksepp, 1998a, pp. 144–163), a command system of undisputed psychobiological and psychodynamic importance. Thus, unequivocal evidence supports bridging core psychoanalytic and neuroscience contributions to understanding dreaming better than any time in recent history.

Because we see dreaming as a learning engine, we start with some observations about learning mechanisms. "Current neuropsychological research strongly supports the idea that motor activity and adaptive learning are fundamentally associated with each other. Jeannerod (1985) reviews the relevant [primary] research in this area, including prominently the work of Hebb, Held, Hubel and Weisel, and Piaget. An interesting question is why adaptive learning does not occur unless the subject initiates motor actions" (Levin, 1991, p. 224).

There are probably a host of factors for why taking an active stance assists learning (Levin, 1991, 1997, 2003): (1) spontaneity[4] activates working memory for what we are learning; (2) activity primes memory generally, adding valuable associations; (3) our actions follow our interests, which facilitates learning by simultaneously activating the primary association cortical areas for the various sensory systems, which facilitates "aha reactions"; and (4) every action is an experiment. One of us (FML) has spent years investigating what is known about learning in terms of mind and brain correlations (Levin, 2003). Some of these factors appear in Fig. 1 (Levin, 2004b, 2005a, 2005c) which summarizes this work illustrating the emotional (psychological) cascade[5] associated with learning, and the corresponding biological cascade associated with the emotional cascade (Kandel, 1983, 1998; Abel et. al., 1998). In this sense there is reason to believe that in the case of adaptive learning, mind creates brain as much as brain creates mind. This is because the new (NMDA) synapses involved in learning are often created by what is emotionally salient (emotional attention) (Levin, 2005a, 2005b, 2005c). These comments are important because they help clarify the psychoanalytic clinical experience from which our model of dreaming has grown, with due respect, of course, to the effects on our theorizing of the explosion of informative neuroscience research on the same subject.

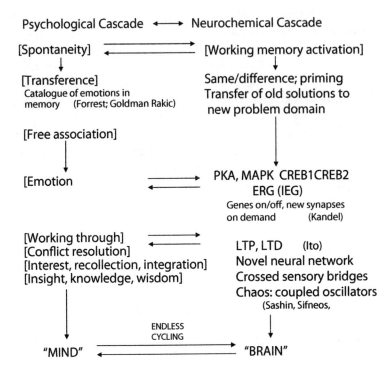

Figure 1. Biological and Psychological Cascades

Our chapter really starts, however, from one question: What is the function of dreaming? This has been a seminal question for NP. We believe that dreams are adaptive for dreamers in at least three interrelated ways: (1) dreams facilitate learning by creating specific emotion-based action plans as probes for the discovery of the exact nature of potential dangers, for guiding the learning about contextual details, and storing this emotionally critical information within implicit (procedural) and explicit (declarative) memory systems during dreaming and waking life, respectively (Talvitie & Ihanus, 2002); (2) dreams exercise the emotional-instinctual potentials of the brain (Panksepp, 1998); and (3) more specifically, dreams can simulate threatening events, rehearse threat perception and threat avoidance, and improve self performance in dealing with threats [and with conflicts], thus ultimately improving the probability of sexual reproduction by the dreamer (i.e. they aid the survival, and we would add, the happiness, of our species) (Revonsuo, 2000). In speculating about the adaptive value of dreams, we are not necessarily restricting ourselves to the dreaming of humans.[6] Indeed, there is a large literature on other animals suggesting that REM sleep is necessary for consolidating memories related to especially stressful learning situations (Panksepp, 1998, Chapter 7).

We shall review the research that bears on our central question. Some important largely neuroscientific evidence appears in Pace-Schott, Solms, Blagrove and Harnad (2003). Other evidence appears in the psychoanalytic literature (Opatow, 1999; Shevrin et. al., 1996; Westen, 1999). A fair conclusion would be that there is an enormous amount of conceptual controversy in the field of sleep and dreaming, ranging from approaches such as ours (that see dreaming as both meaningful and adaptive, especially via dream exploitation of emotions) to those that assert that there is absolutely no reliable evidence supporting such a conclusion (see Walker, 2005).

The problems in sleep and dreaming research relevant to our core hypothesis are both theoretical and practical. On the theoretical side are the obvious difficulties in bridging psychoanalysis and neuroscience. All constructs, psychoanalytic or neuroscientific, need to be based upon evidence and stated in specific testable form. Asserting, for example, that an entire field lacks any scientific basis is dangerous ground. This kind of criticism has been addressed in detail by Opatow (1999) and Westen (1999) in defense of modern psychoanalytic science. Opatow has tackled the philosophy of science issues, making it clear how psychoanalysis helps us gain access to ucs fantasy and thus "acquire valid knowledge of the proximate causes of [individual] ... suffering" (p. 1122). Westen has documented the very large number of independent contemporary articles on the scientific evidence for the existence of a psychological ucs. For example, Westen introduces technical evidence supporting "... that much of mental life is unconscious, including cognitive, affective, and motivational processes" (p. 1061). Westen (1999) cites research articles that are detailed empirical studies relating the ucs to such subjects as subliminal activation, the priming of various kinds of memory (implicit, explicit, associative, etc.), both as manifest in the activity in healthy individuals as well as in amnesics, prosopognosics, and other brain-injured populations (research in these latter areas also appears in depth in Solms, 2000). Westen and Opatow together exemplify the modern psychoanalytic scholarly world, which is often ignored in attacks on Freud's earliest thinking as though it perfectly represents current psychoanalytic scientific opinion (it most certainly does not). There is little doubt that it is easier to attack Freud than deal critically with contemporary psychoanalytic data on scientific grounds. Fortunately, correspondingly ill-argued attacks from psychoanalysis, such as the argument that neuroscience is largely irrelevant to analytic studies, have dramatically decreased in the past decade.

Part of the practical problem for neuroscientific dream research arises from the fact that *we currently have no empirical access to non-REM dreams in animals*. Therefore, among the two major varieties of dreams, REM dreams and non-REM dreams, and the mixed variants combining these two types (as a third variety), it is only for the REM dream category that we can easily identify dreams empirically (because of the obvious eye movements). Therefore, our chapter focuses exclusively on REM dreams. On the positive side, however, there is a *significant consensus* that REM dreaming is more emotional. We should thus be better able to substantiate our points about the meaningfulness and adaptiveness of REM dreaming, which often seems identified by the dreamer's affects. The fact is that most of the hard neuroscience data on REM dreaming and the abundance of well-controlled experiments comes from animal research. In other words, it is to our advantage to deal primarily with emotion-laden REM dreaming because such dream emotions likely express valuable information, or important content issues of interest to neuro-psychoanalysts. It should be equally obvious that it helps that REM dreaming can and has been objectively studied simultaneously at both psychological and hard-neuroscience levels in man and animals.

Although much of the dream research reported in Pace-Schott, Solms, Blagrove, and Harnad (2003) appears to take the importance of emotions for granted, nevertheless, a significant minority feels emotions (and even dream contents) can safely be ignored in examining dreams! Obviously, we disagree with this assertion. "As dream commentators have long noted,[7] with Revonsuo (2000, [Revonsuo & Valli, 2000]) taking the lead among ... present authors, emotionality is a central and consistent aspect of REM dreams" (Panksepp, 2003, p. 200). Contents are also critical for determining the meaning of dreams clinically and experimentally. From our perspective, dreams also have an evolutionary, and not just an individual adaptive effect. Our theorizing and Revonsuo's threat simulation theory (TST) are nearly identical, although TST and our theorizing developed completely independently of each other. We also define "danger" as relating to internal feeling states and conflicts along with external dangers. Dangers have a natural close connection in the dreamer's need to struggle with life events, and maintain various internal equilibria simultaneously (Shevrin & Eiser, 2003, p. 218).

The testing of TST theory (Revonsuo et al. 2000) has involved detailed collections and content analysis of threatening events in dream reports across a wide range of subjects. Attention was paid to the nature and source of the threatening event, its target, severity, as well as to the subject's participation and reaction to the threat (i.e. its consequences). One key prediction was that if TST theory is correct then one should find a high frequency of threatening events in the dreams of normal subjects, relative to the (lower) frequency of such threats in the waking life of the same individuals. This turned out to be exactly the case. Revonsuo et al. further correctly predicted that the dangers would be to the self and to those emotionally close to the self, relatively realistic, and that the dream self should routinely take at least some defensive action against any impending threats. Importantly, Revonsuo et al.'s theorizing, based upon empirical evidence and now significantly experimentally confirmed, contradicts the views of those dream researchers who have insisted that dreaming is chaotic and biologically an epiphenomenon (i.e. functionless, and meaningless) (Hobson, Pace-Schott, & Stickgold, 2003; Pace-Schott & Hobson, 2000). It is also ironic that the critics of the meaningfulness of dreams sometimes attach the word "chaos" to dreams, when in fact the modern technical meaning of the word "chaos" refers to a phenomenon (e.g. chaotic attractors in nonlinear dynamics) that expresses deeper hidden meaning or order that underlies a surface of merely *apparent* meaninglessness or disorder!

The core new element in our contribution is twofold: (1) we are applying modern psychoanalytic learning theory to understanding the adaptive aspects of dreaming, and analyzing things simultaneously from an experiential (psychoanalytic) and a (neuroscientific) empirical perspective (Levin, 1991, 2003); and (2) our idea that deferred action plans are critical, when activated, to the learning from dreams that results in adaptive shifts in the self, is a novel contribution with clinical implications and a biological causation that is increasingly known. We are asserting that one critical way such adaptive learning follows from dreams is that dreaming generates strategies for actively checking upon and thus responding to potential dangers, including those emanating from internal psychological conflicts, and that it is not until certain actions are taken and new important threat-related information discovered (confirmed or disconfirmed) that the final phase of learning occurs in the form of adaptive adjustments in the self. Such adaptive adjustments obviously involve changes at fundamentally different levels of analysis: at the cellular level involving various transcription factor effects on genes; at the level of neural networks, involving memory consolidation[8] and reconsolidation or extinction; and within the personality, involving adjustments to emotional and motivational processes.

II. A clinical example and definition of "deferred action planning" in dreams

Darlene is a 26 year-old medical student in psychoanalytic treatment. She had the following dream: "I am in a kind of SUV. I am with a nutsy friend who is driving, and he decides we will drive over some roadblocks in this desert area. He enters this blocked off area without any concerns for our safety. Finally we come to a military base where we are captured. They take him away and I can tell from how he looks when he comes back that he was tortured. The guy who did it to him was smiling when he took him away. I wish him well, but my status is unclear."

When asked for associations to the dream imagery she comments immediately on her conscious impulse to go against the wishes of a member of her family. The friend in the dream reminds her of her analyst, giving her dangerous permission to proceed against her relative, but Darlene is afraid of taking initiatives. Her relative would be strongly against Darlene's wish to let her classmate fix her up on a date. Her relative's anger over this seems almost paranoid. But how could she go against this relative? She wants to go out on the date, but it's like running the risk of being thrown out of her family. In spite of this, she can see that as her analysis proceeds she is gaining some additional confidence in herself, and there is more of a possibility now than ever before that in the near future she is likely to violate some of the internal rules she sets up for herself, such as her rule never to disobey this particular relative. She can barely stand the pain of feeling so much trapped between her wish to date only people who are acceptable to her family vs. her desire to live her own life! She knows that a decision needs to be made, but it is so very hard to make. She is grateful for the time and space the analysis provides her to make up her own mind, without external pressure. Yet she can see that her analyst's permissiveness, even just to consider her own wishes, is itself dangerous novel terrain for her.

A month later she did indeed reach out to get together with the young man her classmate wished to set her up with, and she was greatly relieved that nothing awful happened. Her anxiety peaked as she ruminated over forming her own action plans, initiating them on her own timing, and being her own person. It took time for her to carry out her particular deferred action plan, but it became more and more precious for her to ponder because it increasingly became something that truly belonged to her, and which could be kept private. It is not coincidental that the context of these developments was also her relationship with her analyst as someone who recognized her wishes, talents, and ambitions, but who respected her need to work through her various conflicts patiently without being pressured. She was able to accept that her analyst was indeed giving her permission to act, and that this in itself was not a setup for disaster, but a kindness that grew from his respect for her long-term welfare, and her judgment. And she was of course also free to decide not to act, if that was her preference.

Our proposed relationship between dreaming and deferred plans for actions hinges on the fact that actions have learning potential. Whether this learning potential is tapped depends of course upon what happens next, including what happens within a person's life or psychoanalysis.[9]

The above vignette reminds us of the importance of our tracing actions (in this case also transference feelings and associated behavior) within psychoanalysis, to their deeper level meanings. It is obvious that this patient's action planning is deeply influenced by her ucs wishes and associated conflicts. We therefore need to define and describe what we mean here by ucs both practically and theoretically. Practically, she worries: How can she possibly carry such wishes into waking life in one form or another, given her fears? It seems obvious to her that her dream-related wishes are extending into her waking life. Theoretically, we will clarify our thinking of the Freudian ucs right after we define "deferred action plans".[10]

"Deferred action plans" in our chapter refers literally to the plans for action, including imagined actions that occur in dreams, and real actions later on in various forms. We think they spring largely from our unconscious (ucs), and become identifiable as such from the analysis of our dreams within a clinical psychoanalysis. Here "action plans" can also be thought of as memories of thinking in the form of images of movements with purpose. A discussion of the possible functions performed by dreaming, followed by related actions after a period of delay, is the core of our chapter. But how are we conceptualizing the ucs?

A definition of the "ucs" will help, since there seems to be a relationship between dreaming and mentation of the ucs variety.[11] The Freudian "ucs" refers to the activity of mind/brain that is unavailable to recollection by mere effort, but which reflects important emotionally-based private musings, wishes, desires and also the hidden conflicting feeling states of the self. Privacy potentially protects this aspect of mental life, which is why these states often surface in any psychoanalysis where we feel protected (i.e. safe): the form taken by these ucs elements includes the emergence of our deeper feelings in various contexts (usually in disguised forms), free-associative thoughts and behaviors (including one's slips of various kinds), transferences, and of course, the experience of dreams, only some of which are recollected consciously. We are not arguing that the dream must be recollected for what happens within the dream to have an adaptive (or other) effect on the dreamer.

Shevrin et al. (1996, pp. 14–19) have described four basic assumptions that underlie thinking about the ucs mind psychoanalytically, and their work should be consulted, especially for their description of quite elegant experiments on ucs phenomenon from a NP perspective. The four assumptions they mention are (1) psychic continuity; (2) psychic determinism; (3) the psychological ucs; and (4) the role of free association. As they state it, "… psychic continuity and psychic determinism … are special versions of two assumptions of scientific endeavors in general, continuity and determinism. To assume continuity is to presume lawfulness (though not necessarily regularity); to assume determinism is to take for granted cause and effect. *Psychic* continuity, then, is the assumption that all psychological events—including those that seem inconsistent, such as symptoms, gaps, slips of the tongue, and other parapraxes—are not only lawful but can be rendered psychologically meaningful. *Psychic* determinism holds that even such apparent psychic discontinuities as symptoms, parapraxes, and gaps are not only caused in general, but often have primary psychological causes in particular, and are capable of being explained, at least in part, on a psychological basis" (p. 15). This does not mean that there are not times or circumstances when biological factors result in such behavior as slips, or failures, which may look psychologically and/or unconsciously motivated. Rather, it means that a search for meaning is needed in each instance, and then evidence needs to be examined carefully to see what this evidence best supports as explanation.

Shevrin et al. continue: "...a psychological unconscious...follows from the first two assumptions. A psychological unconscious is posited, such that if unconscious contents and processes were taken into account, the apparent discontinuity would resolve. The forth assumption tells us that it is through the use of free association that the significant unconscious elements will be revealed or inferred in order to resolve seeming psychic discontinuities" (p. 16). In the case of Darlene noted above, it should be obvious that the patient's first free associations to her dream images were the key steps in identifying her impulse to go against one powerful family member (and what also got her in touch with her fears about doing so). That is, her immediate association to her dating impulse after reporting her dream signifies the important connection in her mind between the two.

In Darlene's case, deferred action planning specifically refers to her plan to allow herself to go out on a date one month after her dream, with a young man she knew her family member would not approve of. In this way she contemplated and actually tested a danger beforehand (mentally), worked over her reservations about being proactive, and began to deal more generally with her fear of taking her own initiatives whether they were approved by a particular authority figure in her life or not. Importantly, one could begin to speculate and then investigate over time to what extent Darlene's initial inhibition towards action represents an unconscious conflict between various wishes: sexual, aggressive, or otherwise, and whether her proactive solution (to try dating in this instance) represents her resolution of such conflicts. This, we assert, could only be known by a deep content analysis of Darlene's thinking on a broad array of subjects, which was in fact carried out by following her free associations within her ongoing psychoanalysis.

Later in Chapter 2 of Part 1, we make some speculations as to where action planning likely occurs in Darlene's brain (what neurological systems might be involved), and provide some further accounting for the chemical matrix (cytokines and various transcription factors) that might specifically be involved in her feeling states. But at this point we will need to consider the research on two related subjects: (1) on the insights of Modell (1993) on nachträglichkeit and après coup (sometimes defined within psychoanalysis as "deferred action" or "the retrospective representation of earlier events", and (2) on memory consolidation and reconsolidation research in neuroscience. In other words, it is possible to bridge mind and brain perspectives on such matters as the specific effects of dreaming, dream-related action plans, and learning within dreams, as exemplified by Darlene's case. Our core hypothesis about dreaming assumes that the learning that occurs during dreaming involves a variety of memory changes: modifications of memories that are consolidated or reconsolidated, and extinction of some memories that are treated as though they are better off deleted.

Modell (1993) begins his discussion (following Freud's understanding) of the two variables we just mentioned, as follows: "nachträglichkeit (and après coup) involve a normative process in which the memories of successive developmental periods are more or less continuously updated, to avoid psychopathological meanings from accumulating" (Modell, 1993, p. 161; Birksted-Breen, 2003; Quinodoz, 2004). Please note, here there is an important difference between the "deferred action" (meaning "delayed [re]actions") in the literature just cited, and "deferred action plans" (which is our term for what dreaming produces that helps us identify dangers and make plans to deal with them adaptively).

When writing about trauma in the case of the so-called Wolf man, Freud (1914–1916, 1918) first referred to nachträglichkeit as deferred [re]action,[12] by which he meant that some trauma occurred when the Wolf man originally observed his parents copulating (at the age of 1½) and then especially when he re-thought about this again (at age 4). His trauma, from the traditional prerspective, involved his being upset in one set of ways at the earlier age, while a different set of concerns played a role when he rethought things at age 4. Freud (1914–1916, 1918) goes to great pains to understand his patient's dream of wolves, and the patient's various fears in relation to such concerns as delayed castration fears (from his re-experience of his memory of earlier viewing his mother nude, i.e. during his experience of the early 'primal scene'). What is important for our consideration is that when Freud was writing about deferred action in this instance, what he meant was that on reflection (that is, after a delay) some mental content(s) can be re-experienced differently than originally, for example, traumatically.

When we refer in our discussion to "deferred action plans", we are clearly not referring to the matter of "nachträglichkeit" or "après-coup" *per se*. However, the reader needs to appreciate that these terms in the English and French technical literature of psychoanalysis are attempts used in the post-Freud period of psychoanalysis to explain aspects of important developmental issues, and as such they are highly pertinent to our discussion of learning in the context of dreams.

To be more specific, *nachtråglichkeit and après coup express the idea that new insights into the meaning of current events significantly change our understanding of past events, just as new insights into the past change our understanding of present events.* Especially important from a neuroscientific viewpoint, there is emerging solid evidence that *such shifts, as we have noted, likely involve the "consolidation" and/ or the "reconsolidation" of memory* (see also section IV). To this extent the literature on "nachträglichkeit" and "après coup" is relevant to our core hypothesis in a number of subtle ways: (1) our chapter deals with the adjustment of memories (knowledge) in relation to various dangers, including, of course, the changing of our insights from the past according to present insights, and vice versa; (2) any learning involving dreams necessarily involves the effects of memory consolidation and reconsolidation (see Alberini, 2005, for various aspects of such memory adjustments, for example, in relation to memory use and disuse); (3) making adjustments to danger via learning and memory consolidation/reconsolidation undoubtedly involves the effects of specific cytokines acting as transcription factors turning genes on or off, for example, the genes that control new synapse formation, and which therefore lead to new long-term memories (LTMs); and (4) there is always the possibility that the experiential state of mind of the person reviewing memories out of awareness during wakefulness may be not dissimilar from the experiential state of mentation associated with REM dreaming. What both would share would be a "dose" of the ucs. The importance of this "dose" deserves neuro-psychoanalytic appreciation.

To create proper neuro-psychoanalytic understanding of learning in relationship to dreaming (and more generally) we certainly need to answer a number of complicated questions about the types, mechanisms, organization (anatomy, chemistry, and physiology), and vicissitudes of memory[13]. But we first need to accomplish two things: to make some predictions based upon our core hypothesis, and to describe experiments to test our theory. This is the subject of Section III. We also delve more deeply into modern dream theory in Section IV.

III. *Predictions based upon our core hypothesis, and specific experiments that might settle the issue*

We propose two experiments. These take into consideration the research that shows that windows for sensitivity to REM deprivation occur, and are related to the fact that for at least some kinds of learning we are unprepared for or which are unusually complicated, there is an increase in REM pressure after training, after which there is an increased retention of the dream work in memory (Pearlman, 1973; Greenberg & Pearlman, 1974). Our experiments are therefore designed around relatively unprepared for or complex learning tasks; in these cases we apply REM deprivation to highlight what is lost without REM-related memory consolidation of learning. We also remind the reader of our position that REM dreams (and not non-REM dreams) are the subject of our chapter, and of these experiments. Although we believe that the really important functional dreams are REM dreams, we affirm this cannot yet be proven since no one yet knows how to systematically deprive humans of non-REM dreams!

Experiment #1

In this we would take fledgling music-performance students who find it a challenge to render well know classical pieces with full affective intensity, and break them down into two randomly assigned groups. One would practice daily at their task, and there would be daily evaluation of their recorded performances by a panel of musical experts for expressive clarity and subtlety and affective impact. The other group practices, as does the first, but they are given systematic REM-deprivation in a sleep lab. The prediction is that the REM-deprived group will have difficulty achieving artistic mastery of the piece as rapidly as the control group.[14] The reason for using fairly inexperienced students is that experienced ones may already have too many cognitive skills, and this would allow them many short-cuts in the arduous affective-cognitive processing that is necessary for one to achieve artistic mastery of new pieces. It also makes sense to set up the experiment so that the group whose sleep is disturbed is allowed extra sleep to avoid the conclusion that they are failing merely because of fatigue. They would thus also receive extra REM, but this is not a serious problem since their additional REM deprivation does not produce a feeling of fatigue; slow wave sleep deprivation does that. We are not arguing that this experiment is necessarily better than many others that one could think of; only that it would prove our point about REM deprivation. Also, without going into detail, we believe a REM-deception control group could be added to this first experiment, for the purpose of demonstrating as well that the effect of REM deprivation is real and thus would not occur in those who would merely think they had experienced REM deprivation, but only in those who would actually be REM deprived.

Experiment #2

A computer-based gambling game, say, the card game poker or the Iowa Gambling Task, would be given to two groups of college students, because of its ability to measure student responses to dangers on a scale that runs from passive to active extremes for financial success or losses. As the students learn the game, it would be predictable that those students who take an active stance would be more successful in speedily mastering the game and less risk adverse, vs. those who operate in a more passive mode. Especially important would be examining the patterns of "attack" according to proactively locating and testing for dangers posed by the other players as part of developing novel methods for winning the card game. During the nights between games, subjects would be followed in the dream lab, and sample dreams collected from each group. On a purely random basis, one group would be REM-deprived. We would predict that the REM-deprived group would be less successful in the game, but in particular, this group would show less activity in locating and dealing proactively with specific dangers, as a generalization, compared to the group not so deprived, which would make more general attempts to overwhelm the other players but without a detailed strategic plan based upon analysis of danger, counting cards played, noticing the reactions of the other players so as to learn when they are bluffing, etc. Those students previously expert in such games would be excluded to avoid having the data skewed by unusual expertise that might overcome the REM-deprivation effect on forming and utilizing creative action plans.

In both of these experiments there is an obvious attempt to deprive subjects of REM and see if the observed effects on mode of problem solving is disturbed. If our predictions are demonstrated, and if the dreams and the pattern of playing music or poker would shift towards the successful employment of various action plans, then this would support our core hypothesis that dreaming itself involves various kinds of active problem solving on the basis of learning from our emotions, and that dreams are meaningful adaptive learning-related "engines" that improve the quality of our life, and serve to promote our survival and reproduction as an evolutionary adaptation as well. This would extend the findings of the REM-deprivation literature. The learning disturbances in each REM deprived group would further demonstrate the already known importance of REM for learning. Details of ratings on the various test batteries noted between REM deprived subjects and those not so deprived will show a shift in the REM deprived group away from various action-related modes of problem solving in favor of more passive approaches to problem identification and solution.

IV. *Solms and Panksepp: Bridging mind and brain on sleep and dreams—The new paradigm for sleep and dreams, and details of memory consolidation, reconsolidation, and extinction*

Recent research has dramatically changed the landscape on sleep and dreaming. We summarize the work by Mark Solms and Jaak Panksepp. Taken together they illuminate critical insights into sleep and dreaming, and the closely related foundations of a science of human and animal emotions.

In a number of publications Solms has presented convincing evidence that (1) REM sleep and dreaming are doubly dissociable, so there can be REM sleep without dreaming, and dreaming without REM sleep. Thus, the equation of REM sleep with dreaming is untenable. This challenges the prevailing theory on dreams for the previous generation which assumes an equation of dreaming and REM sleep (Hobson, 1999, 2004; Hobson, Pace-Schott, & Stickgold, 2000); (2) the REM state is controlled by cholinergic (ACH) brainstem mechanisms, which "can only generate the psychological phenomena of dreaming through the mediation of a second and separate, probably dopaminergic (DA) forebrain mechanism" (Solms, 2003a, p. 54) which indicates higher level mesolimbic/mesocortical control or input into dreaming processes (Solms, p. 55); (3) dreaming can be manipulated by agonists and antagonists with no concomitant changes in REM frequency, duration, and density" (Solms, 2003a, p. 54); (4) dreaming is obliterated by lesions to the ventromesial frontal lobe (VMFL) which is known to have associations with emotion, decision making and psychologically relevant states, underling meaningful non-random input into dreaming; (5) "the central tenet of the [earlier] model (of Hobson et al., op. cit.) is that the causal stimuli for dream imagery arise 'from the pontine brainstem and not in cognitive areas of the cerebrum' (Hobson & McCarley, 1977)" (Solms, p. 52); however, (6) REM sleep is not controlled by forebrain mechanisms, but rather by the brain stem, although, as noted above, damage to the forebrain (e.g. the VMFL) that spares the brain stem unequivocally eliminates dreaming; (7) therefore, although Hobson et. al.'s theory of brain stem control of sleeping is correct, their arguments that dreams are primarily under pontine control and without ideational, psychological, and deeply meaningful imagery and thought seem obviously flawed (Solms, 2003a).[15]

Solms also demonstrates that dreaming is lost by lesions to the PTOCJ,[16] something he feels is not surprising since this region "supports various cognitive processes that are vital for mental imagery" (Solms, 2003a, also citing the work of Kosslyn, 1994; see also: Hau et al. 2004). The region in question has many fibers that connect frontal and limbic structures with DA cells in the ventral tegmental area (VTA), the source cells for the mesolimbic mesocortical DA system. The connections are complex but especially interesting, as described by Solms (who cites especially the work of Panksepp, 1985, 1998) as follows: The DA cells ascend through the forebrain bundles of the lateral hypothalamus (LH), which Panksepp has focused upon in his description of one of the key functional systems of the mind/brain, namely, what he calls the SEEKING (or wanting or curiosity or appetitive) command system (Solms, 2003a, pp. 54-55).

What is important here is that not only is the evidence strong that meso-cortical meso-limbic DA cells contribute to dreaming; there is no doubt that dreaming involves higher cortical centers, mood, object choice, self evaluation, affect regulation, meanings, goals, drives, etc. as well as the participation of lower components, including brainstem multiple reticular activating structures, intralaminar thalamic areas, and as noted, heteromodal cortical areas. In other words, every conscious state involves critical contributions from both so-called higher and lower centers. Two critical conclusions follow: (1) significant evidence supports the psychoanalytic position on dreams as deeply meaningful events, and thus renders Hobson's earlier theory of dreams as controlled from the bottom up by the pons, as imprecise[17]; and (2) it is important to appreciate the interactivity between higher and lower structures in carrying out a variety of important mind/brain functions, a subject we address in Part 2 of this essay.

We are now ready to move on to a consideration of REM dreaming and its effect on memory. We are basically identifying what allows us to not just dream, but to remember as LTM insights from our dreams, including deferred action plans related to various dream concerns about potential dangers. There is strong evidence that dreams allow the dreaming subject to process (consolidate or reconsolidate) memory "off line" as it were (Lee, Everitt, & Thomas, 2004; Stickgold, 2004; Stickgold, Whidbee, Schimer, Patel, & Hobson, 2000; Stickgold, Scott, Rittenhouse, & Hobson, 1999; Atienza, Cantero, &

Stickgold, 2004; Fosse, Fosse, Hobson, & Stickgold, 2003; also see discussions in Levin, 1988, 1991, 2003). A consensus position has emerged and is best expressed by Panksepp (1998) as follows:

> "REM allows the basic emotional circuits of the brain to be accessed in a systematic way, which may permit emotion related information collected during waking hours to be re-accessed and solidified as lasting memories in sleep. REM periods may allow some type of restructuring and stabilization of the information that has been harvested into temporary memory stores. During REM, neural computations may be done on this partially stored information, and consolidation may be strengthened on the basis of reliable predictive relationships that exist between the various events that have been experienced. The dream may reflect the computational solidification process as different emotionally coded memory stores are reactivated, and the web of associated relationships is allowed to unreel once more and to coalesce into long-term memories and plans, depending on the predominant patterns of reevaluation." [Panksepp, 1998, p. 139]

Stickgold (2004), marks the above paradigm shift when he comments as follows upon dream-functionality (though he equates dreaming with REM sleep, thus glossing over the important work of Solms noted above):

> "... a unique physiology of sleep, and perhaps even more so, of REM sleep, shifts the brain/mind into an altered [dreaming] state in which it pulls together disparate, often emotionally charged and weakly associated memories into a narrative structure, and ... this process of memory reactivation and association is, in fact, also a process of memory consolidation and integration, which enhances our ability to function in the world." (italics added, Stickold, 2004, p. 1165)

Research first done in the 1970s by psychoanalysts trained also as neuroscientists, demonstrated that REM dreams are associated with the consolidation of memory (Pearlman, 1971, 1973, 1979; Pearlman & Becker, 1973, 1974; Greenberg & Pearlman, 1974). The specifics of memory consolidation and/or reconsolidation[18] are critical to understanding learning shifts, including, of course, those within dreaming. These terms refer to "a process whereby newly formed [or old] memories become increasingly less susceptible to interference ..." (Walker, 2005). Many signaling molecules are involved in the several stages of memory acquisition, consolidation, and reconsolidation (Abel & Lattal, 2001). In their report in *Science* (304: 829–830), Izquierdo and Cammarota (2004) credit Lee, Everitt, and Thomas (2004), and Frankland, Bontempi, Talton, Kaczmarek, and Silva (2004) for providing fresh insights into the mechanisms of memory consolidation and reconsolidation. *The work of these latter two research groups demonstrates a double dissociation between consolidation and reconsolidation, and between brain derived neurotrophic factor (BDNF) and Zif/268.* Memory consolidation requires BDNF (but not Zif/268), reconsolidation recruits Zif/268 (but not BDNF). Consolidation and reconsolidation are clearly different processes (Bahar, Dorfman, & Dudai, 2004).

On the one hand, BDNF only consolidates those memories that have deteriorated because of memory disuse (inactivity). On the other hand, the activation of long-term memories (LTM's) can also result in memory deterioration and typically requires a separate method for reconsolidation involving Zif/268 (Izquierdo & Cammarota, 2004; Zaraiskaya, et al. 2004). The loss of LTM is generally called "extinction" (whether from use or neglect).[19] Old LTMs, however, apparently do not require reconsolidation after use as much as recently acquired LTMs (Milekic & Alberini, 2002; Dudai & Eisenberg, 2004). We do not know all the important constraints effecting when a reactivated memory requires reconsolidation (Biedenkapp & Rudy, 2004; Bozon, Davis, & Laroche, 2003). We are, however, learning more details about subtle factors such as carboxypeptidase E (CPE) which plays a critical role in delivering the inactive form of BDNF—proBDNF, to the neuron, where it can be converted to its active form, aBDNF (Pang et al. 2004; Lou et al. 2005).

Also, Tononi and Cirelli (2003), cited in Gorman, 2004, p. 5, believe that it is SWS activation that reduces the strength of neural connections, in contrast to REM sleep activations, which increase the strength of connections.[20] They speculate that there may be some optimal level of connectedness which if exceeded taxes the body's energy demands beyond the usual 20% level required to supply what is needed for the brain's maintaining neuronic connections.

Izquierdo and Cammarota contrast the mechanisms of memory extinction in three cases: Pavlovian extinction, Freudian repression, and amnesia. In the first case, extinction involves the activation of enzymatic pathways, gene expression, and protein synthesis in the hippocampus and amygdala (Vianna et al. 2003; Anokhin et al. 2003;

Askenasy, 2002; Bonner, 1999). Freudian repression is seen as inhibition of hippocampal activity on the basis of output from the prefrontal neurons at the time of memory retrieval (Anderson et al. 2004). Amnesia, they believe, results from real neuronal or synaptic loss that can be either morphological or functional.

Agnihotri, Hawkins, Kandel, and Kentros (2004) demonstrate that long-term stability of new hippocampal fields, as in the hippocampal spatial memory system, which forms an internal representation of the environment, requires new protein synthesis. It is not easy to understand what all of this reconsolidation is accomplishing. One possibility is that reconsolidated memories can be re-contextualized (modified) at various levels, for example, at both a cellular (local neuron) and an interactive systems (brain regional) level (Debiec & Ledoux, 2004; Debiec, LeDoux, & Nader, 2002). Without reconsolidation fear memories in the amygdala are headed for extinction after retrieval (i.e. they become labile with use) (Nader, Schafe, & LeDoux, 2000). These authors note that the lateral and basal nuclei of the amygdala [and hippocampus] seem to be the look-up site for memory "storage" in fear learning. One could imagine that extinction of such memories on a selective basis would at times be useful, say in the self-induced recovery from post-traumatic stress disorder (PTSD). Put differently, "the reactivation of memories can initiate genuine processes of reconsolidation and extinction. Such forgetting could depend either on alternations in the neural networks storing the information, or, on active processes which hinder consolidation or block the expression of memories" (Morgado, 2005, p. 289). We would speculate that dreaming mentation initiates a process of reactivation of memories, resulting in a variety of changes in those memories depending upon what neural regions (systems) are activated, what transcription factors involved, and whether the desired goal is extinction or reconsolidation (with possible modification).

We cannot leave this section without noting the work on genetic modulation during sleep (Tononi & Cirelli, 2001; Cirelli & Tononi, 2000, 2004; Cirelli, Gutierrez, & Tononi, 2004) indicating that 10% of gene transcripts in the cerebral cortex change their expression between day and night, and half of them are modulated by sleep and wakefulness independent of the time of day. Molecular correlates of sleep are also found in the cerebellum, not known for generating sleep rhythms, but important for learning (Levin, 1991, 2003).

Approximately 100 known genes show increased expression during sleep, and they are believed to provide molecular support for protein synthesis, membrane trafficking, and neuronal maintenance. The gene products that are more abundant during wakefulness are those in the brain involving high-energy requirements, transmission between nerve cells, and the acquisition of new information. Those gene products abundant during sleep are involved in rebuilding or neuronal maintenance operations (Cirelli, Gutierrez, & Tononi, 2004). It would help for us to know (1) how and why genes are turned on during sleep (and what transcription factors are involved), and (2) exactly how REM activation plays a role.

V. *Our core hypothesis*

From a strict NP perspective, dreaming represents both a mode of thinking, and an expression of the ucs mind.[21] Of course, by ucs we are describing a theory with a very long history. Freud most certainly did not invent the subject, but through his discovery and working out of the many details of the psychoanalytic clinical method he greatly advanced how analysts deal clinically with knowledge without awareness, and the structure and function of fantasizing (Bornstein & Pittman, 1992; Shevrin, Bond, Brakel, Hertel, & Williams, 1996).

It may help to spell out more about the thinking behind our core hypothesis. Although we believe that dreams can give rise to a significant number of deferred action plans expressing the ucs (or if you will, subconscious) wishes, fantasies, costs,[22] or needs (our maximum hypothesis), it is important to recognize that whether this is a correct assertion can only be settled by empirical studies (such as we suggest in the previous chapter). If we would state our reason for believing our hypothesis connecting dreams and deferred action plans, however, we feel it seems intuitively correct from the following clinical psychoanalytic perspective: often spontaneous insights and self-initiated actions go together during analysis in facilitating learning (Levin, 1991, 2003).

Our central speculation also seems to make the following sense: if action plans turn out to be a product that carries our dream goals into the real world, not just in fantasy, then we believe that such action plans would likely be serving a set of adaptive (regulative) functions.

At least three psychological mechanisms would then be at work: First, dreams would work through their stimulation of action plans, that is, spontaneous activity, to learn more about that which seems specifically dangerous to our security, and help us make appropriate adjustments for our own safety. As Levin (2003) has pointed out there is solid evidence that spontaneous activity is itself critical for learning, through its activation of working memory for the subjects considered by the mind/brain. Without working memory activation we would not be able to as easily modify and store away as memory the results of our thinking in the most salient form.[23] Second, if the feelings and actions embedded in our dreams are reflected upon during dream mentation, they could result in emotional insights of adaptive value in dealing with potential dangers or conflicts. Thirdly, by action planning and carrying out even tentative or exploratory actions, we also move closer to more safely realizing our deeper ucs (fantasy) wishes and goals.

In addition, a number of biological mechanisms might obtain regarding such dream-related learning, which would be the counterpart of the psychological mechanisms we are describing. In Figure 1, presented earlier, we try to help the reader connect the two general perspectives (biological and psychological) involved in emotion-based learning.

But for us a decisive line of thought supporting our speculations about the role of action planning must include the following: we can imagine that if dreams only satisfied us in fantasy, that this might not be sufficient to satisfy a large enough number of people, nor to provide our species with an adaptive enough advantage so that dreaming would have survived long in our (or other) species. Logic requires that dreams must do more than satisfying us in fantasy alone, since *fantasy satisfaction is not as fulfilling as satisfaction in reality, and we further know from Revonsuo et. al.'s work that most dreams are simply not that satisfying.*

Please note that in our speculation about deferred action, we are not insisting that all dreams lead to instruction sets for deferred actions (our maximum hypothesis), since such actions expressing the ucs could obviously come from a variety of sources, only one of which is dreams. Yet how can we exclude dreams *a priori* as a significant source of at least some significant action plans (our minimum hypothesis) when everything within the history of psychoanalysis theoretically and clinically has focused upon dreams as the major vehicle by which we gain access to ucs intents? Moreover, every clinical analysis involves dream interpretations to some significant degree; therefore, *if dreams represent the enactive and articulate expression of the ucs mind, then is it not probable that our dreams lead to action plans expressive of our ucs life, and safeguard whatever might threaten it?* One could argue here that action planning is thus a normal concomitant of using our capacity for insight to protect our secret ucs goals and emotional life.

Naturally, all of the above considerations only suggest some possibilities; but they constitute neither evidence nor proof. Yet philosophically, we would argue that it is not necessary to prove our maximum hypothesis; demonstrating our minimum hypothesis would still be useful to clinical psychoanalysis and to neuroscience, as an effort to round out dream theory by tying together older ideas about dreaming with more modern ones, including some speculation about the probable evolutionary advantage of dreaming by means of its role in facilitating learning about dangers, and eliminating or at least mitigating them. In this sense, having made such a postulate, it was exciting to have learned of Revonsuo et al.'s work, and of its experimental confirmation. This, of course, puts our speculations in this area on much firmer footing, for which we are grateful.

To be still more precise, we are suggesting an answer to the question as to why we dream, by asserting that the function of dreaming and its action planning is to eliminate mal-adaptive planning rather than to merely generate adaptive plans. Eliminating mal-adaptive planning seems not really much different from creating adaptive planning, but the former seems a slightly more correct assertion than the latter! And it leads us to the still more detailed considerations (see below) regarding how mal-adaptive plans might specifically be avoided.

VI. *The larger learning system in which dreams and actions plans occur*

In Fig. 2 we portray schematically the larger system in which the ucs and conscious (cs) systems are related to a number of other components that seem important to psychoanalytic learning, as noted earlier. Action and deferred action plans appear in the lower left hand corner of the figure. Dreaming appears at the upper left. On the ucs side we see connections to variables we designate as dreaming, transference, same-difference analysis, and the priming of memory,[24] spontaneity, and free association. On the cs side there are also connections to spontaneity, and such variables as free association, and self-reflection (these subjects are covered in great detail in Donald, 1991, 2001; and Levin, 1991, 2003). Of course, some ideas presented in Fig. 2 are speculative, but many aspects of learning presented schematically in Fig. 2 are solidly based on diverse evidence already accepted within NP.

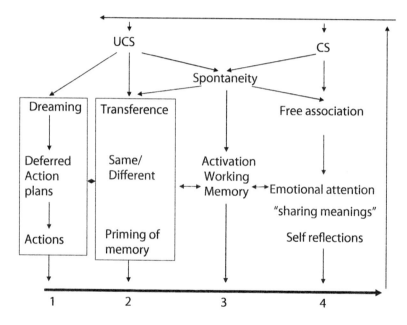

1-Experimentation, imitation; 2-Trans. solutions from past to present; 3-Working with activated memory; 4-sharing meanings with others

Figure 2. Specific Mechanisms of Learning

At the bottom of the diagram is a horizontal arrow that runs to the right, towards the "facilitation of learning". In a previous paper on transference (Levin, 1997), we present evidence that transference has a major adaptive (evolutionary) advantage, namely, it facilitates learning. It does this by helping us in a number of ways (indicated by the numbers 1-4 in Fig. 2. These correlate with the four descriptions at the bottom of the figure). They include learning to operate according to an expert system, in which certain memories are stored away under the category of transference, and they also involve primable states that allow us to remember them, and to transfer and test solutions from earlier relationships (that are selected on the basis of similarity and difference analysis), or from present relationships. This makes some things that would otherwise be relatively inexpressible symbolically, substantially rememberable and/or at least thinkable. Of course, "thinkability" could be considered a kind of action in itself; for example, it is always part of the drama in our experience of our relationships with other "personages" wherever they might be.[25] All such spontaneous activity (whether transferential, free association, or action planning) greatly organizes and facilitates (stimulates or primes) learning.

In the present chapter we are considering the adaptive advantage of dreaming rather than focusing primarily upon the learning-stimulating aspects of transferences or other spontaneous activities. It seems to us that the very same argument made previously elsewhere (Levin, 1997, 2003) for the adaptive advantage (for learning) of transference (specifically) and spontaneity (generally) can be made as well for dreams, and for what we claim are one of our dream's mechanisms or products, namely, deferred action plans. This argument reasons that both transferences and dream products are derivatives of the ucs mind/brain. It therefore seems probable that in each case, the down arrows in Fig. 2 logically run into the horizontal arrow (at the bottom of the figure) leading towards the right, namely, towards the facilitation of learning. *The mind/brain has simply evolved multiple pathways that assist learning. And research supports the contention that the SEEKING system is critical for individuals learning of how rewards are likely to be obtained (in relation to what contingencies, actions, etc).*

Our earlier arguments seem even stronger, however, than our reasoning above by analogy between transferences and dream products. This follows because we know for sure the various transcription factors, for example, Zif/268 and BDNF, play an active role in some forms of memory reconsolidation and consolidation, which obviously supports learning. And in our discussion above (and as elaborated in Part 2, our companion chapter to Chapter 1) we identify the clear ability of dreams to create action plans based upon the dreamer's access to a number of critical brain structures: the anterior cingulate cortex (ACC) with its connection to limbic system emotions and wishes; the supplementary motor cortex (SMC), which obviously is a pathway towards action instructions (action plans) (see Levin, Gedo, Ito, & Trevarthen, 2003 and Trevarthen, 2003 for more details); and with the periaqueductal gray (PAG) and the centromedian nucleus of the thalamus (CNT).

VII. *Summary and conclusions*

As for why we dream, our answer is *dreams are deeply meaningful, psychological and cognitive problem solving engines that are adaptive for the dreamer and his species*. We have presented a NP model of dreaming as a unique kind of mentation that integrates affective wishes (cs and ucs) and cognitive concerns, while creating what we call "deferred action plans". Deferred action plans (1) capture what we identify in our dreams as potential dangers or conflicts, (2) stimulates and simulates our learning about such threats, and, (3) when the time is right, carry these specific plans formulated during the dream into our waking mental life for the purpose of dealing more effectively with dangers or conflicts.

Our model developed from two inspirations: (1) the vast research on sleep and dreams, including the most recent work of Panksepp, Solms, and others, explaining the relationship between REM sleep and dreaming. Now it is clear that the pedunculopontine nucleus (cholinergic) system (that turns on during REM periods) helps to facilitate REM sleep, while the MVFL, which like many prefrontal systems has extensive dopaminergic afferentation, is proven essential for dreaming (see also Yu, 2001); and (2) an emerging psychoanalytic learning theory which highlights the importance of activity for learning: via the effects of spontaneity on working memory activation, for the effect of priming on recovering associative memories, for the effect of spontaneous metaphors on facilitating aha reactions, and for the critical role of emotion in supporting active attentional mechanisms that appear essential to the creation of new synapses on demand.

We have described the controversies in the older sleep and dreaming literature, and their resolution in the form of the new paradigm in which *dreams are now readily seen as psychologically meaningful and distinctly non-random events*. Revonsuo et al.'s work on the evolutionary value of dreaming is reviewed; it is our viewpoint as well, developed independently, and appears solidly grounded. Thus, Freud's insights about the possibility of a dynamic ucs remain a very real probability, though not yet accepted by at least some neuroscientists, yet a shrinking minority.

The dream of a psychoanalytic patient has been discussed to help the reader see what we call deferred action planning. We then define the psychological ucs (Shevrin, op. cit.), and include supporting arguments and research for this idea. We also define Nachträglichkeit and après coup and consider its importance for learning within psychoanalysis seen from the perspective of the new model of dreaming as a learning engine (Birksted-Breen, 2003). This lead us directly to considerations of memory consolidation and reconsolidation, phenomena related to learning and associated with unique transcription factor effects (from Zif/268 and BDNF, respectively, and undoubtedly, many other transcription factors). Obviously, here we are presenting a modern expansion on the older understanding that REM sleep consolidates memory. We leave for Sleep and Dreaming, Part 2, our companion chapter a further discussion of related interdisciplinary details of how dreaming is processed in the new perspective.

We have presented a number of predictions, based upon our dreaming model, and we hope to demonstrate these predictions experimentally. The research of Solms and of Panksepp is the principal source of the dreaming model presented here. The critical recent result (by Solms) demonstrates that REM dreams and sleeping are doubly dissociable, and that the VMFL and POTCJ are the two primary telencephalic areas that appear required for dreaming to occur, whereas damage to the pontine sleep control centers (operating at the behest of the hypothalamus) only affect sleep, and dreaming only indirectly. Therefore DA and AC are both important, the former for dreaming, and the latter for REM sleep.[26] DA pathways are important for their relationship to higher centers that involve feelings, object choice, self evaluation, goals, wishes, conflict resolution, etc. (i.e. variables that are psychologically important). The work of Panksepp is decisive because he has elegantly described the SEEKING system which is obviously playing a key role in dreaming, a role relatable to the workings of what analysts call the ucs mind. REM mechanisms are important in relation to the research on memory consolidation, reconsolidation and extinction. Some descriptions of cytokine transcription factors are also made, as noted above (Zif/268 and BDNF) to alert us to the complexity of the systems involved both locally and regionally; obviously, we have a lot yet to learn.

In conclusion, dreams allow satisfaction in fantasy, but perhaps more important, they help us deal with potential ucs dangers or conflicts. This may be their principal adaptive purpose. There is very good reason to believe that the learning occurring during and after dreaming essentially involves simulations of situations to determine the nature of these dangers, and help us decide how best to deal with them. The simulation-related learning seems itself to depend to some significant degree on the formation of deferred action plans spawned from the dream. Our conclusion is that dreams, together with their plans for deferred actions, result in learning about dangers the solution to which provides their adaptive evolutionary function (see also Revonsuo,[27] 2000).

In our companion chapter, we explore details relating to which mind/brain systems regulate or structure dreaming. Eventually it should be possible to make tighter correlations regarding the psychoanalytic, psychological and neuroscientific (neuro-chemical and anatomic) perspectives on learning and better develop a NP learning theory that is broad enough to encompass both sleep and dreams, and the perspectives of modern psychoanalysis.

Notes

1. Thanks to Jhuma Basak, Alice B. Colonna, Patrizia Giampieri-Deutsch, Eric Johnson, Carlos Macedo, David Olds, Jorge Schneider, David Terman, Douglas F. Watt, and Arnold Wilson for their commentaries on chapters 1 and 2. The authors, however, take sole responsibility for these chapters final form.
2. See also footnote 12.
3. Recall, "learning how " (vs "learning that") suggests involvement by the implicit memory system, which is controlled by the CB and basal ganglia.
4. "Spontaneous" here means without effort or premeditation.

5. "Cascade" refers to a sequence of events, in this case, either psycho-
    logical or biological. Figure 1 shows the psychological sequence on the
    left, and the biological sequence on the right, proceeding in each case
    from the top downwards. These are like the long arms of a ladder. The
    "steps" of the ladder are the bidirectional arrows connecting each long
    arm. Although inference goes into this depiction, and much work needs
    to be done to prove the connections made, there is a formidable body of
    evidence accumulating that suggests what is depicted in Fig. 1 is close
    to the truth.

6. Karl von Frisch, Konrad Lorenz, and Nikolaas Tinbergen won a Nobel
    Prize in 1973 for exactly such a perspective: their ethological approach
    "highlighted the importance of interpreting animal behavior in the
    context of its survival value and showed that much could be gained by
    comparing behaviors across species" (Miller, 2004).

7. It is impossible to review the history of dreaming research without men-
    tioning the seminal work of Panksepp (1998, 2005) and others on the
    affective organization of mind, brain, and behavior. Reiser (2001) also
    highlights the pioneering research of Mishkin and Appenzeller (1987)
    on primates "identify[ing] the neural (corticolimbic) circuitry that is
    involved in matching newly registered (strange) patterns of sensory
    stimuli to previously registered emotionally meaningful patterns that
    have been retained in memory…[A] perceptual pattern…initially regis-
    ters in the primary visual cortex and, by means of processing in the pre-
    striate cortex, reaches area TE of the inferior temporal cortex… *[But this
    pattern] is not yet available in (declarative-type) [explicit] memory for match-
    ing until is has been linked, by limbic and paralimbic structures, to the memory
    circuits of the prefrontal and association cortices…[It therefore seems that
    the act of passing] through the limbic structures…[generates and regulates]
    emotion…supporting the idea…[that] enduring neural networks of memory
    [are indeed] organized by emotion* [italics added].This idea is…isomorphic
    with the psychoanalytically derived concept …[that] enduring nodal
    memory networks are organized by emotion" (Mishkin and Appenzel-
    ler, op. cit.) and by motives for action, which emotions animate and
    regulate. Reiser notes parenthetically that in these same experiments
    it was shown that for instrumental conditioned responses (presuma-
    bly involving some gestural actions) "information [was] routed from
    area TE directly to the basal ganglia without passing through the limbic
    system" (Reiser, op. cit.).

8. A recent article (Ganguly-Fitzgerald, Donlea, & Shaw, 2006) shows why
    sleep is vital by demonstrating the role of sleep (we think via dreaming)

in the consolidation of memories for what is experienced during the daytime that is adaptive.

9. There is a large literature on the learning-cognition and brain action systems. Readers will also appreciate one recent contribution (Jacob & Jeannerod, 2005) criticizing the over-use of such theories.

10. Stern (2004), and Levin (2003; 1991/2003) further elaborate on our particular attempt to understand emotionally significant moments such as our patient's from an interdisciplinary mind/brain perspective.

11. For an alternative perspective on the nature of the ucs the reader should see: (Talvitie, 2003, 2006; Talvitie & Ihanus, 2003).

12. Although Freud thought of nachträglichkeit invariably as "deferred [re]action" it is important to recognize that, just as was the case with the Wolf man, usually the impact of trauma is immediate, although, obviously, some effects are indeed delayed (Harold Blum, personal communication).

13. We further agree that both explicit and implicit memory play an important role in ucs life (see: Levin, 2004c; Mancia, 2003). Both need founding on motivating/developmental processes at biological and psychological levels. Specifically, *some ucs activity, namely that represented in implicit memory, is not rememberable as such, but is nevertheless recoverable in psychoanalysis by priming shared experiences of events or discussions, and through reconstructions using the results of priming.* We will discuss this frequently misunderstood aspect of dream-related learning later in this essay.

14. Possible confounding factors need to be mentioned, for the sake of completeness. There is a possibility, given the fact that REM deprivation can make people more labile, that this might contribute to this group showing more affective intensity in their playing than the control group; however, the counter argument might be that this labilty or affective intensity would actually be a disadvantage, since such effects would detract from learning musical subtleties. A second potential complication is the fact that in making artistic mastery a dependent variable we are courting disaster, since music theorists have been arguing about such things for millennia. We disagree: in our opinion, the identification of mastery can be identified correctly in this case because expert judges would be involved, and they could easily be shown to demonstrate consistency among themselves in their judgments.

15. We have tried hard not to conflate two issues: that certain regions of the telencephalon are essential to dreaming, versus "disapproving" the upper brainstem-hypothalamic control of sleep and sleep stages.

16. "Right-sided lesions of the PTOCJ cause complete cessation of dreaming

in association with disorders of spatial cognition..." Left sided lesions of this area cause cessation of dreaming in association with disorders of "quasi-spatial (symbolic) operations. In this way the PTOCJ of both hemispheres contribute to slightly different inputs.

17. To be sure, Hobson's theory, at least in its more recent iterations, is not simple, so perhaps another way to summarize the current situation is that it is shifting in ways that enable an accommodation of psychoanalytic perspectives on dreams much more so than in the past.

18. Work on memory reconsolidation (Suzuki et. al., 2004) indicates that the rate is complicated by (dependent upon) the strength and age of the memory: younger and weaker memories are more easily reconsolidated than older and stronger memories.

19. We are aware that "extinction" may not be entirely equivalent to "forgetting"; that the animal literature considers it a motivational situation in which animals stop responding because some frustrations are demotivating. Obviously, bringing the animal and human research into proper alignment is a difficult goal at present. Thus we chose, in this section, to try to envision a credible temporary compromise in methodology, to see where it takes us, by which we mean no disrespect.

20. It may seem from this that there is a paradox in that REM sleep is understood to provide a "loosening of connections", versus the idea that REM is also providing "memory consolidation"; but here there is no problem because the loosening of connections is a reference only to associations (i.e. a psychological perspective on the availability of memories to consciousness), whereas consolidation here refers to the firming up of memories themselves (i.e. a biological perspective on memory strength or weakness).

21. The paradox here is that both conscious and ucs activity are expressible in dreaming. Psychoanalysis explains this in terms of a layering of experience, so that what we experience superficially is only one level of what we are feeling or meaning, while a number of other levels remain out of awareness.

22. By "costs" we refer to the costs of taking action(s) versus the costs of not taking action(s).

23. Working memory is probably the primary if not exclusive gateway into short-term memory (STM) and ultimately declarative STM.

24. Levin and Kent (1994a, 1994b) presented arguments that transference, similarity/difference psychology, and the priming of memory represent one phenomenon seen from three different yet closely related per-

spectives (by psychoanalysis, cognitive psychology, and neuroscience, respectively).

25. "Where ever they might be" refers to the fact that thinking within transference states involves relating, of course, to people who are somewhere else, some one else, or some mixture of identities.

26. As Solms puts it (2005a, p. 57) "This implies a two stage process, involving (1) cerebral activation during sleep and (2) dreaming. The first stage can take various forms, none of which is specific to dreaming itself, since reliable dissociations can be demonstrated between dreaming and all of these states (including REM). The second stage (dreaming itself) occurs only if and when the initial activation stage engages the dopaminergic circuits of the ventromesial forebrain."

27. Revonsuo (2004) sees dreams as having adaptive evolutionary value, but believes that the simulation of the current concerns of modern humans probably has little if any biological value. Our view differs in that we see dreams as generative of action plans, testing our working assumptions, putting the ucs through a reality loop (i.e. experimenting to allow better reality testing), and working through our fears, all of which have obvious psychobiological adaptive value as the self-organization grows.

CHAPTER TWO

Sleep and dreaming, Part 2: The importance of the SEEKING system for dream-related learning and the complex contributions to dreaming of memory mechanisms, transcription factors, sleep activation events, reentrant architecture, the anterior cingulate cortex (ACC), periaqueductal gray (PAG), and the centromedian nucleus of the thalamus (CNT)

Fred M. Levin, Colwyn Trevarthen, Tiziano Colibazzi, Juhani Ihanus, Vesa Talvitie, Jean K. Carney, and Jaak Panksepp[1]

"I like the talky talky happy talk/Talk about things you like to do/
You got to have a dream/ If you don't have a dream/
How you gonna have a dream come true?"
Rogers and Hammerstein (*South Pacific*)

Précis: In Chapter One we make use of the new model of dreaming as active, psychologically meaningful, and adaptive: a unique blend of mentation that integrates affective wishes and fears with cognitive concerns, while at the same time creating what we call "deferred action plans". These plans seem born in dreams where they help simulate what has been identified as potentially dangerous, and are activated later in waking life where they help us explore and reduce the dangers noted.

In Chapter Two we start with the SEEKING system (Panskepp, 1998) and elaborate its relevance for the study of dreaming, especially the effect of the dopamine related neural systems on the creation of predictive error signals, and the assignment of incentive salience (a state of both wanting something, and figuring out at the same time how best to get it) (Hyman, 2005). Along the way we attempt to integrate the contributions to dreaming of memory mechanisms, transcription factors, sleep activation events, reentrant architecture, and a variety of neuroanatomical subsystems and functions. Along with the VMFL and PTOCJ with their emerging importance for dreaming (see Chapter One), the other brain subsystems "of interest" as dream contributors include the anterior cingulate cortex (ACC), the periaqueductal gray (PAG), the centromedian nucleus of the thalamus (CNT), the cerebellum (CB), hypothalamus (HT), various basal ganglia and upper brainstem structures, and inferotemporal cortex (ITC) (supramarginal gyrus) (Yu, 2001). The amygdala (A) and hippocampus (H) are also important for processing dangerous stimuli perceived in the environment, and for processing or encoding the contextual features of emotional experience (Brendel et al. 2004). For example, the CB is critical for the coordination of thoughts and also actions, as well the prediction of events and assignments of their emotional meanings based upon need assessments (the research of Masao Ito, cited in Levin, 1991, 2003), while the ITC is important for connecting motivational systems and the visual cortex, including the tracking of meaningful objects in space. Because of space limitations, in Chapter Two we concentrate primarily on the ACC and PAG, and leave for later a more detailed consideration of the other brain systems noted.

Along with discussing the SEEKING system, we consider a role for pleasure in anticipation and the effect of dopamine on using perceptual information to motivate behaviors to obtain what we want and/or need (Panksepp, 1998, 2005a, 2005b; Hyman, 2005). We are well aware of the danger of plying our "net" too broadly in attempting to nail down how various brain subsystems

might influence dreaming. But given the complex underpinnings of dreams
it pays to speculate about possible relationships and mechanisms if we are to
construct a cogent and comprehensive theory of dreaming.

1. Introduction to the SEEKING system

I n our companion discussion (Chapter One) we describe the
roles of functional systems for learning and memory, for sleep
and dreaming, for the expression of the unconscious (ucs) in
fantasy,[2] for the detection of dangers or conflicts and their resolution,
and for the utilization of deferred action plans as a way of imple-
menting the evolutionary and personal requirements of protecting
our wishes and avoiding unnecessary risks. In Chapter Two we are
now ready to explore our sleep and dreaming model in more detail.

One way to deepen our model of dreaming is to introduce
readers to what Panksepp calls the SEEKING system. A significant
part of what we are considering in our two companion chapters
about dreaming could potentially be related to myriad details of
the SEEKING system as conceptualized by Panksepp over many
years (Panksepp, 1998, Chapter 8). Panksepp begins with a quotation from Oliver Sack's 1973 book *Awakenings* where Leonard L. feels
"saved, resurrected, reborn … a sense of Grace … like a man in love"
(Panksepp, 1998, p. 144). Previously Leonard L. had been trapped
in his body, in a brain without a fully functioning SEEKING system,
as the aftermath of the influenza-related Parkinsonism he suffered
in childhood during the Great Influenza Pandemic of 1918. Leonard
L's dopamine (DA) circuits were knocked out and had ceased to
function until Sacks tried him on L-DOPA, a precursor to DA. The
results were remarkable; Panksepp describes the SEEKING system
functions that returned for people like Leonard L. as follows:

> "Without DA, human aspirations remain frozen, as it were, in an
> endless winter of discontent. DA synapses resemble gatekeepers
> rather than couriers that convey detailed messages. When they are not
> active at their posts, many potentials of the brain cannot readily be
> manifested in thought or action. Without DA, only the strongest emo-
> tional messages instigate behavior. When DA synapses are active in
> abundance, a person feels as if he or she can do anything" (Panksepp,
> op. cit., p. 144). He continues: "These chemistries lead [us] to set out

energetically to investigate and explore [the] world, to seek resources and make sense of contingencies in [our] environment…[and] to extract meaning from our various circumstances" (p. 145). Panksepp feels that the SEEKING system, which is concentrated anatomically in the extended lateral hypothalamic (LH) corridor (p. 145), meets the most stringent neural criteria for defining a *basic emotional system*. By this he means that the SEEKING system (1) is innate and not dependent upon higher brain functions; (2) organizes behavior "by activating or inhibiting motor subroutines…that have proved adaptive in the face of life-challenging circumstances during the evolutionary history of the species" (p. 150); (3) this system is built so that emotive circuits change the sensory systems relevant for the behaviors that are aroused; for example, there can be more effective cortical arousal, in the hemisphere which is ipsilateral to the side of the stimulation[3]; (4) "neural activity of emotive systems [in the case of the SEEKING system] outlast the precipitating circumstances" (p. 150); (5) *the SEEKING system cells exhibit spontaneous learning,* and the ventral tegmental DA source cells "exhibit anticipatory learning during appetitive conditioning…" (Ibid.; italics added); and (6) "The emotive circuits have reciprocal interactions with brain mechanisms that elaborate higher decision-making processes and consciousness" (Ibid.).

The emotive power of this DA controlled system [although other neurotransmitters are also involved, as they are in many coordinated brain functions] is that it is not simply driven by "pleasure" but rather, *what is "pleasurable" is the energized state of psychic power and engagement in goal directed activities and the correlated-cognitive expectations that basic needs will be met when the system is properly functioning.* In other words, the SEEKING system is a built-in mechanism in man and animals for "foraging, exploration, investigation, curiosity, interest, [and] expectancy", one that "leads organisms to eagerly pursue the fruits of their environment—from nuts to knowledge, so to speak" (op. cit., p. 145). These energetic states of mind are tightly integrated with the spontaneous emergence of positive expectations about world events. Obviously, much of what we have just described for the SEEKING system, also applies to dreaming, and the ucs mind.

Reviewing the history of the SEEKING system, Panksepp makes clear (p. 151) the original assumption was that when experimental animals were observed to self administer electrical stimulation to their brains (ESB) within the lateral hypothalamic (LH) corridor, that they did so because the ESB was "activating brain reinforcement or consummatory pleasure processes. In fact, however, this assumption was wrong; rather, the observed behavior was really the primary reflection of the arousal of a built-in exploratory urge. Quoting Panksepp: "Just as the sea hare Aplysia ... goes into a search mode to find a stable footing when it is suspended in a tank of water, *all mammals go into a search mode when their bodies are hungry, thirsty, cold or desirous of social/sexual companionship*. Indeed, it is hard to imagine that an organism could survive if such an appetitive function was not well ingrained within its basic neural structure. *Since nature [does] not always provide the necessary resources for survival immediately at hand, each animal has a spontaneous tendency to explore and learn about its environment*" (op. cit., p. 151, italics added).

Two more introductory comments on the SEEKING system may help orient the reader to what follows about dreaming: (1) "there are now reasons to believe that forethoughts...do in fact emerge from the interactions of the SEEKING system with higher brain mechanisms, such as the frontal cortex and hippocampus, that generate plans by mediating higher-order temporal and spatial information processing. Indeed, circuits coursing through the LH can trigger hippocampal theta rhythm, which ... is an elemental signal of information processing in that structure. At the peak of the theta wave, there is a glutamate-induced strengthening of the hippocampal marker of learning known as long-term potentiation [LTP]. The hippocampus also has strong downward connections with the hypothalamus via the descending fiber bundle of the fornix (and these connections may convey cues from spatial maps to foraging impulses). Other projection zones of this system, such as those in the basal ganglia, also have strong downward influences onto the hypothalamic sources of the SEEKING system" (Panksepp, op. cit. pp. 152–153). And (2) the SEEKING system "responds not simply to positive incentives, but also to many other emotional challenges where animals must *seek* solutions" (op. cit., p 155).

Hyman's research (2005) completely supports Panksepp's viewpoint, making it clear that the dopamine effect on the nucleus acumbens (NA) enables the individual to use perceptual information about reward availability and contingencies to begin to plan appropriate actions for obtaining what is desired and/or needed.

Therefore, it would seem possible, based upon our theorizing in Chapter One, and the above considerations, to tie together the

SEEKING system and dreaming, that is, the neuroscientific perspective and the psychoanalytic perspective on dreams, as follows: (1) that dreaming is an emotionally meaningful experience and neither random nor a mere stimulus response; (2) that dream affective and cognitive activity has survival value; (3) that dreaming involves learning; and (4) that this learning likely expresses itself in action plans with adaptive value for individual and species. From the perspective of NP these propositions follow exactly because the SEEKING system overlaps with what we have already described (in Chapter One) as the MVFL system without which there would be no dreaming. So in describing dreaming, we are also describing in effect how the DA system of the LH is continuously preparing to find "supplies" in the environment which are important biologically and emotionally, and how it carefully anticipates dangers that might disturb their availability, and does so in real time. Moreover, psychoanalysts will recognize that what they have been describing in dreams as wishes, are closely related to basic mental states that we depend upon for survival biologically and psychologically, as is described so well in Panksepp's SEEKING system. And the neural distribution of this LH system, suggests which brain subsystems are therefore likely involved in dream mentation. With this integrating perspective in mind, we can now elaborate further upon our neuro-psychoanalytic view on dreaming.

II. Complications of learning and memory: Recalling events as memories or as reconstructions

In order to make some of the arguments from Chapter One more intelligible, it may help to provide further background on the subject of memory typolgy. As most readers may appreciate, some spontaneous early aspects of mental life are encoded as implicit memories—memories that are not easily remembered consciously and which generally do not involve conscious experience (Levin, 2004c). Unlike explicit memories that involve the hippocampus and neocortex of each hemisphere, plus supporting structures such as the amygdala and mammilary bodies, implicit memories are more critically dependent upon the basal ganglia and the CB. And, as noted, these memories (implicit) have to do with "knowing how"[4] to accomplish something, rather than merely remembering facts ("knowing that" something is so).

That implicit memories are not rememberable as such, however, does not mean that they cannot be recovered. In fact, they can be recalled in the following manner: First they express themselves in transferences, dreams, free association patterns, slips, and various observable action patterns and associated feeling states. Second, they can be primed by various means. For example, once the various component parts of important implicit memories are primed, and these fragments identified and catalogued as it were (by which we mean, once they come to be at least partially understood within explicit memory systems), they can then be reconstructed like the pieces of a puzzle that are potentially rearrangeable into a unique and intelligible pattern (Levin, 2004c; Mancia, 2003; Talvitie & Ihanus, 2002). Of course, this kind of "reconstruction" of implicit memories into explicit memory formatting is a common event during virtually every psychoanalysis. Such reconstructions can then be confirmed or disconfirmed by the presence or absence of collateral testimony or other evidence, internal consistency or the lack thereof, etc.

Why are the above comments on implicit memory important to this discussion of dreaming? The priming of implicit memory, as through action, is another way of appreciating our hypothesis that dreams are learning facilitators by way of their connection to action planning. Namely, dreams lead to a variety of possible useful outcomes. For instance, action plans can lead to actions, which may help prime ucs (implicit) memories, which may in turn facilitate the critical reconstructions of past events, as well as insights associated with these reconstructions.[5] During analysis such reconstructions often need (at first) another person (the analyst, as primer) for their successful discovery; however, after an analysis, individuals learn that they have acquired the capacity to carry out such analysis by themselves, or in tandem with someone other than their analyst, or via the mental imaging of another person (as a kind of internalized "Muse"). Of course, there is no reason to assume that the only way to learn psychologically about the ucs is via psychoanalysis. But for many of us, analysis has substantially facilitated our psychological growth and development (including the priming of highly relevant personal memories), because it is an approach that facilitates the overcoming of emotionally defensive resistances to insight, psycho-logical development, and to change in general.

One final comment about the explicit/implicit dichotomy: the explicit and implicit memory systems are quite complementary and obviously intimately interconnected, even though it may well be that it is mostly the implicit system that is involved in the disturb-ing aspects of dreams (the parts that worry us, and "keep us awake at night"). We further believe that such implicit memories pervade dreaming extensively, and certainly contribute greatly to human adaptation while expressing our unconscious wishes and fears. However, for now it remains a major challenge to envision how the products of implicit memories are so pervasive in our lives, our minds and brains, while remaining much less "visible" to the expe-riencing self. Perhaps through an interweaving of the complicated "tapestry" of dreams and neuropsychology, we can better appreciate how adaptive learning is served through hidden action planning that may emerge from dreamwork. In the final chapters of this book we will tie implicit and explicit systems together in a much more satis-factory manner around the CB capacity to make models. In essence, this will involve showing that explicit and implicit systems can take "snapshots" of each other, and combine these two great memory systems.

III. *Reentrant architecture[6] and further complexities*

The brain's reentrant architechture, according to some, invalidates some arguments about the neurodynamic "origination" of dreams, since dreams could only be the product of complex continuously interactive systems. Moreover, the same critics argue that seeing "arousal" frequently correlated with the highly distributed brain-stem and reticular regions begs many questions about how the reticular activating system underwrites conscious states and inte-grated activity in the forebrain. But before one gets involved in such thinking one needs to be very careful about how one decides what is controlling what in the brain. Nevertheless, our preference here is to believe that the Solms' updated view of dreams facilitates a more productive form of thinking in this arena, as when they describe the new neuroanatomy of dreaming as we report their work on Sleep and Dreaming in Chapter One, in particular, the importance of the medial ventral frontal lobe (MVFL) and the parietal temporal occipital cortical junction (PTOCJ).

In particular, Watt (2003) describes how *the brainstem, thalamus, and multiple forebrain regions communicate with each other via reentrant architecture, thus making it unreasonable to think of one area controlling the others*; rather, the multiple component regions need to be seen as highly interactive systems, that function more like "committees" that sometimes produce products quite different than what might be expected by examining their "chair-person". This is certainly true for routine activities, but as we shall see later, it is not the case for matters of particular concern, where errors are not permitted. In addition, the evidence suggests that the dreaming contents of REM sleep are actually controlled more by the lateral hypothalamic SEEKING system (which monitors our sleep debt just as much as it monitors our other homeostatic needs) than by the pontine REM generators. Yet there appears to be no doubt that multiple brainstem regions shift in various ways, again pivoting, so to speak, around a complex set of poorly understood axes, to initiate the various global state shifts involved in all the stages of sleep, which obviously influence dreaming.[7]

It should be obvious from the above statements, integrating our understanding of dreams can be most difficult and costly in areas where each specialty viewpoint is struggling to adequately describe its state-of-the-art thinking. Yet in spite of knowledge limitations, we believe that the model of dreaming we are presenting actually fits the facts quite well, and in particular, strongly suggests that *action plans and dreams are directly related*. Second, we feel our assumption that *such plans carry out an adaptive function together, namely, facilitating our learning about dangers*,[8] has of course also been well developed and confirmed by the research of Revonsuo et al.. After all, what good would it be to have unconscious wishes if they were never enacted, even in substitute or semi-disguised forms? Here we would argue that such actions are basically functioning as tests of working assumptions, probes for the discovery of dangers and pleasures, and a means of appreciating affectively what we want, what we need, and what is truly indifferent to us. Given a clear knowledge of wishes and needs, we can begin, as stated above, to make plans for reducing the dangers (and conflicts) in our lives. However, to round out our understanding of what dreams are accomplishing, we need to further consider the functional contribution of specific brain areas that contribute to dreamwork.

IV. *The Anterior Cingulate Cortex (ACC)*

As we noted in Chapter One (citing Izquerdo & Cammarota et al.) the hippocampus and ACC are needed for the retrieval of memories associated with contextual fear conditioning. Frankland et al. (2004) show the ACC is particularly crucial for retrieval of remote fear memory which is accompanied by an increase in Zif/268 and the production of another activity dependent gene, c-fos, in the ACC and other brain areas. Obviously, there are many neuronal growth and gene transcription factors, and many protein pathways that need to be considered before any reasonably comprehensive understanding of dreaming can be achieved (Riva, et al. 2005).

As for how action planning actually comes about, there is good reason to believe that during dreams, input to the supplementary motor area (SMA) from both sensory associative areas and from the ACC (Ito, cited in Levin, Gedo, Ito, & Trevarthen, 2003, Chapter 9, p. 195) is decisive because in this way allowance is made for two critical inputs, namely, sensory and emotional signals "… as [expected] instruction signals for [later] voluntary movement" (op. cit.), that is, for "prospective control".[9] Moreover, it is well known that movement is attenuated during sleep,[10] so actions that are contemplated during dreams necessarily are deferred. On this basis one could postulate that while our dreams are taking place in their characteristic forms during sleep, information from sensory input and emotional longings are entering into the imaginative planning for future actions that are, we assume, based upon originally ucs wishes, detached from somatic and visceral regulation.[11] And, of course, "actions" in our dream world simulate what might happen in the external world.

A further word about the role of the ACC seems in order. The ACC is part of a circuit that involves a form of attention that regulates both cognitive and emotional processing. Anatomically and functionally, the ACC has been conceptualized as an interface between limbic structures such as the amygdala, higher order cortices such as the dorsolateral prefrontal cortex (DLPFC), the mediolateral prefrontal cortex (MLPFC), and the hypothalamus. It has also been show that different regions of the ACC are activated by different tasks. Busch et al. have cogently reviewed studies supporting the functional segregation of the ACC into ventral affective and more dorsally located cognitive subdivisions (vACC versus dACC). The affective division is activated by emotion-related tasks and so-called "symptom provocation studies". The cognitive division handles stimulus-response selection in the face of conflicting information (Busch et al. 2000).

According to current conflict-resolution theory, the ACC (more specifically its dorsal portion) detects and signals conflicts in information processing (Botvinick, Nystrom, Carter, & Cohen, 1999), allowing compensatory adjustments in cognitive control (Botvinick, Cohen, & Carter, 2004). The ACC may also be involved in evaluating error-likelihood, i.e. the predicted likelihood of an error in response to a given task (Brown & Braver, 2005). Therefore, along with the CB, the ACC seems to play a crucial role in handling conflicting streams of information, detecting errors and discrepancies, and in anticipating errors or likely mismatches between behaviors and intended goals even before the errors have occurred. In addition, and as an aside, attention allocation within the posterior cingulate may well be responsible for reduced performance on executive tasks, as is evident in those with ADHD (Rubia, Smith, Brammer, et al. 2005). As Rubia et al. indicate, citing Mesalum et al. (2001) *the cingulate cortex may thus be an important neural interface between attention and motivation.*

Thus, given its central role in information processing and behavioral adaptation, it is not surprising that the ACC has been shown over the past decade to be relevant to mood states in general, and to depression in particular (Mayberg, et al. 1999; Bench et al. 1992; George et al. 1997). Clinical phenomenology associated with cingulate seizures and tumors further supports *a role for vACC in the regulation of mood* (Mayberg et al. 1999; Bench et al. 1992; George et al. 1997).

Based upon the above considerations, we believe the ACC plays an important role in the learning we are discussing in relation to dreams. If dreaming is a way that the brain creates deferred action plans to deal with dangers, then the role of the cingulate gyrus could possibly be as follows: the ACC would mediate conflict resolution between one set of automatized solutions and another set that is less automatized (and possibly more creative). In this case, decreased cingulate function could be reflected in one not being able to suppress more automatic responses, that is, getting cognitively "stuck". It may also play a role in the tolerance seen in dreams for opposites (a reflection of a unique kind of conflict non-resolution, or patience, depending upon one's point of view).[12] Indeed, dreams may just be one way that the mind/brain goes through various action planning configurations" simulating different patterns of activation in an attempt to resolve conflict between mind/brain areas and between incoming data sets. The cingulate cortex may be a central node for facilitating and coordinating such activities.

It is also possible that the bias towards actions when rewards are expected, is balanced by a complex system that complements the action impulse (Ikemoto & Panksepp, 1999), and works out alternatives (to action) when events are detected that do not appear as expected (i.e. are not propitious of success, or, where there is more than a suggestion of failure and complications) (Minamoto, Hori, & Kimura, 2005). These same authors suggest that under such contingencies, the complex decision balancing system involves the striatum, limbic system, and cerebral cortex, in tandem with the centromedian nucleus of the thalamus (CNT) and basal ganglia (in other words, a thalamostriatal projection and cortico-basal ganglia loops). This would then allow for the balancing of the midbrain dopamine signals (biased towards actions) with a complementary process "mediated by signals transmitted by [CNT] efferents" (Minamimoto, Hori, & Kimura, 2005, p. 1800).

We would further suggest a role for a coordination of higher cortical centers, along with the lower centers including the pons. It seems obvious that there must be an integration between the highest cortical levels of cognitive activity, with their refined evaluation of self-in-the-world, complex conflicts, narcissistic-equilibria, balancing of emotion and psychological insights, and the effectiveness of the so-called lower systems, particularly those in the dispersed limbic system (see below) which focus on much the same things but likely from a more intensely emotional perspective (see Greenberg, 1999, 2003; Panksepp, 1985, 1998, 2003, 2005; Panksepp & Burgdorf, 2003; Shevrin & Eiser, 2003; Shevrin, et al. 1996; Solms & Turnbull, 2002). In other words, dreaming could not be as adaptive as we believe it to be, nor the experience of it as beautiful, scary, and profound, without a comprehensive and vast physiological and neurochemical integration across brain systems. On the one hand, we can respect both the pons for its cholinergic generation of REM sleep and its associated assist for memory consolidation, and on the other, as noted earlier, we can respect the SEEKING system for its dopaminergic dream-facilitation contribution[13] from meso-limbic mesocortical areas including the VTA on up, ultimately including the highest cortical areas with their contribution relating to dream contents, associations from a life history and future plans, etc. Obviously, we need many parts of our brain working together to create one so-called "simple" dream.

V. *The Periaqueductal Gray (PAG)*

At this point, it may further our understanding of the neural control of movement, affect, and other relevant variables involved in dreaming, to comment on the PAG. Research demonstrates that the PAG "plays an essential role in making emotion an active motoric process" (Watt, 2003, p. 106; see also Panksepp, 1998, especially Fig. 16.1). What exactly does this mean?

First of all, the PAG is closer to the bottom of the staggeringly complex concatenation of systems in the brain contributing to instinctual actions. Such integrated movements involve literally a symphony of systems, such that any definitive treatment of action programs has yet to be written. Although the PAG plays a role in making emotion an active motoric process, we do not attribute to it any role in planning, which has to do with much more dorsally and rostrally placed cortical systems.[14] What we mean by "plays a role" in emotional movement is the idea of a kind of primitive "motor gating" function. In essence, differential columnar activation of several columns within the PAG may be what distinguishes the various prototype emotional states from each other as we experience them (see below). The resulting differential activations appear to somehow link to pontine and other brainstem motor systems (possibly other reticular activating subsystems as well), such that when we are frightened we either freeze, run like hell, and avoid sexuality and other consummatory delights; when we are sufficiently angry we attack; when we are sad we have distress vocalizations but never attack; and when we are playful we engage in wrestling and tickling, etc. but rarely freeze or run away.

Overall, the PAG mainly constrains the state space of the motor system in fundamental ways, such that angry behaviors are virtually never available when we're playful, and playful behaviors disappear when we're angry.[15] Positive states may involve differential activation of 4 or 5 more columns within the PAG than negative states. The latter also typically involve more dorsal PAG activation. In other words, the prototype states most activated determine which "large domains" within the total "affective movement state space" we are going to land in, and what large group of behaviors will become increasingly available as a result.

The PAG receives (recruits?) all kinds of inputs from upper brainstem, diencephalic and basal forebrain systems, and based upon this input somehow (for want of a better word) "computes" which primary affective action state best fits those inputs. Then, in conjunction, perhaps with several other systems, the PAG participates in the appropriate motor, reticular and monoamnergic adjustments. This is another way of saying the PAG is "part of" the regulation of a number of basic emotional processes, including social behavioral regulations. Massive lesions of the system knock out emotion in the brain, and this is true for most all animals (including primates and humans) suggesting that its operations are essential for valence and for other primitive core components of emotion (Watt, 2003).

To complete our comments on the PAG, particular emotional states likely activate or are components of an enormous range of potentially associated actions based on our personal history, and each of those potential actions in turn "tickle" brain emotional systems in various ways including orbital frontal cortical systems. The result is the generation of a vast "internal array" of felt or anticipated consequences or "outcome potentials". Further selection or editing of prospective actions (behavioral outputs) probably comes at this stage, and orbital frontal systems "thin" or "trim" the initial array of behavioral options because a large number of them have contingencies in our history that make us feel that they are likely dangerous. We suspect that this is exactly the problem we are modeling in our work with the fascinating dream analysis of Darlene (described in Chapter One, our companion chapter), where she is reworking her contingency space of independent initiatives, while worrying at the same time about not violating the wishes of a powerful authority figure. An interesting question here is the role that orbital frontal systems might have in dreaming, a subject for which Solms' research (1997, 2003) has great relevance.

If our neuroscientific reasoning is on the right track to this point, then we might imagine that analytically dreams have the potential for setting up future actions which, no matter how neutral they may look when they occur in the real world, are clandestinely expressing emotional wishes stemming from the feeling states in our dynamic ucs. In this way, fantasizing or dreaming has the potential to disguise our true intentions while also covertly carrying our dream life and our concerns about safety into the "reality" of our waking life. Obviously, this would involve many real and potential emotional/motor reaction patterns, as described above, and favor adaptation by the creation of plans which provide probes (potential actions) and response patterns for further analysis of and mitigation of dangers.

Of course, each psychoanalytic session is generally set up to limit the completion of most enactments beyond a trivial level, and to thus set individuals up for learning from uncompleted rather than completed impulses. Before psychoanalysis came about, mental enactments probably supported our need to try out various possibilities in action, but hopefully, not carry them too far. In other words, actions of ucs origin attempt to satisfy wishes in real relations, but without insight as to their emotional or interpersonal complexity or origin. But we are arguing here that alongside enactments (so-called acting out and acting in) are also "actions pure and simple", where the goal is an important one, and where the action constitutes a potentially adaptive and valuable learning experience in itself, through which danger is actually reduced over time.

Another way of putting our idea is to say that actions can sometimes serve as a means of putting our ucs through a reality loop or check. (i.e. by means of "carrying them out" or "releasing them" within some limited contexts).

VI. *Summary and conclusions*

In Chapter One, we present the modern model of dreaming worked out by Solms, and others, as a meaningful, adaptive, proactive learning process. Our contribution is to note (1) how dreams explore and mitigate possible dangers, and (2) how dreaming creates deferred action plans which when carried out in later waking life, serve as the step-wise mechanism by which dangers are minimized, eliminated, or maladaptive approaches corrected in time to avoid disasters. The neuroscientific evidence from the new model of sleep and dreaming allows more integration of psychoanalytic and neuroscientific thinking on dreaming than envisioned during the past century.

In Chapter One we discuss neuro-psychoanalytic perspectives to round out the theory we are presenting by applying what is known about the SEEKING system to dreaming. We then go into more detail about possible relationships and complex mechanisms within the mind and brain. We cover the importance of recalling events as memories vs. reconstruction, the significance of the reentrant architechture of the mind/brain, and possible roles in dreaming for various parts of the mind/brain, especially including the ACC, CNT, and PAG.

We explain that although implicit memories are not rememberable as such, that this does not mean they are irretrievable by other means. We describe how such retrieval can be achieved, focusing upon the conversion of bits and pieces of implicit memory, glimpsed from various priming events, or identified via tracking patterns of free association, dreaming patterns, mental slips, transferences, and the like, which are then finally placed into something akin to a psychoanalytic "reconstruction" based upon matching up the "snap shots" taken by explicit memory of the above components of implicit memory "elements". Such reconstructions can of course later be confirmed or disconfirmed by various kinds of external evidence or independent testimony. This series of steps is important because dreams often contain meaningful information as implicit memories, which needs to be properly decoded by the dreamer before he or she can understand the dream's deeper-level meaning(s) and achieve further insights. So the decoding of implicit memory, we believe, is one of the critical steps in identifying what is intuitively identified as possibly dangerous; in this manner various dangers are placed under a mental "microscope" during dreams. Thereby, deferred action(s), executed after the dreamer awakens, may allow individuals to investigate dangers proactively so as to protect the self more effectively.

Our discussion on reentrant architecture and other complexities highlighted the issue of brainstem vs. forebrain regarding dreaming origination. There seems to be a consensus that we need to be cautious about deciding prematurely that one area vs. another is controlling some process when we know quite well how much the brain is constructed of interactive elements organized into subsystems that themselves dovetail with still larger system units, and ultimately even into super-systems.[16] Nevertheless, if we hesitate to make reasonable speculations about the possible contributions of the various elements in any larger system how could we make progress in understanding the highly complex subject of dream and sleep relations? This is why we have focused in Chapter Two of our essay on the contributions to dreaming from particular subunits.

In the section on the ACC we focus primarily on the ACC's dual role in retrieving memories for contextual fear conditioning events. Obviously, the ACC has different sub-regions, some devoted more to cognition, the others for emotion, with various intermediary levels of integration. We describe these differences between the vACC (for affect evaluation) and the dACC (for cognition) and the connections with other participating structures: the amygdala (involved in fear conditioning), higher order cortices such as the DLPFC and MLPFC, and the hypothalamus. Based upon our review of the literature, we believe the ACC is critical to the learning that is linked to dreaming.[17] More specifically, we think its position as part of the executive control network enables the ACC to mediate conflicts (especially those in which there is a bias towards actions) by sometimes suppressing automatic response patterns or in encouraging tolerance (a kind of creative conflict non-resolution). We have described how this may involve circuits balancing midbrain dopamine signals with a loop involving the ACC, CNT, basal ganglia, cerebral cortex, and limbic system. In other words, sometimes, as in dreaming, we let something happen without taking immediate action, and as a result we allow a moment or two for reflection, or deferred action. The latter, from our current perspective, needs to be elaborated in a number of significant ways. It is possible the ACC coordinates these kinds of mental activities and thereby helps facilitate planning for the successful resolution of various perceived threats.

Our section on the PAG is important for our overall model because the PAG is known to play an important role in regulating essentially all basic emotional responses. Most important, PAG regulation of emotion is determined in relation to our personal history to which the PAG has access in its decision-making contributions. This would appear to make the PAG an important element in the decision-making that relates to appreciating possible dangers, and determining the most expeditious way to test these out in the future, and thus improve our judgments about safety.

To summarize, dreams allow satisfaction in fantasy, but also help us deal with potential dangers in reality; more precisely, dreams may help reduce what is maladaptive during waking behavior. There are good reasons to believe that the learning occurring during and after dreaming[18] essentially involves dream simulations of situations to determine the exact nature of dangers, which help us decide how best to deal with them in waking life. This simulation-related learning seems itself to depend to some significant degree on the formation of deferred action plans spawned during the dream. Our provisional conclusion is that dreams, together with their plans for deferred actions, ultimately result in learning about potential solutions for various specific danger situations, which, if successful, would explain the adaptive evolutionary function of dreaming (see also Revonsuo,[19] 2000).

Of course, the fact that dreams may also protect sleep and provide some degree of ucs fantasy satisfaction should not be downplayed. It is just that we do not know precisely all that these ucs functions accomplish, and thus they deserve continuing investigation. But that dreams might well include deferred action plans seems particularly important in helping to explain how learning in relation to dreaming occurs. In our estimation, the essence seems to hinge on the following: (1) dreaming represents for the psyche the possibility of expressing deep ucs wishes and fears; it is especially important for (2) the priming of implicit memories involved ontogenetically and phylogenetically in critical decision making; (3) implicit memories are latently present in many of our actions (transference, free association, and other spontaneous behavior); (4) when the action planning created by our dreams is no longer deferred, the ucs wishes are carried into reality to varying degrees; (5) these actions have a dual purpose: they are partial satisfactions in themselves, and they further serve as experiments that stimulate reality testing, working through of neurotic and reality based fears, the recall (via priming) and reconstruction of past events; and (6) such action plans generally facilitate learning about our deepest hopes and fears, in personally meaningful contexts, thus satisfying the built-in requirements expressed by the SEEKING system of helping us obtain important goals without damaging ourselves too excessively. In our estimation, research on the SEEKING system goes a long way towards clarifying what dreams are about, and what subsystems of the mind/brain are likely involved in their genesis. In this view, the privileged role of REM in the arousal of dreaming is not disputed, nor is the possibility of dreaming without the energization of the REM-sleep process.

Notes

1. Thanks also to Jhuma Basak, Alice B. Colonna, Patrizia Giampieri-Deutsch, Eric Johnson, Carlos Macedo, David Olds, Jorge Schneider, David Terman, Douglas F. Watt, and Arnold Wilson for their useful commentary on this chapter. The authors, however, take sole responsibility for this chapter's final form.

2. Fantasy is "a product of mental activity which…represents an attempt at the fulfillment of a wish…[It] represents one form of thinking and so is a normal concomitant of the development of the mental apparatus. It [further] serves [as]…preparation for realistic action appropriate to the requirements of the environment" (Moore & Fine, 1968).

3. See Levy and Trevarthen (1976) where they describe "metacontrol" involving channeling processes and consciousness between hemispheres, even sometimes without regard to the special processing competence of the selected half of the cortex. Also see G. Klein, 1974.

4. In German "wissen wie" vs. "wissen das" ("knowing how" vs. "knowing that"). Obviously both systems are needed for either to work.

5. Another consideration on actions: We don't remember how we do things so expertly in the moment of doing them, but we can become aware of how better to attend to such events, so as to learn how to do them better the next time, or even, how best to teach such skills to others (see also Rogoff et. al., 2003, for her "intent participation model of learning").

6. The term "reentrant" describes a system in which a large number of functions have concurrent access to the computational product. This has been applied to computers and nervous systems.

7. A complication here is how much of visceral regulation is altered during sleep. For example, we know that 30 second autonomic cycles

of heart rate and respiration continue in sleep, and one of us (CT) has even related this timing of an intrinsic activity cycle to the ordinary childhood "feeling" of narrative time, e.g. in the verse of a song shared by infant and mother (Delamont et al. 1999; Trevarthen, 2003).

8. Donald (1991, 2001) (see also Levin, 1991, 2003) makes clear that day dreaming and "auto-cuing" are also important to learning, as man passed through stages, first learning as H. Erectus did, mimetically (pre-symbolically), and only later on in modern humans, utilizing a "theoretic mind".

9. "Prospective control" means control guided by sensory input so that action already takes knowledge of the world into account in making plans, and this principle of control is formulated by "tau" theory (Lee, 1998). Studies at the University of Edinburgh by Delafield-Butt, as yet unpublished, examine whether Paramecia use perception-in-action forms of motor control (also see Herrick, 1948; Trevarthen, 1986).

10. We refer here to pontine atonia that inhibits actual movement, but action, and some basic experience of movement, presumably based on intact proprioceptive ability while dreaming, nonetheless remains critical to the dreaming phenomenology.

11. There is no space for a full discussion of consciousness (cs) which is relevant to the discussion of emotion, so the reader is referred to Porges (2003), for his "polyvagal theory" which deals with the evolution of special visceral efferents for communication of emotions. By this account cs originated when the brain evolved from reptilian to mammalian structure; reptiles were reactive, mammals are proactive (consider also our similar comments on Panksepp's SEEKING system).

12. Here too, as in the case of the DLPFC, the ACC contribution seems to us involving some "detached/disengaged" orientation and regulation.

13. Panksepp (1998) also makes clear glutamate, GABA, and other neurotransmitters play a role in the SEEKING system. The arousal of the DA during REM sleep has recently been demonstrated (Lena et al. 2005).

14. If we would ask how lower vertebrates manage, and whether they need forebrain and diencephalic activation of plans, our answer would be "probably".

15. An interesting question that we cannot currently answer, is how the PAG connects to the special visceral efferent nuclei (face and voice) and the motor nuclei for the hands.

16. One contributor to the problem of identifying system elements as contributory to particular functions is the existence of neuronal coherence (NC) (Schoffelen, Oostenveld, & Fries, 2005). NC is when neuronal

groups interact with each other even if they are widely separated because one group modulates its internal oscillatory frequency to synchronize with and thus influence another group on the basis of cognitive demand. So proximity is not the only pointer to connectedness.

17. One of us (FML) has written extensively on a corresponding role for the cerebellum (CB), amygdala (A) and hippocampus (H). The CB is involved in the resolution of conflict in relation to the core self, and in the anticipation and prediction of events There is no doubt that a discussion of these additional three areas would be needed to round out our discussion of the management of affect in the face of dangers (please consult Levin, 2003a, 2003b for elaboration on these contributions, which is beyond the scope of this chapter).

18. Walker (2005) discusses learning within sleep, but does so without acknowledging that such sleep involves dreaming (and thus emotions, adaptation, and integration at cortical as well as limbic levels); Greenberg (2005) politely points out this overly cognitive approach of Walker.

19. Revonsuo (2004) sees dreams as having adaptive evolutionary value, but believes that the simulation of the current concerns of modern humans probably has little if any biological value. Our view differs in that we see dreams as generative of action plans, testing our working assumptions, putting our ucs through a reality loop (i.e. experimenting to allow better reality testing), and working through our fears, all of which have obvious biological adaptive value.

PART II

EMOTION: TOWARDS UNDERSTANDING ITS PLACE AND PURPOSE IN MIND/BRAIN

CHAPTER THREE

A neuro-psychoanalytic theory of emotion, Part 1: The basis for a serious interdisciplinary approach, or, how we are trying to clarify the ways brain and mind create each other.[1]

Fred M. Levin

Précis: This chapter builds upon Chapters One and Two on "emotion". The word is so common it is surprising to begin to define it, and to thereby become objective about such an important part of our subjectivity! Yet this careful thoughtful approach of NP is that which not uncommonly tries to re-examine mind/brain phenomena that appear self-evident but are not. This is especially critical if we are to properly appreciate mental phenomena scientifically. Moreover, in spite of the fact that the approaches of psychoanalysis and of neuroscience are often different, it seems to this author that there is still a large common ground between these disciplines, and thus the hope of integrating studies of mind and brain.

I. *Introduction*

I n the year 1999, volume 1, number 1 of the journal *Neuro-Psy-choanalysis* appeared. With this inaugural issue dedicated to the subject of emotion, it is hard to think of a subject more central to psychoanalysis, as well as neuroscience. This remarkable new journal, edited by Edward Nersessian and Mark Solms, has, in my opinion, played a major role in helping those scholars interested in both neuroscience and psychoanalysis create a serious venue for the integration of research on mind and brain. It will pay to review what was written in the beginning regarding interdisciplinary approaches.

In what follows I first present the essence of the following contributions from the inaugural issue of NP noted above: (1) Solms' and Nersessian's target article on "Freud's theory of affect: Questions for neuroscience"; and (2) Panksepp's target article on "Emotions as viewed by psychoanalysis and neuroscience: An exercise in consilience". Then in Chapter Four I review those articles following the first two articles in the inaugural issue, which include important commentaries by Antonio Damasio, Andre Green, Joseph LeDoux, Allan Schore, Howard Shevrin, and Clifford Yorke.

II. *Solms and Nersessian*

In their article Solms and Nersession describe how Freud believed in the centrality of emotions, as expressive of the state of the experiencing subject's inner needs (drives), seen as either frustrated or satisfied. Freud's famous so-called "pleasure principle" thus becomes the context for appreciating how mental events are regulated, and invariably set in motion by frustration, where keeping the level (quantity) of unpleasurable tension as low as possible becomes the goal. From this core perspective, pleasure flows from the successful meeting of inner needs and is uniformly associated with the reduction of drive tension; whereas pain is associated with the lack of success and invariably results from increasing drive tension (frustration). Solms and Nersessian state that "this feedback of affect…modifies (motivates) [all of] the subsequent behavior of the individual" (p. 5), and this is the adaptive value or evolutionary advantage of emotion.

Solms and Nersessian next ask specifically, how emotions are understood by neuroscience? The answer begins with an idea: "perhaps the most fundamental of Freud's ideas about affect is the notion that felt emotions are a conscious *perception* of something which is, in itself, unconscious" [by which they mean non-conscious, rather than something descriptively (dynamically) unconscious in the Freudian sense] (p. 5). As noted above, the qualities of pleasure are obviously measured in degrees of pleasure and unpleasure. But such perceptual experience, is, according to Solms and Nersessian, importantly different from the qualia of the sensory modalities (e.g. vision, hearing, touch); that is to say, emotions do not appear to be triggered by external events by themselves, but rather as a subjective response to a complex endopsychic situation (the state of the person). But if feelings represent the state of the person, what does this state consist of neuroscientifically? And what brain systems or structures are necessarily involved in such conscious perceptual experience?

It is no accident that Solms and Nersession begin with Freud's reference to an unconscious, which when referring to the dynamic unconscious, is probably the sine qua non of psychoanalysis. By constructing his definition of emotion as he does, Freud is obviously implying the presence of a psychodynamic unconscious in relation to the fundamental importance of drives. But Solms and Nersessian appear intent on moving stepwise from a descriptive consideration of the perception of feelings, to the deeper question of what is the nature of emotion from a multidisciplinary perspective (read this as a neuroscientific perspective). It should be obvious then that by closely following Freud's seminal articles introducing his ideas on drive theory, these authors show that Freud never specifies precisely what the neural mechanisms are for the system he is describing. Obviously, Freud's reason is not hard to guess: neuroscience had not developed sufficiently enough during Freud's day to allow him to do more than speculate on the biology, so he used an evocative language that skirted this limitation, and speculated as only he could, elegantly describing the signaling effects of forbidden or conflictual emotions (which eventually come into the awareness of the experiencing self, as well as to the awareness of participating others (see below for an elaboration on this theme). One colorful way of putting this was his description that affects are "oscillations in the tension of [hidden] instinctual needs" (p. 6). Consider also the following quotation: "It is the therapeutic technique [of psychoanalysis] alone that is purely psychological; the theory does not by any means fail to point out that neuroses have an organic [meaning, a neurochemical, neuroanatomical] basis" (Freud, 1905, cited on p. 7, Solms & Nersessian, 1999). Moreover, it becomes clear from the citation used by the authors that Freud was thinking specifically of sexuality, and this included a presumption that would later prove correct, though was not documentable during his day, that sexual hormones exist that play important roles in our sexual drives.

But where are Solms and Nersessian headed? I believe they are aiming at three critical ideas. The first is the notion, as they describe it, that "... the state dependent functions of the cortex [which they note Freud believed were critically involved in the perceptual/conscious (Pcpt.-Cs.) system, and thus likely the sense organ for emotional perception, (p. 6)] are modulated by endogenous [?implicit memory] processes. We are referring to the pivotal role that is increasingly assigned to *peptides* and *hormones*, which unlike the classical neurotransmitter systems [they have already discussed], partly influence brain activity through nonnervous circulatory mechanisms which seem to create an unexpectedly direct link between the brain and the body ..." (p. 8). For this latter idea they credit Damasio (1994).

They continue: "It would therefore be important for us to know what role quantitative variations in these endogenous secretory processes [i.e. chemical processes, as postulated by Freud] play in the neuromodulation of affective processes. Of course, as they note, we now know that emotional processes within the brain give rise to chemical modulation for the body via numerous pathways, for example, the hypothalamic pituitary adrenal axis, and that the endocrine target organs (including the gonads) themselves produce chemicals (hormones) which in turn feeback on the brain [hypothalamus] and body itself. A second example of such a regulatory system would be our modern knowledge of the emotional activation of selective attention, leading to cytokines acting as transcription factors, leading to the activation of the genes for producing new synapses on demand. As everyone knows, Eric Kandel won the Nobel Prize for his work on short-term memory (STM), and along the way solved the problem of long-term memory (LTM) as well, that is, for understanding the neuroscientific basis for explicit memory.

The second major idea is that "affective perceptions release ide-omotor patterns of discharge [which are usually called the expression of the emotions]" (p. 9), with complex interactive communicative implications for the experiencing subject and those relating to him or her. Solms and Nersessian call our attention here to Freud's sense of both quantitative and qualitative aspects of mental functioning in the area of emotions, wondering if these distinctions have a neurological equivalent. Their first approximation is to state the equivalence might be that the quantitative dimension possibly correlates neurologically with the differential degree of neuronal activation, while the qualitative dimension might correlate best with differences in neuronal connectivity. This, they note is similar to Mesulam's (1985) distinction between "channel" and "state" functions of the brain, where "channel" functions would be "the modalities of external perception and the various representational processes derived from them (e.g. memory and cognition)" (p. 8), while the "state" functions would include emotions themselves together with the internal perception of emotions. They conclude: "since these two aspects of consciousness are mediated by two different anatomical and physiological systems (namely, the relatively discrete modality-specific and relatively diffuse nonspecific systems, respectively), this distinction might have some considerable bearing on our quest for putative anatomical and physiological correlates of Freud's affect theory" (p. 8).

Obviously, Solms and Nersessian have concluded that affect perception is linked to the modality of nonspecific nuclei and other neuromodulatory mechanisms which regulate state dependent functions of the cortex (p. 8). In a footnote they state more specifically, that the core brain nuclei that produce the circuits of neurotransmitters such as serotonin, acetyl choline, norepinephrine, and dopamine deserve study, as do their projections to the cortical surface, which are in each case extensive, finally including as well "many limbic, paralimbic, and heteromodal cortical areas" (p. 8). Solms and Nersessian's roadmap is clear.

It may help to emphasize that the ideomotor discharge patterns noted above are conceptualized as stereotyped in our species, and in this sense "[they] define the various basic emotions" (see also the work of Darwin (1858, 1862/1899, 1871), Tomkins (1962a, 1962b; Tomkins, Smith, & Demos, 1995), and Basch (1983) on this same subject). Of course, Solms and Nersessian also make clear to others what the experiencing subject might be feeling. So the next question, the third and final major idea of their paper deals with questions relating to the neuro-psychoanalytic basis for the expression, inhibition, and general management of affects.

In their conclusion, the authors remind us that Freud thought of thinking as experimental action (and surely this applies to his theory of dreaming as well, since dreams most often involve thought during REM sleep). The critical corollary is that experiments, such as thinking in place of taking immediate action, from the authors' perspective, obviously involve some "taming of affect"[2] (p. 10). In other words, psychological defenses are involved, as well as a working through process. And when these processes are less than successful, and affect escapes, psychopathology can, in the authors' opinion, occur as a means of containing thoughts, behavior, and further affect from becoming public, or coming into awareness (p. 10) where it might provoke reactions. Naturally Solms and Nersessian make reference to how control over impulsivity and affective inner life gradually becomes established (with due reference to Schore, 1994). The formal Freudian position is of course that the ego gradually gets control over the Id through its own maturation (what this precisely means, however, could be seen as the subject of a large portion of the research agenda of NP). The authors final statement is: "We see the intimate connection in Freud's affect theory between visceral functions, endogenous drives, instinctual behaviors, personal memories, and emotional feelings" [or states]. It would be of considerable interest to know whether these same functional interdependencies are evident from or contradicted by the available neuroscientific evidence" (p. 11). Our best way to approach this question is to move on to the next presentation, that of Jaak Panksepp.

III. *Jaak Panksepp*

Panksepp agrees with most of the conclusions of Nersessian and Solms; he places their comments in the context of what he calls "affective neuroscience" (a synonym for NP), current work in neuroscience bridging mind and brain. However, he sees problems looming in the bridging of psychoanalysis and neuroscience, problems that require significant changes in both fields. Neuroscientists, he believes, need "to take emotional dynamics and defenses more seriously than in the past" (p. 15), and "mainstream neuroscience should ... become more conversant with the fact that *the mammalian brain can generate a variety of affective feelings which probably reflect long-term causes of behavior rather than epiphenomenal flotsam*" (Ibid., italics added). Moreover, analysts need to orient themselves towards more quantitative and empirical inquiries, and be willing to embrace the new neuroscientific knowledge they will acquire, seeing it as potentially deepening their understanding of the phenomena they usually consider merely psychological rather than psychobiological.

On the positive side, according to Panksepp "*throughout the twentieth century psychoanalysis remained the bastion among the human sciences that acknowledged the deeper emotional currents of the human mind*" (p. 15, italics added) while neuroscientists can contribute to a better understanding of how "neuroscientific, psychoanalytic, psychobiological, and sociobiological modes of thought can intersect and evolve" (p. 15). Panksepp believes that Freud's contributions were unique, and have not been proven incorrect, though often criticized. He notes that "indeed, many of the spectacular new findings from modern neuroscience and psychobiology can be interpreted in ways that are generally coherent with many of Freud's ideas. *However, all proposed relationships must be deemed provisional until they are subjected to rigorous empirical evaluation*" [Italics in the original] (p. 16).

After such an introduction, Panksepp launches into an essay in four parts: first is a discussion of modern emotion theory, and related premises and biases; the second, clarification of the importance of subcortical (vs. cortical) emotional circuits; the third, his description of the significance of "distinct neurodynamic resonances" for the "primal self" (p. 26); and the fourth, his overview in which neuroaffective brain systems are seen as orchestrating "various coherent internal and external expressions called the Basic Emotions" (p. 29). I will make some comments on each section of Panksepp's essay.

Panksepp summarizes how best to approach emotional matters objectively, as follows: "...I believe it can be probed credibly ... by (1) seeking essential brain processes that *synchronize* the visceral and somatic motor expressions of emotions; which (2) are also ingredients in the cognitive and memorial aspects of emotions; and (3) combining these findings experimentally with a study of the subject reports of humans [about these same feeling states]" (p. 17).

From Panksepp's perspective cognitive and affective/emotional systems are not usually sharply separated. For example, he states "my personal assumptions, harmonious with Freud's, are as follows: I believe that biological values and the affective neural processes via which they are instantiated penetrate all of the cognitive structures of the mammalian mind/brain. Although certain sensory-perceptual processes may be free of affect, all the higher association areas of the brain, at least as they operate in [Nature], are permeated by the sustaining and guiding effects of biological values... [In other words] ...most of the emotional behavior we see in the world is probably modulated by the background effects of low-level emotions (i.e. moods), and it is within these longer-term influences that affective experience may be critical" (p. 17).

Developmentally, Panksepp further sees affects as making a major contribution in the following manner: "...In early childhood there is no sustained line of thought without a sustained line of affect" and understanding man and animals requires our proper analysis of their respective "emotional feelings" (pp. 17–18). He continues: "...In adulthood, when long-term behavior patterns and habits of thinking and defenses have [then] been established, ... the obvious linkages between affect and behavior diminish...[but in fact] the affective regulators may have simply descended to preconscious levels of neural processing, still exerting fundamental controls over mind and behavior..." (p. 18).

For Panksepp "... a variety of executive systems for distinct emotional processes...exist within the mammalian brain... [These systems] are not simple and modular [however], but widely ramifying, interacting with many other specific and nonspecific processes of the brain" (p. 18). He designates these systems either "instinctual id energies", after Freud, or, "emotional command systems" (Ibid.), and sees one key issue to be their precise characterization neuroscientifically. He recognizes that some of the emotional regulation undoubtedly comes from "the various [psychological] defenses conceptualized by Freud" (Ibid.), but that others are reflections of the product of associative learning. Importantly, and in sharp contrast to modern psychological theories of emotion, Panksepp sides with Freud for "[placing] affect...at the center of his scheme. This can still be deemed courageously controversial, but in my estimation, it is the correct point of view" (Panksepp, op. cit., p. 18).

Panksepp's suggestion for approaching the necessary research into the nature of the brain systems involved in emotion is to "...[triangulate] between mammalian brain research, the study of animal behavior, and the systematic analysis of human [subjectivity]..." (p. 18). This will involve the exploitation of research on (1) localized brain stimulation, including the "noninvasive stimulation of the cortical surfaces with rapid transcranial magnetic stimulation (rTMS)", (2) modern brain imaging techniques (p. 19), and (3), by implication, the careful study of human affectivity via psychoanalysis. Panksepp's conclusion from reviewing these kinds of efforts is that we have neglected the role of many subcortical systems in favor of various cortical systems, which are not anywhere near as important as the subcortex is for emotion. He states: "My personal view is that the shared subcortical heritage, from which the various id energies emerge across mammalian species, provides an essential and solid foundation for understanding the nature of affective processes as well as higher emotion-regulating functions of the brain" (p. 20).

What then can we conclude about the function of emotions, as seen by Panksepp? According to this amazing affective neuroscience scholar, Freud "recognized that the assignment of value to behavioral and higher psychological processes was the key function of emotions... [He saw] that affect registers the importance of salient world events, and thereby permeates the higher conscious functions of the mind-brain. He also viewed affect as arising from fundamental biological mechanisms (presumably brain circuits), which guide instinctual action tendencies. The affect programs of the brain that have now been revealed are probably the immediate infrastructures of such processes (Panksepp, 1998). At the heart of these systems there are a variety of chemical codes (largely neuropeptidergic) that may eventually permit powerful new modes of psychiatric intervention, and new ways to evaluate how feelings are constructed in the brain" (p. 20, italics added).

As noted above, Panksepp's second section deals with affect as "internally generated neurodynamic processes...related to subcortical emotional circuits" (p. 20). Panksepp starts with a speculation that during the evolution of our mind/brains "...the neural process 'that affect is a perception of' has to be fundamentally unconscious [at first]... and that it [later in evolution] became preconscious and then conscious as certain types of additional neural systems evolved [in man]" (p. 20). In other words, as Panksepp puts it: "...*all higher forms of consciousness may still be grounded on the most primitive forms of consciousness, which I am assuming were affective in nature...[so that] rational thought may only be a relatively fragile tip on the iceberg of affective experience*" (Ibid., italics added).[3]

Panksepp's next step is to describe the source of ego, as something that "[sprouts] from rather primitive areas of the brain where basic emotional systems interact with basic neural representations of the body" (Ibid.). The SELF (his acronym for simple ego-type of life form) "may correspond to the most primitive aspect of Freud's ego structure...grounded within the centromedian areas of the brain stem—areas such as the periaqueductal gray (PAG) and surrounding collicular and tegmental zones—but its influence broadcasts widely in the brain through many direct and indirect influences such as the strong two-way connections with frontal executive areas of the brain and widespread influences on sensory cortices through the extended reticular and thalamic activating systems (ERTAS) conceptualized by Newman and Baars (1993)" (p. 21). Panksepp sees the result of these integrations to be a homeostatic epicenter in which the various emotional and SELF systems ebb and flow. In this way perceptual input and internal emotional states interact with "coherent and stable motor representations of the body" and other elements to create what psychoanalysts would designate, along with Panksepp, "a core of our being" (op. cit.). This appears in Figure 2, p. 22 of Panksepp's essay, in two parts. The first, part (A), depicts feelings such as panic, fear and rage, along with seeking expectancies (reflecting drives), feeding into or merging within the level of the superior colliculus in the PAG; the second, (B), shows the emergence of the SELF from the integration of the same information inputs within the mesencephalon, including importantly sensory input (e.g. touch, vision, hearing) and motor planning.[4] As Panksepp states: "with such an extended neural entity, it is easy to imagine how emotional and motivational values could percolate throughout the neuraxis, and how ...[this] may be the foundation for higher forms of consciousness, and its various satisfactions and discontents. All that is required is strong modulation of ascending ERTAS components [as noted above] (including cholinergic and catecholinergic [inputs]) from the PAG/SELF system [as described], *and such neural connections have been [already] demonstrated*" (p. 22, emphasis added).

Panksepp knows a lot, but concedes that there is obviously much work remaining to be done to fine tune and fill out any detailed interdisciplinary understanding of what contributes to a "SELF system", and what directs our emotional behavior at the deepest levels. Some of his personally finest work in this area involves, but is not limited to, his delineation of the SEEKING system (Panksepp, 1998b) which clarifies the purposefulness of the medial forebrain bundle (MFB) [and hypothalamic] corridor arising from the ventral tegmental area (VTA). These important circuits are bidirectional and interconnect areas such as the PAG "and a variety of higher limbic areas (especially the amygdala, cingulate, frontal and insular areas)" (p. 23). We are essentially considering what analysts originally called drives, and which are now most often understood as motivational systems or largely instinctual urges aiming towards the satisfaction of a variety of needs.

What then do we need to expand upon? One area deserving attention is Panksepp's insightful discovery of intrinsic ludic circuits, by means of which the mammalian brain generates play and laughter, something Freud did not anticipate although he intuitively appreciated the importance of jokes and their relationship to the unconscious. Panksepp asserts these same circuits likely also play a role in development, and thus deserve our attention, for he has demonstrated experimentally that mice, for example, are actually capable of genuine laughter (1998), a finding that supports his contention that the mammalian mind/brain ground plan is an enormously complex entity mirroring much of the human core.

A second area needing study is learning how the different kinds of anxiety relate to the variations in circuitry that generate this affect (in other words, why the different types of anxiety are necessary): for example, some input to the PAG comes from the central amygdala, while a second input comes from the cingulate and preoptic/ventral septal regions, via the dorsomedial thalamus. Here Panksepp points out that "the PAG is involved in the bonding processes that characterize all mammals, and suggests further that variations in this process over time may be an important part of what predisposes us to depressions" (p. 22). A third area deserving study, in his judgment, is understanding clearly "which brain areas mediate which affective qualities" (p. 23). In other words, *Panksepp sees our basic emotions as linked to "our basic instinctual action readiness systems"* (p. 23, italics added). But such studies regarding, for example, how one discerns the precise neurochemical-neurophysiological basis for something as basic as pleasures, displeasures and their subtle variations, as difficult as it is, does not come close to the difficulty of distinguishing the basis for differentiating the neural matrix responsible for the more complex feelings states, such as envy, guilt, jealousy, and shame.

Part of what Panksepp is getting at is that while the "…thalamo-cortical systems mediate the basic qualia arising from exteroceptive sensations…these systems do not functionally interact at many places in the brain, allowing values to permeate perceptions as external stimuli gain access to internal value systems [and] help establish more sophisticated learned behavior patterns" (p. 24), and create the more complex feelings noted at the end of the previous paragraph. Citing the work of many researchers, including most notably LeDoux (1996), Panksepp is elaborating on his personal working hypothesis that *we could begin to answer the question about "which brain areas mediate which affective qualities" if we can better appreciate the interactivity between inner values and sensory perceptions, between higher cortical and executive control networks such as the frontal cortical and anterior cingulate cortex, on the one hand, and subcortical systems such as the amygdala, PAG, VTA and SEEKING system on the other* (italics added). In this way Panksepp sees "values" permeating "perceptions", resulting in phobias, defenses, and all the "neurotic" disorders Freud has corralled for us (p. 24). And he obviously subscribes to the belief that lower subcortical centers are more determinative of emotion than higher centers, noting that these subcortical centers, such as the PAG and VTA are much more strongly stimulated (rewarded) by opiates than the higher areas are, such as the amygdala and frontal cortex (p. 25).

To simplify, we might say Panksepp is exploring two key questions: [1] "how the more subtle psychological defenses may be constructed in the brain", and [2] "the manner in which the various affective states are represented in the brain" (p. 24) and then need defending against. On the one hand, it is most interesting that he is referring to defenses in the very same way Freud referred to them, "such as condensations, displacements, projections, and [even] transferences" (p. 24). On the other hand, Panksepp is obviously not aware of prior work connecting psychological defenses and neuroanatomical mechanisms (for example, Levin, 1980, and Levin & Vuckovich, 1983). But we can easily forgive him, since many neuroscientists during the 1980s were simply not expecting any significant contribution towards bridging neuroscience and psychoanalysis to come from psychoanalysts! So it makes sense that in this 1999 discussion Panksepp makes no mention of prior bridging psychoanalytic research, except those much earlier researchers whose work was dealing with general questions regarding how the more complex adaptive defensive strategies involving emotions are learned and/or released, and, from a neuroscientific perspective, trying to flush out exactly what neural subsystems are involved, and what chemistry.

On these latter points, Panksepp is, as always, deeply imaginative and original. He reminds us particularly about work involving substance P (and aggression), corticotropin releasing factor (CRF) (mediating what he calls a "very basic form of anxiety") (p. 25), ß-endorphin (counteracting homeostatic imbalance…[and] creating pleasure" (Fig. 3, p. 25), vasopressin/oxytocin (the former promoting "male-typical persistence" and the latter "female-type nurturance and acceptance" (Fig. 3, p. 25), and cholecystokinin (CCK) regulating emotional systems that have to do with feeding, sex, exploration, anxiety, and pain (Fig. 3, p. 25). Neuropeptides obviously play an important role in emotions, such as glucagon-like peptide-1 (GLP-1) and urocontin, that he believes control feeding behavior indirectly by modulating emotional processes (Panksepp, 1997a). Thus, as do Solms and Nersessian, Panksepp is creating an ingenious outline for us to follow so that we can better appreciate how the lower level (subcortical) systems, and their unique chemistry, fit into the well known and over-emphasized upper level (cortical) systems, and how these two systems might work together to create the complexity of felt affectivity. In this way he is trying to square what he intuits as correct in Freud with what he feels positive about from neuroscience research, that is, to integrate (1) what is biologically programmed into us but needing to be released, (2) what has thus been learned by our ancestors, and favored their survival as a species, and (3) what is being learned by us, and extends our personal repertoire.

But one more qualification is important to Panksepp: the neurotransmitters participating in emotional systems need to be seen as either non-specific or specific in their activity. For example, norepinephrine (NE), serotonin (known also as 5 hydroxytryptamine) (5-HT), acetylcholine (ACh), and glutamate, participate in "practically all emotional and cognitive responses" (p. 26), and are thus non-specific agents. In contrast, the neuropeptides noted above (ß-endorphin, vasopressin/oxytocin, CRF, and CCK) each have more discrete emotional effects, as described, and are thus specific. Panksepp further agrees that if one wants to distinguish between the quantitative vs. the qualitative aspects of emotion, then, "as suggested by Solms and Nersessian, a provocative way [to do so] ... may be to focus on the generalized (i.e. non-specific) systems (e.g., NE, 5-HT, and ACh) [which all] share ... the discrete functional systems of the brain which contribute substantially to a quantitative dimension of affect, while the more specific neuromodulators, like many of the neuropeptides systems, are more influential in establishing the qualitative differences among affects. This [to Panksepp] seems highly promising" (p. 27).

However, if we make such a conclusion, according to Panksepp, we then lose sight that each of the so-called general neurotransmitters also make specific contributions to how brain systems operate! For example, "... NE increases the effects of incoming signals as compared to background noise" and thus makes the cortical processing of information more efficient (p. 27), while 5-HT works by reducing the "impact of information on the cortex" (Ibid.), and ACh "focuses attentional resources" (p. 27). Thus, neuroscientists have their own preferred ways of thinking about the effects even of these general categories of neurotransmitters, and Panksepp feels they are unlikely to see any advantage to thinking of these substances as related to Freud's concept of drive. Here, however, I beg to differ, since I believe it is more than likely that as scientists become more cross-trained (in psychoanalysis and neuroscience), as Panksepp has become himself, it then becomes easier to think of something from multiple simultaneous perspectives. In fact, is Panksepp not discussing times and events where we suddenly feel that insights have occurred that genuinely bridge across disciplines that otherwise previously felt hardly bridgeable at all?

To Panksepp's great credit, later in his discussion, he rethinks arguments, and comes to the same conclusion as I have (!), criticizing his earlier position as follows: "The possibility that a single chemical system can have both qualitative and quantitative consequences is also a reasonable conceptual alternative" (pp. 27–28). He then goes on to elaborate on the very same mixed aspects of the neuropeptides glutamate, and a parallel process with "its metabolically related cousin gamma-aminobutyric acid (GABA)" (p. 28).

IV. *Concluding comments as a preview of where we might be going*

It should be obvious to the reader that Panksepp, like Solms and Nersessian, is trying to find a touchstone that can be utilized to provide a decisive linkage between the two disciplinary *weltanschauungen* under consideration. Equally obvious is the likelihood that given current limitations such a touchstone will be very hard to discover and reach any consensus upon. Nevertheless, each of us is trying very hard to find it anyway! To this end, I would like to complete my comments with a suggestion, that I will follow-up on in the next essays I have promised, as to what I believe may prove to be an important set of possibilities that will help us understand the central concerns of these investigators and put our study of human emotion on a more solid footing.

My suggestion flows from my re-reading the discussions of Solms and Nersessian, and Panksepp, in the context of doing clinical psychoanalytic work on a daily basis, while also attempting to keep current in developments within neuroscience generally, especially as reported in various journals. I would like to refer to a paper (of experimental work on rats) by Bruno and Sakman (2006), and a discussion of it in the same journal *Science* by Alonso (2006). To keep it brief, Bruno and Sakman did some original research in which they show the mechanism by which sensory stimuli are able to reach and drive the cortex in spite of the fact that this input pathway, which comes to the cortex neurons in layer 4 (L4) from the thalamus, involves a small number of neurons that seem, as measured electrochemically, barely able to "elicit or 'drive' neuronal activity" at the cortical level (Alonso, p. 1604)! The key discovery, however, is that the thalamic neuronal input involves the synchronous activity of this small cadre of neurons, and it is the synchrony that increases the efficacy of the thalamic to cortical input.

What I would like to add is the following question: is it not probable that this simple insight of Bruno and Sakman probably explains, under the rubric of synchrony, the way in which most connections within the brain are created at the proper level of efficacy, so that in essence, it is the synchrony of neuronal firing that allows neural networks of great complexity and importance to function? Another way to put it is that synchrony of neuronal activity can raise the impact of affective states, and help provide "committees" of neurons (including, as well, supporting glial cells) that connect the affective and the cognitive core, and all the other aspects of our complex mental life into a unity. More to follow, including some ideas on how the CB may help out, when extended neural networks may not be the most efficacious way to go to solve important but complex problems, such as integrating the activities of extended neural networks.

Notes

1. An earlier version of this chapter appeared in *Samiksa: The Journal of the Indian Psychoanalytical Society*, 2006.
2. Levin and Vuckovich (1983) speculated about the neurobiology of psychological defenses, their relationship to development and to the CB. They also defined at least two defenses (repression and disavowal) in neurophysiological terms, as interhemispheric blocks in precisely different directions, the result of which is to keep the memory of events, and the feelings that assign personal meaning to events separated, at times, for the purpose of psychological defense. It should be understood, that there are many ways the brain could defend itself in this way. Later on, in this book, it will be suggested that by making models of the brain, and using them defensively, not just adaptively, the CB could allow us to live in "parallel worlds" (i.e. allow us to avoid mourning the loss of others, and avoid dealing with other unpleasant realities in our lives). The CB is part of the executive control system of the brain, and it has considerable "power" to determine the "reality" we live in at any given time.
3. Here Panksepp touches on a critical issue about emotion, namely its relationship to awareness, a subject that will be discussed in the concluding section of this book, especially as it relates to the research of Langer.
4. The reference to motor planning might have suggested a role for the CB in core self experience, since the CB is active from before birth, whereas the cerebral cortex is not functional (myelinated) until much later.

CHAPTER FOUR

A neuro-psychoanalytic theory of emotion, Part 2: Comments on Critical commentaries by Antonio Damasio, Andre Green, Joseph LeDoux, Allan Schore, Howard Shevrin, and Clifford Yorke

Fred M. Levin

Précis: In the previous chapter we considered the lead articles in the inaugural issue of the journal Neuro-Psychoanalysis (NP), the ones by Mark Solms and Edward Nersessian, and by Jaak Panksepp. This chapter comments on the commentaries by those listed in the title above. Each of these individuals reacts personally and creatively, clarifying what is salient for himself. By examining their commentaries we can better appreciate their thinking on NP, and the nature of the ongoing debate between how best to integrate neuroscience and psychoanalysis, or even, whether they see this as a desirable goal. We need to be careful, however, because serious scholars, out of their intensity to calibrate their own opinions and the opinions of others, and meet complex philosophical requirements within their disciplines, often sound unfriendly to "outsiders". I believe this happens not because they are so much unfriendly as intense, which can be difficult for others to deal with. I hope the reader also gives me the benefit of the doubt when I take what may appear to be too strong a position against one or another commentator in what follows, out of my own intensity to at least find good questions, if not yet good answers.

Antonio R. Damasio

At the time of the article cited, Damasio is the M. N. Van Allen Professor and Head of the Department of Neurology at the University of Iowa College of Medicine, as well as the author of *Descartes' Error* (1994), and *The Feeling of What Happens* (1999). He makes clear in his first paragraph that he read Freud primarily 30 years earlier while in College, but rarely since then, yet insists that he appreciates "the helpful Freud quotes in Solms and Nersessian's interesting [target] article … and the thoughtful reaction to it prepared by Panksepp" (1999, p. 38). The shortness of his commentary, however, is troubling, along with his contradictory statements about Freud ("Freud did not propose [any] testable hypotheses" [p. 39], vs. "I believe … Freud's insights on the nature of affect are consonant with the most advanced contemporary neuroscience views" [p. 38]!). These contradictions suggest on the one hand, that he is hardly impressed at all by psychoanalysis as a science; yet, on the other, he is respectful of the difficulty for neuroscience, in solving the various conundrums mentioned: about affect, mind/brain correlations, theories of consciousness and the dynamic unconscious, etc.. Not surprisingly, Damasio appears to this writer to doubt that any significant integration of neuroscience and psychoanalysis is likely to help matters. Perhaps even more troubling, he states that even if it [an NP integration] could be accomplished, he fears "premature closure" (p. 39), which seems to mean he wouldn't trust any such results, no matter what their basis. So what, then, is important to him, and what in his remarks helpful for those who are interested in NP?

The following seem important to Damasio: (1) If we are to create a neuroscience of emotions, then we need the attend to the "missing perspectives of evolution and homeostasis in the conceptualization of the emotions" (Ibid.); (2) we need to attend to the role of the body and its representations in the brain; (3) we must more broadly conceive of the neural correlates of emotion than we are currently doing; (4) "...the body, real, and as represented in the brain, is the theater for the emotions, and ... feelings are largely read-outs of body changes 'really' enacted in the body and 'really' constructed in an 'as-if' mode in body-mapping brain structures...[where] the body-mapping structures begin in the spinal cord but coalesce most dramatically in the brain stem and hypothalamus before continuing on in the telencephalon. This idea underlies the argument in *Descartes' Error* and is central to my proposals on consciousness in [my forthcoming book]..." (p. 39). What Damasio is headed towards is (5) his belief that the self is essentially a "protoself" formed from the collectivity of a number of neural structures and systems, including the subcortical brain stem elements, hypothalamus, and basal forebrain, "as well as cortical elements in areas such as the somatosensory cortices" (p. 39). To Damasio this means understanding connectivity "in a cross-regional and supraregional manner" (Ibid.).

My take here is that Damasio is either holding back some insights, or has nothing much to add to the present controversies in this area. His first points have all been covered quite well by well known neuropsychoanalytic research, which Damasio may not be aware of, does not much value, or choses not to mention, such as we have reviewed in the first two chapters of this book, which consider the importance of evolution, that is, the adaptive perspectives (Levin, 1991, 2003; Levin et al., 2005). Work within psychoanalysis, especially within interpersonal and self-psychological frameworks, have also greatly contributed to the psychological/experiential understanding of emotional and cognitive self-development, which Damasio is obviously focused upon, and properly so. Yet there is little evidence in his commentary that even he believes the neuroscientific perspectives he is so at home with regarding "self" might, as he suggests, be merely the external observer perspective on the very same emotional/experiential phenomenon the psychoanalysts, including Freud have been deeply emersed in. Still, one can only hope he continues to make successful bridging efforts, such as he has, whatever his level of skepticism about collaboration. I am also surprised he hasn't any thoughts about the CB; but neither do the others in this section, so he is surely not alone. It is also possible that each of the commentators only had copies of the two target articles, and not copies of the presentations of the other commentators.

André Green

André Green is a Training and Supervising Psychoanalyst, and member of the Paris Psychoanalytic Society. To summarize in advance, however, although a psychoanalyst, Green's thinking clearly has something in common with Damasio, namely, a feeling about the independence of neuroscience and psychoanalysis and the "impossibility of reducing any one of the two to the other" (p. 41). Where he differs with Damasio, however, is that for Green this does not mean that dialogue is impossible or without value. Rather, he feels that each side needs to be open to learning something new in the process, and that much learning will be needed for any true synthesis across disciplinary boundaries. For example, although Green feels that analysts can rely of the importance of emotion, the unconscious mind, and the fact of biological drives (a position that eventually separated him from his countryman Jacques Lacan [see Kohon, 1999]), a fair amount of Freud's thinking, in his opinion, is doubtful "in the light of neuroscience" (p. 40). And yet he equally criticizes the neuroscientists for "deliberately … underestimating the importance of affect" as though "they are ruled by some unspoken prohibition on being interested in understanding the nature of affective experience" (Ibid.). And Green also takes E. O. Wilson to task for asserting that Freud's work was not scientific while never applying the same criticism to scientists in any other domain. In other words, Green sees the same kinds of divergence of viewpoints between the two neuroscientists Panksepp and Damasio, as exists between the differing schools of psychoanalysis. Scholars have learned to be careful before agreeing; for Green this is especially so.

It will help to examine Green's criticism of Panksepp more carefully. In particular he cites Panksepp's suggestion of "triangulating mammalian brain research, the study of animal behavior, and the systematic analysis of human subjective experience" to find common ground (p. 40), reasoning that Panksepp's suggested approach could only level down our knowledge of affects. I feel his attack on Panksepp in this case, however, is not justified. Panksepp is not, as Green suggests, arguing that we ignore psychoanalytic insights regarding affective experience; rather, Panksepp is correctly asserting that we need to think of ways to pursue our study of the phenomenon of emotion in other life forms, especially those we are close to (namely, other mammals), and see how to operationalize the affective patterns we see in terms of reproducible behavior patterns within fixed anatomical and neurochemical pathways. In my opinion, Panksepp has some important criticisms of psychoanalytic theorizing, but he is friendly to the field, and respectful of its unique efforts to study what no other field has studied as intently: the unconscious mind and its affective experience.

But what then is Green asserting here that we might otherwise miss? I think he feels strongly that psychoanalytic science is just as strong as neuroscientific science, and that both approaches are on a par. "[The methods of psychoanalysis]... are [not] subordinate to the findings of [neuroscience] experiments..." (p. 41). Or, another way he puts this: "What [psychoanalysts] learn from intersubjective relationships...[is a method]... that has reached the same level of complexity [that neuroscientific experimentation has reached]. It is the result of relying on observation in a setting ... involving two human beings under more or less constant conditions for a long period of time" (Ibid.). He is making a commentary on the uniqueness of the database psychoanalysis contends with, and the phenomena analysts study daily, for years on end: "We can see what problems arise for neurobiology, when it tries to assess psychical phenomena for which there are no equivalents in consciousness" (p. 41). He means here the distinction between what is dynamically unconscious, and what is merely not conscious, and the important implications for the self of the former. Remember also, that Green is famous for giving importance to biology, and also for noting what he has called "the negative", meaning "that which is absent, that which is lost, and that which is latent, much like the unconscious itself" (Simmel, 2004). To further quote Simmel on Green: "Repression and representation are critical variables and in this way, Green enfolds Freud's basic elements and actions of the mind to explain his own model. For Green, the negative is a normal, necessary aspect to development, [similar] ... to Winnicott's interest in the absence of the mother in ordinary ways and Bion's use of the representation of the maternal container to master separation [from the mother]" (op. cit.).

But a still more important criticism is Green's quarrel with Solms' and Nersessian's way of describing Freud's basic theoretical orientation, on the one hand, and Jaak Panksepp's way of describing Freud's thinking on the other. Basically, his criticism is that both are trying to "complete Freud by neuroscience" (p. 42). What he means is that Solms and Nersessian are changing Freud's mental apparatus into something that subserves a biological purpose, emphasizing the maintenance of inner tension to within certain limits (the so-called Nirvana, Constancy, or Pleasure Principle) while at the same time missing Freud's personal intention to focus not upon the representational processes Solms and Nersessian see, but rather on perceptions and their associated feelings, especially in relation to the drives of the unconscious, such as sexuality, aggression, and so forth. The same for Panksepp's relegating the drive concept to "such factors as hunger, thirst, and thermoregulation...[But then asking:] What is left of the references [in Freud] to sexuality and destructiveness?" (Ibid.).

Yet the reader needs to appreciate that Green is entirely aware of the importance of the neuroscientific viewpoints of his targets, and their usefulness; he merely cannot tolerate the misrepresentation of Freud on the subjects of the dynamic unconscious and impulses, sexual or destructive. But he can readily applaud, for example, Panksepp's appreciation of the role of the lower brainstem areas such as the periaqueductal gray (PAG) for affect regulation, which involves "the long-term effects and modulatory influences of affects" as opposed to higher centers "such as the amygdala, hippocampus, and the rest" (Ibid.). Here Green's urgent voicing is quite clarifying: "...*what Freud meant by the cardinal role attributed to the drives is [just as Panksepp notes in the terminology of neuroscience, and Panksepp's emphasis on the motor organization of the brain] ... [namely, that they, the drives] are always active*" (Ibid., italics added). We can conclude that Green sees feelings/emotions/affects as representing the activity of the Freudian unconscious, something deeply meaningful to the self, a point of view he feels Damasio shares with him more than Panksepp. I suspect that he is misjudging both Damasio and Panksepp in this final assertion. But I like his conclusions about Freud, which seem accurate.

Joseph LeDoux

Joseph LeDoux is Professor of the Center for Neural Science of New York University. Just as the other discussants of the Solms/Nersessian presentation, LeDoux attempts his own translation of psychoanalytic affect theory. He begins with an historical perspective of Freud's "pleasure principle" as a form of hedonism, introduces Thorn-dike (1913) and his "law of effect" (behaviors followed by rewards recur, those punished get stamped out), and then combines Jeremy Bentham's 18th century ideas about "hedonism" in an interesting comparison by E. G. Boring (1950) as follows: "that Thorndike's 'law' was a hedonism based upon past events, whereas Freud's 'principle' [is] based on future expectations" (p. 45). Ledoux then continues that since the two major traditions within psychology, clinical and experimental, have hedonism as the point of departure for understanding mental/behavioral functions and thus share a common core, perhaps this core "can be used as a conceptual bridge between psychoanalysis and neuroscience" (p. 45).

LeDoux also mentions Matt Erdelyi's 1985 book *Psychoanalysis: Freud's Cognitive Psychology*, but fails to elaborate on this fine contribution, except for the following passing remark: "but as far as I know not much has happened since [the cognitive revolution]" (p. 45). What he means by "not much has happened" is that as far as the field of academic psychology is concerned, "the unconscious (in this case the cognitive unconscious rather than the repressed unconscious of psychoanalytic theory) became a scientifically legitimate concept with broad acceptance..." (Ibid.). Sadly, by virtue of overlooking the likes of Erdelyi's contributions, which take into account both psychology and psychoanalysis, the field of academic psychology has been missing something important, given the unusual talents and insights of a significant cadre of psychologists (e.g. Erdelyi, 1996, 2004, 2006) for such subjects as how emotions and cognition relate.

One section of LeDoux's discussion is entitled "feelings as the conscious perception of something [dynamically] unconscious"; this makes clear how Ledoux is putting things together, using his own precious research knowledge of the amygdala to great advantage. He begins: "Freud's notion, described by Solms and Nersessian, that felt emotions are a conscious perception of something—something which is, in itself, 'unconscious' [meaning non-conscious, and that] is compatible with the working memory concept" (p. 45). In this regard he notes that "When electrical stimuli applied to the amygdala of humans elicits feelings of fear...it is not because the amygdala 'feels' fear, but instead because the various networks that the amygdala activates ultimately provide working memory with inputs that are labeled as fear" (p. 46). LeDoux has already stated his belief that there is a consensus within neuroscience that "working memory is a staging area for consciousness" (Ibid.). He then makes a helpful elaboration: "For example, we now know that the amygdala is an important component of the brain system that detects and responds to danger. However, the amygdala is not directly responsible for conscious feelings of fear. Building on the working memory notion, I have proposed that conscious feelings of fear come about when working memory is occupied with the fact that the amygdala has detected and begun to respond to danger" (LeDoux, 1996, p. 45).

It will help us understand LeDoux if we draw briefly from his book (LeDoux, 1996), especially as regards the word emotion and its neuroscientific referents. LeDoux describes his work with Gazzaniga after the latter had worked with Sperry on split-brain studies. In Chapter 1 of his book LeDoux notes this collaboration as the time he became interested in emotions (LeDoux, 1996, p. 13). What interested LeDoux at that time was that if stimuli were experimentally presented to someone with a split-brain, where the right hemisphere was disconnected from their left hemisphere to treat intractable epilepsy, then one could experimentally show that when the two hemispheres were tested post-surgically, the left hemisphere could not correctly identify what had been presented (in contrast to the right hemisphere), but it could consistently make correct emotional appraisals of the object presented (good, bad, etc.)! That is, the parts of the right hemisphere "that determine the emotional implications of a stimulus" could still communicate to its counterpart in the left hemisphere (op. cit. p. 15). From this Ledoux concludes that "the left hemisphere...was making emotional judgments without knowing what was being judged," and importantly, this mental activity obviously "[took place] outside of the [left hemisphere's realm of awareness]...[that is] unconsciously" (Ibid.).

On the basis of such systematic observations in split-brain patients, LeDoux thus came to the conclusion that the word "emotion" does not really name a function, but rather "it is only a label, a convenient way of talking about aspects of the brain and its mind. Psychology textbooks often carve the mind up into functional pieces, such as perception, memory, and emotion. These are useful for organizing information into general areas... [But there is no such thing as the 'emotion' faculty and there is no single brain system dedicated to

[it]… [So if] we are interested in understanding [emotion], we have to focus on specific classes of emotion (anger, sexuality, etc.) since each such system is different" (LeDoux, 1996, p. 16; see also Panksepp, 1998).

LeDoux essentially sees modern neuroscience as diverging from the classical Freudian notion that conscious emotion is the awareness of something that is basically unconscious; in this new perspective "affect is a separate modality of consciousness" (p. 46). Here, as I stated above, by unconscious LeDoux is not meaning the Freudian unconscious, but non-conscious mental/brain activity. If we keep this definition of his of the unconscious in mind, then it is not hard to agree with him, that emotion picks up on important internal events in various networks, including those of working memory, which carry the history of previous experiences, intentions, wishes, etc. He then makes an interesting and I believe important contrast: "Consciousness (working memory) can be occupied with mundane or significant events, depending on the system that is controlling the occupation. [In contrast] emotional states of consciousness tend to be more prolonged and intense because of the greater variety of brain systems that are called into play to contribute in various ways to working memory … [Brainstem neurochemical inputs, feedback from bodily responses including hormonal feedback] help lock us into the state we are in and ensure that our perceptions, attentions, and memories stay focused on the significant event and make it harder for other things to bump this event out of working memory" (p. 46). He concludes that multiple overlapping networks involving the amygdala "and other subcortical areas, suggests there could be some affective compartmentalization in working memory that could constitute something like a modality for affective consciousness" (Ibid.).

Regarding the question of quantity vs. quality LeDoux speculates that "the amygdala is presynaptic to the reticular formation in the triggering of nonspecific arousal. The sensory systems and their representations in the thalamus and cortex provide the amygdala with 'quality' and the amygdala, by way of triggering the brainstem participates in the generation of 'quantity'" [meaning intensity] (p. 46). This is important for LeDoux's subsequent speculations regarding where talking therapies might have their important impact. LeDoux's research in rats supports the theory that the cerebral cortex (specifically, the anterior cingulate/infra-limbic system) inhibits sub-cortical regions, suggesting that these very same structures are what regulate our emotions. "In studies...aimed at understanding how learned fear is extinguished, we found evidence consistent with this view (Morgan, Romanski, & LeDoux, 1993). In brief, when the medial prefrontal cortex...was damaged, the rats took much longer to extinguish their fear reactions.... [In comparison] when the medial prefrontal region is damaged, the control is lost, and fear remains unchecked" (p. 47). Since the lateral prefrontal cortex "is critically involved in working memory (Fuster, 1989; Goldman-Rakic, 1993)" (Ibid.) LeDoux singles it out as the likely target of successful "talking therapy" (Ibid.).

LeDoux next tackles the psychological defense "repression", which he notes is central to psychoanalytic theory. His take is that psychoanalysis may be wrong here, since he is aware of possible mechanisms which do not involve anything necessarily meaningful psychoanalytically. That is, he thinks what analysts call repression may be merely normal brain activity that is misinterpreted. His key argument is that stress is known to alter the function of the medial temporal lobe memory system. So in that case, the hippocampus is presumably shut down by stress, rather than the mind/brain protect-ing the self via shifts in the availability of memory. In this regard I think LeDoux's argument suffers greatly from his lack of familiar-ity with the psychoanalytic literature on the subject of psychologi-cal defenses, and their likely neurophysiological mechanisms. Most relevant is the work of Basch (1983), Levin and Vuckovich (1983) and Levin (1991, 2003) on the subjects of repression and disavowal. In a nutshell, these authors have shown the utility in understanding other brain mechanisms, not mentioned by LeDoux, that in fact define "defense" in terms of the sequestration of information between the hemispheres (based upon the CB), knowledge LeDoux obviously is aware of (see my references above, to his using this in explaining his deep interest in what happens with emotions in split-brain patients). Thus, a better argument here would have been that information can be shared between the hemispheres once the corpus callosum is myelinated, which incidentally occurs around the Oedipal period. Before this time the developing individual is protected from prema-turely appreciating the meaning of their affects; but after this time, people can only protect themselves psychologically by creating a functional interhemispheric disconnect on an as needed basis. And this is not to say that there are not also situations where because of brain injury that the hemispheres are not communicating properly with each other, or that this cannot show up and be misinterpreted psychoanalytically when a neuroscientific explanation would be more complete.

Finally, LeDoux has a mixed reaction to Panksepp's target article. First, he agrees with Panksepp's position that there are emotional command systems, different for the different emotions, and that these have survival value for the individual and species. Where he differs is regarding Panksepp's interpretation that since the command systems for the different emotions are the same in humans and animals, it is likely that the experience of these emotions is the same between humans and animals. LeDoux insists "there is no way to know" (p. 48), and adds two comments: (1) "I prefer to restrict my theorizing to human brains" and (2) "We are far from bridging psychoanalysis and neuroscience" (Ibid.).

Although I respect LeDoux greatly, I differ with him on the issue of the significance of the great similarity between humans and the great apes. After I learned sign language and once found myself entranced in witnessing on TV a "conversation" I could follow perfectly in sign language between a human researcher, and an experimental ape (Washo) my mind was changed forever. Thus although one could argue as LeDoux does that "there is no way to know", I believe that Panksepp is more correct when he asserts that the command systems in humans and [such] animals are essentially the same, [therefore,] it is likely the experience of these emotions is not that different, if it is different at all!

Allan Schore

Allan Schore is Assistant Clinical Professor at the University of California Los Angeles School of Medicine, and on the Faculty of the Los Angeles Institute of Contemporary Psychoanalysis. It is fairly easy to summarize Schore's commentary on the target articles: the development of the self is critically dependent upon affects that are reflective of the limbic system, which is preferentially connected to the right hemisphere, and, according to Schore, reflects the Freudian dynamic unconscious. Naturally Schore finds support from most sources, since there is a long history of research acknowledging the importance of affects, their relationship to the limbic system, the right hemisphere, and the dynamic unconscious mind. However, as Schore continues his attempts to "get it right" (pun intended), I feel that to some extent he side steps a number of questions that have challenged researchers for some time; these include some of the following:[1] (1) Exactly how are relations within the limbic system regulated? (2) What is the exact relation between the hemispheres as regards the various kinds of affects? And what is the emotional role for the CB? (3) What is the exact relationship between the higher cortical level systems and the subcortical structures, of which there are many, as regards the various affects? (4) What is the relationship between the various parts of the limbic system? And what is the role of the so-called limbic lobe of the CB? (5) What can be said specifically about the role of the periaqueductal gray (PAG), the amygdala, the ventral part of the anterior cingulate cortex, the thalamus, and the limbic cortex? (6) How do the limbic subsystems change as we shift from one affect-related system to another, say from one that expresses anger to the system that regulates sexuality? This is important since it seems generally, as LeDoux points out in his discussion, that we are considering "affect" or "emotion" not just in the abstract, but also the specific affects, the systems that create them, and, as noted, these systems are not identical. (7) What is the precise timetable of development regarding the formation of self? And how can work in this area of development be related to what is known about the scientific maturation of mind/brain functions, including our ability to experience and communicate affects? (8) What are the important theories within psychoanalysis regarding developmental models of the mind (e.g. Gedo & Goldberg, 1973)? (9) If individuals trained in psychoanalysis and/or neuroscience are going to speculate as to which systems of the mind/brain are likely involved in change during psychoanalysis or analytically-oriented psychotherapy, how are we to best understand, compare and test these theories? (10) How has analytic technique been changing in response to the new insights from NP on affect and emotion? (11) From the perspectives of NP, what can be said about the connection between emotion on the one hand and consciousness and psychological defenses on the other? And what is the relationship between consciousness and Freud's dynamic unconscious?[2] Obviously, we do not yet have anything approaching complete answers to such questions, but as noted earlier each of these important questions are taken up in Levin (1991, 2003) and Levin and Vuckovich (1980, 1983) as well as in the present volume (e.g. Chapters One and Two). And some of them have been entered into significantly in the target articles (Chapter Three) and the commentaries reviewed in this chapter.

For those more interested in some additional thoughts on Allan Schore's interesting thinking, let me quote from some earlier comments of mine (Levin, 2006) reviewing for the journal NP a chapter Schore wrote for *Revolutionary Connections* [RC] as follows: "Schore sets the stage for what will follow by explicating ... the decisive role of the caretaker(s) early in life in the formation and further development of the infant's and child's immature nervous system. As Gedo (1999) has pointed out so well [in his own review of Schore's work], one key is Schore's focus on the structuralization of the ventro-mesial frontal lobes (VMFL). [This structuralization] (particularly in the right hemisphere), with its connections to the limbic system ... [provides] circuits that are essential for the development of emotions, and, consequently, of motivations; [for example], through the hypothalamic connections, they regulate the autonomic nervous system and thus play a decisive role in psychobiology. This subsystem of the brain [including especially the VMFL], through neuroendocrine mechanisms, activates the centers for pleasure and pain (reward and punishment), and it forms the apex of the hierarchy of psychosomatic control [Gedo, 1999, p. 96]. The authors of the book [RC] would add that the VMFL constitutes core self—or, as Schore puts it, "the structural development of the right hemisphere mediates the functional development of the unconscious mind" (p. 9). Along the way of spelling out the history of this insight within neuro-psychology, Schore is careful to credit especially Freud, Bowlby, and Stern, along with untold numbers of researchers and clinicians (neurologists, psychotherapists/psychoanalysts, psychologists, and creative others from various disciplines) who have helped us appreciate the critical centrality and many details of attachment. In effect, this volume [RC] is about the VMFL, and its many tributaries, in terms anatomical, chemical, and physiological; in terms of homeostasis, emotion, and cognition; and in terms of human suffering and victory over adversity—that is, in terms psychological, familial, cultural, and psychoanalytic" (Levin, 2006).

Howard Shevrin

Howard Shevrin is Professor of Psychology in the Department of Psychiatry of the University of Michigan Medical School. Typically, Shevrin aims straight at his target: "the relationship of affect to consciousness, motivation, and action" (Shevrin, 1999, p. 55). Regarding the first issue, Shevrin states: "If I follow Solms and Nersessian in their understanding of Freud, affects cannot be preconscious or unconscious, but are quintessentially conscious. [But] there is a disconnect here that must be addressed..." (p. 56). The problem is that unlike what Panksepp has stated about consciousness relating primarily to the pleasurable or unpleasurable aspects of feeling, the first problem Shevrin sees is that logically and experientially, everyone who experiences some emotion consciously, not only can tell whether it is pleasurable or not; they can also identify the type of emotion involved. So obviously the consciousness system involves more than just pleasure identification. According to Shevrin, one way this might work, from the perspective of Solms and Nersessian, is that the experiencing subject can observe the bodily sensations that go along with inner drive states, and this obviously provides a clue as to what the drive is about. Yet if Panksepp is thinking of some hierarchical regulatory motivational system of mind/brain that controls emotions, the question naturally remains regarding how things work within the hierarchy. The answer for Shevrin is different. He imagines that "each higher level 'detects' and in this sense 'represents' what is going on at a lower level" (p. 57).[3]

As for the relationship of affect to motivation, Shevrin questions Panksepp for linking [too tightly] "basic emotional affects" to basic instinctual action readiness systems, and "motivational affects" to sensory systems. Shevrin argues: "it is hard to see how experiences of desire and power, which appear to be motivational affects, are more closely linked to sensory rather than action readiness systems" (p. 57). One way out of the dilemma would be, according to Shevrin, for us to "identify a class of experiences as motivational which is independent of another class of experiences called affective. Each such class would [then] have its unconscious aspects so that we could speak of unconscious motives becoming conscious, and conscious affects becoming unconscious. This alternative allows for a more flexible and varied relationship between affect and motivation, conscious and unconscious, than the view attributed to Freud by Solms and Nersessian" (Ibid., italics added). He adds (p. 58) it also shifts conscious experiences from pleasure/unpleasure towards gratification vs. frustration. Clinically, one sees states of pleasure and unpleasure in various mixtures, and Shevrin points out this new view would also help explain that, namely, the pleasurable frustrations vs. the unpleasurable gratifications of urges.

Before discussing the relation of affect to action, Shevrin raises a most interesting question. Why is affect or emotion built into experience any way? Could we not function without it, as he imagines many lower life forms do? Shevrin's answer underscores some of Solms and Nersessian's perspectives, along with those of Panksepp, with the viewpoint of psychoanalysis. Namely, affect/emotion facilitates adaptation by signaling a successful engagement with our environment in the sense that we have engaged in some successful compromise between our ego, our id [and superego], and this signal function of emotion also tells us when we are getting close to dangers, such as acting on unacceptable wishes. He states clearly: "I am suggesting that all affects have this purpose. They are signals, sometimes subtle and unconscious, sometimes gross and conscious, which indicate the import of the internal battle for what we must or must not do next" (p. 58). Therefore, there is no doubt that affect gives us "breathing space" in which to make the proper decisions about actions. Shevrin doesn't use the expression "delayed action plans" but in keeping with Chapter One of this book, he is clearly arguing the same points that we make in that chapter, in relation to the affects within dreams.

In his final comments, Shevrin reminds us that the unconscious of Freud is not good at dealing with reality ("it is a poor learner", p. 59), but one could say that it tries hard to come up with effective measures, sometimes knowing when to inhibit actions, and at other times when to take them. Bridging psychoanalysis and neuroscience obviously will involve having a much better understanding of how the unconscious mind does this, and how this is actually instantiated in brain. As Shevrin notes in his last sentence, "it is this [very discovery of] complexity at the neuroscience level that is the best harbinger of future success in building bridges between neuroscience and psychoanalysis" (p. 59).

Clifford Yorke

Clifford Yorke is a Training and Supervising Psychoanalyst of the British Psychoanalytic Society. Yorke begins his complicated commentary with a reminiscence of his once having made a comment at a psychoanalytic meeting early in his career in which he asserted "that the understanding of affects [within psychoanalysis] was perhaps the weakest part of the psychoanalytic theory of the way the mind worked" (Yorke, 1999, p. 60). That no one criticized him first surprised him, but then made him think in retrospect that no one knew he was wrong! He explains as follows. First, as Solms and Nersessian point out in their target article, Freud's comments on affect appear in a vast array of Freud's articles, so it is easy for those who might miss a few of the details to develop some misunderstandings. Second, some specialists outside of psychoanalysis have willfully distorted Freud's ideas and denigrated their value for various reasons, not always scientific; moreover, some "uninformed criticism [comes] from inside [psychoanalysis]" (p. 60), and both of these complications need to be set right. According to Yorke, this has involved those analysts who believe that affects can be easily theoretically separated from the idea of drives, even though these drives are in effect what originated them. As he puts it: "It is widely believed today that affects can replace drives rather than be linked with them. If Freud's theory of affects is misunderstood, so is his theory of drives. So I want to underline, in the course of what follows, his definition of drives as emphasized by Solms and Nersessian in their paper, adding one or two points" (Ibid.).

In other words, Yorke greatly appreciates what Solms and Nersessian have accomplished in stating the basic principles of Freud's drive theory, which he feels, in spite of the many contributions since Freud's day, "stand up remarkably well nearly 60 years after his death" (p. 61). And thirdly, it is obvious that just as Yorke praises Solms and Nersessian for stating Freud's affect theory in a form that is "succinct, predigested, and readily assimilable" (Ibid.) so can we praise Yorke for his making explicit precisely what could easily be misunderstood in Freud's fundamental conceptualization of affects and drives. Yorke also has a completely different take on drives, as compared to Panksepp, who notes in his target commentary that "the Freudian drive concept retains little value, and ... should be put to rest" (p. 61). Here Yorke believes that Panksepp "has not fully understood the meaning and significance of that usage [of the word 'drive']" (Ibid.). It will pay for us to further examine the matter of drives more carefully.

To Yorke, the synopsis on Freud's views on affective process involves "the concept of drives...[as] an indispensable part" (p. 62). He points out that when Panksepp rejects drive theory in relation to affects "[Panksepp] made no mention of footnote (4). [He then adds] Let me repeat an essential part of it, adding a few words that preceded the passage quoted: *'The id, cut off from the external world, has a world of perceptions of its own. It detects with extraordinary acuteness certain changes in its interior, especially oscillations in the tension of its instinctual needs, and these changes become conscious as feelings in the pleasure-unpleasure series"* (Freud, 1940, italics added) (p. 62). Yorke then emphasizes: "This was written by a man nearing the end of his life, who wanted to set on record, however briefly, his views on psychoanalysis as he understood it at that time; and it is clear that he had not altered his opinion on the relationship between drives and affects. The fact seems to be that *if you accept the groundwork of Freud's theory of affect, whether subject to Panksepp's provisions or not, you accept, to the same degree, his concept of drives. Without that concept, the entire theory falls to the ground"* (Yorke, p. 63, italics added). Yorke then goes on to clarify, that when Panksepp understands Freud's drive concept in terms of generalized tension states that accompany homeostatic imbalances he is mistaken, and that in reality *Freud is talking about something quite different. Namely, Freud was describing drives as something clinical, yet intrinsically unknowable [at least in terms of the state of biology at the time of his theorizing], yet [something nevertheless] definable in terms of "a source [meaning a somatic process], an aim [meaning something needed in a psychobiological sense], a pressure [that is, with significant intensity], and an object [this means that the goal states are meaningfully defined in relationship to other human beings]"* (p. 63 italics added). Here Yorke further cites Freud for clarifying that such drives are inferable by their mental representations ["ideas and images as representatives of 'drives'" is Yorke's favorite way of thinking of this], and [by] the actions that they may lead to. Such differing drives/instincts might also be [eventually] traced to their differing somatic sources" (p. 63).

All this would seem clear enough, so where is the disagreement with Panksepp? It comes out clearest in Yorke's final comments comparing his feelings about the differing scientific methods of neuroscience and psychoanalysis. Yorke states: "...there is to my mind, an unfortunate equation of *empiricism* with research methods involving *quantification*" (p. 66). Next, Yorke notes that *"[the] analyst works with the instrument of an analyzed mind, but it is also a mind in touch with the patient in a way denied an outside observer. Only the analyst can relate a current thought or affect to information given him by the patient days or weeks ago..."* (italics added, p. 67). I am reminded here of Einstein's distrust of both empirical and inductive approaches to scientific problems! Einstein preferred to try various "Gedanken Experimente" in association with a rich mixture of both methods, seeing where imagination and feelings took him, then following up on his intuitions with more formal experiments. In this same sense I think in Panksepp, and in Solms and Nersessian on the one hand, and in Yorke, on the other, we are seeing a mature frustration over how best to tap what is salient behaviorally about human emotions and the unconscious (vs. mere conscious experience of them), and how to match the unbelievable psychological complexity involved in mind properly with our deepening knowledge of the "working brain", to use a phrase Luria appreciated. Yorke respects Luria deeply, as he shows when he states that "Luria pointed to the difficulties in both empirical and inductive procedures" (p. 66). Perhaps Yorke's problem is thus believing, as Panksepp does, that anyone could have equal commitment to, and respect for neuroscience and psychoanalysis, and therefore strive towards integrating these fields, especially around the complex subjects of drives and emotion.

Notes

1. One author who has addressed most of the questions indicated above, is Pally (2005). Regarding the neuroscience model of emotion she states her conclusion that "imbedded with emotion itself is the organization of adaptive behavior (Damasio, 1995; LeDoux, 1994, 1996)" (p. 179). Essentially, emotion organizes the behaviors [i.e. actions] to help us adapt to our environment. For her this involves the cerebral cortex, amygdala, orbital frontal cortex, hypothalamus, thalamus, autonomic nervous system, and brainstem. It also involves norepinephrine (NE),

oxytocin and vasopressin, HPA axis-cortisol, and endorphins. Her summary is quite correct, although we obviously believe it a mistake to leave out the CB. Alas, so do most other researchers, including Schore.

2. This last question is a key question for this book, since this author believes that consciousness is usually a marker for the explicit memory system; however, as we shall see, especially in later chapters of this book, consciousness itself may be less important, in terms of outcome, than the nature of the relationship at any given moment between implicit and explicit memory systems. This is the "Holy Grail" we are seeking.

3. From a clinical psychoanalytic perspective, however, there is no doubt that often feelings remain unknown to the experiencing subject. It therefore seems a problem to put too much weight on the matter of consciousness, except perhaps to recognize that the experiencing self likes to believe (falsely at times) that it knows and intends various events.

PART III

MORE ABOUT GENE ACTIVATION, SPONTANEITY, AND THE PRIMING OF MEMORY FOR PSYCHOANALYTIC LEARNING

Synapses, cytokines and long-term memory networks: an interdisciplinary look at how psychoanalysis activates learning via its effects on emotional attention[1][2]

Fred M. Levin

"Weeds grow and animals slip about in the night Where no man dares to hunt them down."

Loren Eiseley, *The Night Country*, p. 3

Précis: We have already discussed the activation of genes in relation to emotional attention in Part I, Chapters One and Two. However, here we are taking the time and space to review more of the details of this perspective, so as to put learning into a clear context: that of emotional events with special meaning to the self. One key, however, is recognizing that emotion does not merely contextualize our experience, as critical as this function is; emotion also expresses our meanings to our self, and to the world, in ways that invite further elaboration of our fundamental drive states through fantasy, and eventually through various need-related actions.

I. *Introduction*

I begin with a quote from Loren Eiseley about the darker side of mental life. Unfortunately, all of our increasing knowledge of mind/brain cannot neutralize our human limitations. Obviously, a lot depends upon how any new knowledge we develop or acquire would be applied. My hope is that our neuropsychoanalytic insights will lead to the improved application of psychoanalysis clinically, especially to matters of the human heart, which Eiseley wrote about so movingly.

Eiseley was an only child, the son of a deaf mother during an age when deaf people were ostracized as "deaf and dumb". He lost his father early in his life, was picked upon frequently by playmates, eventually leaving home in his youth and riding freight trains across the U.S.A. during the Great Depression. His vagabond years lasted until he found an island of hope in the "night country" of his mind, and started upward movements. Against all odds, Eiseley ultimately became the distinguished chair of anthropology at the University of Pennsylvania, and one of America's great writer-scientists![3] He had learned to collaborate with feared others, and it touched his fundamental sense of aloneness, but he never forgot the inner darkness.

From time to time in what follows I will illustrate the human side of my discussion of the potentially dry technical details of memory and learning by imagining that Eiseley, long dead, is in analysis with me (really, no such thing ever happened), and I shall describe aspects of a completely imaginary interchange with him![4]

Psychoanalysis, psychology, and neuroscience each contribute to learning theory. This chapter discusses some of the details that make this so, and aims towards a more unified theory of learning. It also considers the value of interdisciplinary studies that I believe are significantly changing psychoanalytic theory and practice, and impacting as well on neuroscience and psychology.

There are three parts to my chapter: I begin with a summary of Horst Ibelgauft's webpage (1999) on the Neuroimmune Network (NIN) (Levin, 2002a). One leitmotif of Ibelgauft's webpage and this chapter is the role of cytokines (CK) on synaptic plasticity, via their ability to activate and inactivate genes. To quote Abel, Martin, Bartsch, and Kandel (1998):

the neuronal activation of genes means simply that the molecular basis of memory may hinge on the balance between chemical factors that establish versus those which inhibit synaptic plasticity (Ibid., 338).

For a long time the Holy Grail of neuroscience depended upon determining the cellular and molecular chemistry of memory and learning, including the synaptic matrix in which CK act. I believe that psychoanalysts can participate in this quest, along with brain scientists, through the search for apt mind/brain correspondences (Solms, 1999). Such correspondences are required for the creation of comprehensive evidence-based learning theories that also cross disciplinary boundaries. Therefore, in the second part of this chapter I revisit my personal interest in research into how psychoanalysis facilitates learning readiness (Levin, 1991, 2002b). Because our theories and our techniques are inseparable we owe it to our patients to develop both as carefully and objectively as possible.[5]

Learning is an inherently emotional phenomenon, that is, a highly motivated action that satisfies vital needs, and which has its affective origins deep within the brain; it is not a receptive or passive cognition. That learning involves a core emotional self is particularly important because there is reason to believe that cognitive neuropsychological research approaches to learning are not sufficient in themselves, for two reasons: (1) they often downplay emotions because emotions can be hard to quantify, and (2) they are sometimes restricted primarily to those brain surface structures which can be seen on scans. Thus deep structures such as the periaqueductal gray (PAG), and the hypothalamus within the brain's core tend to get short shrift because of the dominance of cognitive/cortical theories of learning and memory, and for this reason we need to learn more about how the deeper structures contribute to the sense of self and related learning. Obviously, both emotions and their substrates deserve our attention.

The biology of learning and memory thus involves macro-, micro-, and submicroscopic levels of brain organization. A major problem is that any presentation that goes deeply into such subjects as synapses, ion channels, chemical signaling, receptors, and second messengers is likely to lose the audience's attention. Yet how can we avoid such considerations if our goal is to set the stage for a serious neuropsychoanalytic consideration of learning and memory, and particularly if we wish to comprehend the complex role of CKs?

From a cognitive perspective memory comes in at least two flavors (explicit and implicit), each further dividing into short vs. long-term forms. Memory-related gross anatomical structures associated with explicit memory include the medial temporal lobe, (including of course the hippocampuses and related structures, such as the amygdala's), while those associated with implicit memory are principally the product of the cerebellum and basal ganglia.

Psychoanalytically-oriented research in the area of learning and memory has benefited greatly from the work of the late Niels Lassen (on working memory), Michael Posner and Tim Shallice (on executive control), Jaak Panksepp (on core affective systems), John Gedo (on the hierarchical-developmental model), Arnold Modell and Fred Levin (on the holding environment and metaphors), Howard Shevrin (on subliminal perception), Colwyn Trevarthen (on mother-infant interaction), Merton Gill, Karl Pribram, and Karen Kaplan-Solms and Mark Solms (on mind-brain correlations), and Eric Kandel and Masao Ito (on synaptic chemistry and mechanisms and important differences between the two systems, such as long-term potentiation, LTP, in the case of explicit memory [characteristic of the brain outside the CB], vs. long-term depression, LTD, in the case of implicit memory) [characteristic of the CB] (Levin, 2000b; also see Panksepp, 2000, 2001).

Standing on the shoulders of these scholars and many others, a picture is slowly emerging regarding how the different levels of mind/brain organization are integrated. For example, I believe in the following important correlation: that during any meaningful psychoanalysis learning-readiness is created by the analyst's provision of a proper holding environment, especially as this invites the analysand's spontaneity. But what gets learned within psychoanalysis is more than the consequence of interpretations per se;[6] analytic learning involves conditioning (procedural learning) as well (Fonagy, 1998; Levin, 1991, 2002b), so that in the final result, both emotion and insight play critical roles. And if learning is involved, obviously, synaptic plasticity is also.

The spontaneity I am considering is invited by two aspects of psychoanalysis: (1) the patient's free associations in the context of a trusting (i.e. safe) relationship with his or her analyst, and (2) his or her allowing various spontaneous transference enactment's to manifest themselves. Spontaneity, in whatever form, appears to activate working memory for the subjects that are remembered or enacted in treatment. These memories and enactment's can then be interpreted to the patient beneficially, begin to effect the patient's response patterns, and ultimately enter emotional attention more pervasively. Most important, this process of learning via emotional attention occurs whether or not the decisive analytically observed behavioral or affective patterns ever actually enter the patient's or analyst's consciousness; this follows from what we now know about subliminal perception and knowledge without awareness (see Levin, 1997, 2002b for review of Shevrin's important work on this subject).

But even more critical for our consideration today, the emotional attention and the learning stimulated within a psychoanalysis obviously have a direct relationship to the neurochemical changes occurring within the brain during such states. I would argue in fact that the learning and the neurochemical changes are in fact dependent concomitants. To give credit where it is due, it seems important to note that what Freud called the drive organization of memory is his intuitively correct depiction of an adaptive learning process[7] in which we now know that synaptic plasticity is altered by affective experience (and vice versa).

I use the expression *emotional attention* for precise reasons. Emotional because I feel that what becomes new long-term memory (LTM) starts from our being moved by the emotional significance of events, and from our multiple emotional needs, e.g. for companionship, affection, novelty, and so forth. It seems reasonable to conclude that it is this emotionality that then becomes the trigger for new learning (see below). And I use attention rather than consciousness because, as I noted, many important observations enter into our thinking subliminally.

I shall report in this chapter upon details of the chemical and neurophysiological changes associated with neural networks and LTM. Our ultimate goal, of course, is to connect, as much as possible, psychoanalytic learning and those factors contributing to new LTM (Levin, 1995). My intuition is that the key to understanding learning within psychoanalysis lies in two general approaches: (1) better understanding those practical procedures within psychoanalysis that invite the activation of working memory and emotional attention, together with (2) appreciating exactly how such emotional attention and insights alter synaptic plasticity chemically, especially via their effects on CK-mediated gene activation.

When I mention practical procedures within psychoanalysis I mean the following (all of which stimulate learning-readiness): giving attention to what the patient is moved by; respecting the patient's methods of learning; taking care to avoid humiliation and shame; carefully proceeding from what the patient already knows to what is for him or her new knowledge; considering our role, as analysts, in contributing, along with the patient, to the patient's transference enactment's, and seeking to understand better both the patient's and our own such contributions; and so forth (Levin, 1995).

Finally, in the third part of this chapter I comment upon the current profusion of schools within psychoanalysis. My suggestion is that this reflects interdisciplinary and collaborative efforts that are currently informing psychoanalysis with the viewpoints of various specialized areas of knowledge; but, in addition, *they are also helping establish several new fields, and not just schools*. For example, in the case of efforts that bridge psychoanalysis and neuroscience, they have created neuro-psychoanalysis.

Collaboration across disciplinary, cultural, philosophical and language boundaries represents a much needed effort to reduce the complexity of thinking generally by introducing novel testable scientific paradigms, as suggested by Patrizia Gianpieri-Deutsch (personal communication). In the future, progress will not be accomplished without larger groups of specialists working together. Our meeting in Vienna, under her leadership, is a fine example of such a process at work.[8]

Paradoxically there seems to be a growing affinity, within psychoanalytic discourse, for the application of two divergent, but I would argue, nonetheless complementary philosophical positions: on the one hand there is Pragmatism, recently explicated by Arnold Goldberg (2002).[9] Practical approaches appeal whenever the subject matter of research interest reaches a critical level of complexity. This is surely the case for our current interest in studying mind or brain both in depth and in tandem. On the other hand, as suggested by John Gedo (personal communication), there is also a place for creatively thinking matters through deeply, in a mode where discovering the deepest truths is the primary consideration (as in the example of Einstein's theories of General and Special Relativity). Combining the search for deep truths with practical real time experimentation and verification seems the best of both worlds.

II. *The Neuroimmune Network and immunity*

Horst Ibelgauft (1999) at the University of Munich has created a Cytokines Online Pathfinder Encyclopedia (COPE), containing over fifteen thousand scientific references and 50,000 hyperlinks to the thousands of CKs listed. He makes clear that the nervous system (NS) and the immune system (IS) (including the neuroendocrine system) essentially constitute a single, integrated overarching system, the *neuroimmune network* (NIN). His conclusion is based upon evidence such as the following: (1) "Neural targets controlling thermogenesis, behavior, sleep, and mood are affected by the so-called pro-inflammatory CKs [namely, interleukin 1 (IL-1), interleukin 6 (IL-6), and tumor necrosis factor Alfa (TNFalpha)] which are released by macrophages and monocytes during infection; (2) within the NS "production of CK has been detected as a result of brain injury, during viral and bacterial infections, and in neurodegenerative processes". In other words, communication between the nervous system and the soma is two way (Ibelgauft, cited in Levin, 2000a). Moreover, (3) research on the details of synaptic transmission confirms Ibelgauft's conclusion that CKs play a critical role (for details see Abel, Martin, Bartsch, & Kandel, 1998); and (4) there are structural chemical similarities between the NS and IS; for example, Agrin, an aggregating protein, is expressed in lymphocytes (where it plays a role in T cell signaling and so-called "lipid raft formation", the latter subject mentioned below), as well as in neuronal signaling, and even in the functionality of the myoneural junction (Khan, Bose, Yam, Solski, & Rupp, 2001).

So what are CKs? They are "a diverse group of soluble proteins and peptides which act as humoral regulators at nano- to picomolar concentrations … and which act on a wider spectrum of target cells than do hormones" (Ibelgauft, 1999, section on cytokines, p. 2). CKs [are produced by] cells of the immune system, from glial cells, neurons, and from skin cells" (Levin, 2000a). You will recall that skin cells and neurons began life as neuroectoderm, that is, they derive from the same tissue.

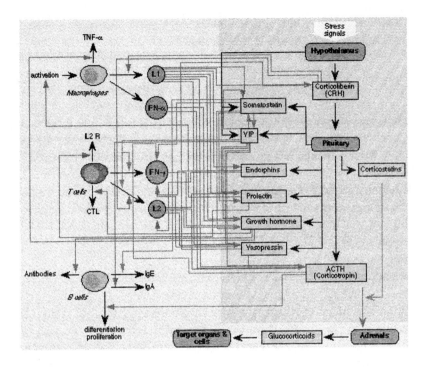

Fig. 1. (from Ibelgauft, reproduced with permission of the author) presents a simplified scheme of the hypothalamic-pituitary axis (HPA). IS and CNS are captured in a snapshot that shows as well a bit of the complexity of the NIN.

According to Maier and Watkins (1998), there are at least three pathways between the periphery and the brain. Unidirectional pathways include Pathways A and B. Pathway A is the autonomic nervous system, the sympathetic part of which enervates immune organs. In Pathway A, catecholamines (largely epinephrine and norepinephrine [NE]) are released from sympathetic nerves, controlling various organs (e.g. the spleen, thymus, etc.).

Pathway B is the hypothalamic-pituitary axis (HPA) itself. In Pathway B various releasing factors (e.g. corticotropin releasing factor [CRF] whose source is the hypothalamus) enter into the bloodstream heading from hypothalamus to pituitary, which in response releases various hormones on demand (e.g. adreno-corticotropin releasing hormone, or ACTH). These pituitary hormones then travel via the blood stream and effect both the peripheral endocrine organs (e.g. the adrenal cortex, which then releases cortisol) and the immune system.

The reader may detect that we are slowly moving towards a discussion of the bidirectional immune pathways between the brain and the periphery. One arm of Pathway C is composed of *immune cells* (i.e. largely macrophages, and some other cells) that release IL-1 (as an example), that can stimulate sensory paraganglia of the vagus nerve, which in turn carries impulses to the nucleus tractus solitarius (NTS) and the area postrema (AP) in the brain-stem. We do not often think of the vagus nerve as having a sensory component, but it does. A neural cascade then occurs which at least theoretically could result in the release into the blood of CK such as IL-1. There is a real question, however, whether any of this blood born IL-1 actually reaches the brain itself or crosses the relatively impervious blood-brain barrier. Thus, most important for CNS CK production, a second arm of pathway C starts as does the first in the vagus nerve, reaches the NTS and AP, but then heads into two different brain areas, the hippocampus and the hypothalamus, wherein IL-1, for example, is generated within brain cells (Levin, 2000a). I believe it is this pathway that is involved in new synapse formation on emotional demand (see below).

Once so generated within the CNS, the IL-1 in our example, (or any other CK in principle) is capable of interacting with any neuron that carries the appropriate CK receptors. Any of three further different results then become possible. One is simple neurotransmission, i.e. the generation of a postsynaptic depolarization. Second, for the case of the interleukins released within the CNS secondary to vagus nerve stimulation, there could also be the so-called proinflammatory response, namely sickness reactions, fever, fatigue, anorexia, etc.

The third possibility is that once CKs become bound to postsynaptic receptors, they can induce gene transcription and translation (see below),[10] which obviously can profoundly effect neural network formation, memory and learning (Levin, 2002a). In effect CKs are obviously part of the mechanism for LTM formation, which I intend to review in more detail. Before doing so, however, let me comment briefly on the subject of immunity for those who might not be that familiar with the subject.

III. *Kinds of immunity*

In a recent review of the subject (Levin, 2000a) I cite Maier and Watkin's (1998) description of immunity as follows:

> There are two kinds of immunity, either specific or nonspecific. The specific type, also called "humoral", is slow; the nonspecific type, also called "cellular", is relatively rapid. Both are secondary to the detection of foreign invaders (either viral, bacterial, or toxic-chemical) and they follow distinctly different pathways.
>
> Nonspecific cellular immunity occurs within 1-2 hours of the invasion, and depends upon phagocytes such as macrophages or neutrophils. Later, when I summarize specific immunity, I will note the role of macrophages in that process as well, where they serve as antigen presenting cells (APCs); however, in the present discussion of rapid, nonspecific immune response the goal is three fold: (1) the nonspecific recognition of foreign material (antigen, none self, "stressor", "toxin"), (2) the transfer of this material into phagocytes ("eating cells"), and (3) its destruction by various intracellular means, including exposure to enzymes, nitric oxide, and/or various CK (e.g. IL-1, IL-6, TNFalpha, etc.). These defensive proteins and other transmitters create the so-called proinflammatory reaction noted above, that further attracts other immune cells.
>
> Specific humoral immunity is more complex, generates antibodies, and takes 3-5 days because a number of cell reproductive cycles are required to create enough of those cells making the specific antibody targeted at particular antigenic stimuli. First the foreign substance (antigen) is engulfed within the APCs. Parts of the invader are then moved to the surface of the APC. This display of these parts is recognized by T cells that carry appropriate surface receptor sites. Recognition involves a binding between the T cell receptor site and the displayed antigenic part, a process that stimulates the T cell to differentiate and proliferate, increasing the number of T cells which can then target the specific antigen (invader).
>
> Some T cells are cytotoxic, and kill specific antigen producing cells. Others are T-helper cells, which help a separate class of B cells expand their number, and begin to detect antigen, differentiate, and proliferate just as the original T cells did, thus joining the battle against antigen. From our point of view, what is important is that the substances secreted by the APC and which assist their performing complex antigen-site matching and intercellular communication

among the T-helper cells, and the B cells, are basically CKs (e.g. the interleukins already mentioned).

IV. *CK and synaptic plasticity*

"CKs are involved in the amplification, coordination, and regulation of communication pathways within the NIN" (Ibelgauft, 1999, section on the neuroimmune system or network, p. 2). Gene activation refers to the processes of both gene transcription and translation. The first step involves Messenger RNA (mRNA) forming from DNA in a process mediated by specific RNA polymerases active at the ribosomes (Ibelgauft, 1999, section on Gene expression, p. 1). The second step involves RNA being translated into proteins that express specific gene functions.

As we shall see, many complex factors effect gene expression, including the CKs I am highlighting in this chapter (Levin, 2002a). For example, all genes have *promotor regions* that contain special DNA that regulates transcription and processing of the genetic codes. Transcription factors that aggregate in the promotor regions[11] are referred to as *response elements*. Some of these transcription factors are required for the transcription of all genes, but others are important primarily or exclusively for specific classes of genes. One subgroup of transcription factors or so-called nuclear receptors is also designated *early response genes* (ERGs). We will return to ERG later when we consider the cascade leading to LTM, but first I need to describe more about the synapse and types of memory.

V. *The synapse[12] and types of memory*

Everyone knows that synapses are the spaces (clefts) into which neurotransmitters are released, thus providing chemical contact between neurons. These neurotransmitters are released from pre-synaptic vesicles; they then traverse the synaptic cleft and attach themselves to receptor sites on the postsynaptic membrane (that is, the membrane of the second neuron). This usually allows the first neuron to depolarize the second neuron and continue a nervous excitation wave in a particular direction.[13] There may be as many as a trillion synapses within the CNS. What may not be readily appreciated, however, is that the actual structure and functional relationships of synapses belie the simple description just given! For example, it is now known that synapses do not just preexist, but are created on emotional demand by the activity of cytokines, that is, in relation to the drive towards learning, and various other drives.

Let's take a brief pause. If I imagine Loren Eiseley in psychoanalysis with me, I believe the critical issue for him might be whether or not I would carefully listen to him and remember what he has told me. Only then would he be reassured that he exists for me, i.e. in an important emotional sense. My hunch is that this kind of emotional awareness or attention is exactly what serves as a decisive trigger for the induction of new synapses and the use of these in the service of new learning. Whether we are properly seen, heard, appreciated, and especially loved and respected, is never neutral.

Emotional attention in psychoanalysis may be particularly useful because it feels to us as if it is not guided, that is, it is something felt to be independent of outside agency and thus of immediate interest to the self. During spontaneous activity emotional attention and executive functions seem less in play than they would be otherwise; and perhaps that is why this kind of attention feels important; that is, it seems particularly salient for our survival. Selective attention may therefore be a precursor to emotional attention. Csikszentmihalyi argued long ago (1975), and I agree, that emotional attention plays a central role in learning, especially when it falls in some optimal effective range.[14]

Returning to synapses, we still need to make our way through the very dense subject of what happens in the synaptic cleft, as well as at the pre- and postsynaptic membrane levels, that influences synaptic weights and the related learning in networks of neurons. Exploring this complicatedness of synapses will help us better appreciate the daunting task of placing CK activity within the context of neural transmission, memory and emotional learning.

It will help to consider the categories of memory and say something as well about receptors.[15] Understanding neural transmission involves distinguishing at least between the two major types of memory already noted, implicit and explicit (sometimes called procedural and declarative), their receptors (AMPA or NMDA receptors[16]), their neuroanatomy (lateral temporal lobe, amygdala and hippocampal vs. the cerebellum and basal ganglia), and their time course of activity (in the case of explicit memory, multiple repetitions seem required for learning, and memories are read out by merely asking conscious questions. Nonconscious or unconscious methods can also result in or tap explicit memory. In the case of implicit memory, however, learning usually occurs with a smaller number of passes,[17] and recall is usually obtained by priming, i.e. without consciousness being required). Children do as well as adults in the case of implicit learning.

Let's take another time out. My hypothetical treatment with Eiseley would involve both explicit and implicit memory systems. The implicit system would especially be involved whenever I would prime his memory by reminding him of things he told me earlier, and which might be related to his here and now feelings. For example, imagine that he was talking in the previous session about people who interrupt him with stupid comments instead of patiently listening to him. Suppose I ask him, towards the end of his spontaneous comments, if, when he was complaining about bad listeners last time, he was also thinking that I fit into this category! This could be seen both as an interpretation, but also as a case of my priming his memory. Another kind of priming, might be to let him know what I think he seems to be feeling, and ask if this might be the case or not. Or priming could be my mentioning a song that is running through my mind, or I might sing it to him or wonder aloud with him if it reflects something in him that I might be tuning in upon. Priming connects past and present feelings in complex ways.[18] Priming is also the critical mutual activity that connects the minds and brains of two individuals, that is, which puts and keeps them in resonance with each other.

Long-term-potentiation (LTP) has been eloquently reviewed by Bliss (1998, pp. 78–82; see also Johnston, 1997, and Malenka & Nicoll, 1999), and seems often a prelude to long-term memory formation. Bliss feels it definitely is.[19] LTP is the enhancement or easier neural firing secondary to neuronal use or stimulation. LTP is also characterized by so-called specificity and associativity. These are defined as follows:

In terms of the hippocampus, for example, if two sets of converging electrodes are placed on either side of a recording electrode in the CA1 region of the hippocampus, say to activate pyramidal cell axons of the neighboring CA3 region, LTP will be produced in either of the two pathways providing only that it is active at the time of the stimulating input. In other words, each synapse, in principle acts as an "independent computing device" (this is *input sensitivity*; Bliss, p. 80). *Associativity* refers to the ability to induce LTP in the second pathway of the above example, that is, even in the face of a weak tetanus in this pathway, when a strong stimulus is given at the same time to the first pathway. Bliss sees this form of associative memory as coinciding with classical conditioning (Bliss, p. 81).[20]

Each form of memory, implicit or explicit, is also recordable in two phases: short-term and long-term. However, only long-term memory requires the synthesis of new proteins (Albright, Jessell, Kandel, & Posner, 2000, p. S13). "Short-term synaptic enhancement ... results from a covalent modification of preexisting proteins mediated by the cAMP-dependent protein kinase A (PKA) and by protein kinase C (PKC)" (Albright et. al., p. S13). In contrast, *long-term memory involves "the translocation of PKA and mitogen-activating protein kinase (MAPK) to the nucleus of the sensory neurons where these kinases activate CREB1 and derepress CREB2, leading to the induction of a set of immediate or early response genes [ERG], ultimately resulting in the growth of new synaptic connections"* [emphasis added] (Bartsch, et al. 1995, 1998, cited in Albright et al., p. S13).[21] The point here is that at a molecular level all of the known memory systems likely involve roughly the same set of molecular [cytokine] markers (Michael Posner, personal communication).[22] These complex steps will be covered again, so don't worry about committing them to memory just yet!

Returning to the implicit/explicit memory distinction, it is important that in spite of the differences noted, the explicit and implicit memory systems should not be thought of as wholly separate and competitive; rather, they are judged to be highly complementary to each other in the brain and usually create a mosaic of integrated memory formats, i.e. "they ordinarily cooperate with each other in learning" (Squire, 1998, p. 68). This is part of the complexity of memory alluded to.

Putting this all together in his classical early paper on CNS plasticity Floyd Bloom (1985) describes the neural cascade, culminating in LTM, as follows: it begins when NE alters the firing of particular neurons by activating cyclic AMP (an intracellular second messenger), which then activates the enzyme protein kinase (noted above), which leads to the phosphorylation of macromolecular substrates (such as pre- and postsynaptic ion channels) and the enhance-ment of transmission. Obviously, by the mid 1980s, synapses were understood to be fairly complex structures even though the wrinkle of gene activation and CK was less well understood compared to now.

Contemporary articles on synaptic activity clearly show the grow-ing appreciation and complexity of CK in synaptic changes (and make clear the large number of cofactors involved—see below on Ito's work). I will now review two studies in particular. The first is by an American research group, Beattie et al. (2002) which I introduce to make clear the role of glial cells; the second paper, on the CB, by Masao Ito (2001) is introduced to explain LTD and various important synaptic subtleties.

The American group describes how activity-dependent modulation of synaptic efficacy in the brain contributes to neural circuit develop-ment and experience-dependent plasticity. They further remark on the decisive role of glial cells as follows: although glia [supporting cells] are affected by activity and ensheathe synapses, their influence on synaptic strength has largely been ignored.[23] One key is that a protein produced by glia, tumor necrosis factor alpha (TNFalpha) [a CK] enhances synaptic efficacy by increasing surface expression of AMPA receptors thus playing a role in synaptic plasticity. Another key is that neurons and glia have complex communications (Fields & Stevens-Graham, 2002; see also Chapter 6, part II.).

To be more precise, however, in spite of explicating the role of glial TNFalpha in activating genes and thus altering AMPA recep-tors, these researchers did not conclude, at least in their particular set of experiments, that gene activation played a major role in mod-ifying synaptic plasticity; rather, they felt that neural activity was responsible for the changes in AMPA receptors. Nevertheless, they believe gene activation could not be ruled out absolutely (personal communication).[24] Obviously, it is not easy to tell when gene acti-vation is a direct factor in synaptic enhancement, or when indirect. The distinction may not be that critical to our synopsis of learning changes, however, for if CKs increase synapses by increasing neural activity, or by directly enhancing the synapese, in either case neural network formation (and LTM) is clearly enhanced.

The complexity of the synapse, as regards CK, emerges still more clearly if we shift to Ito's work (2001). He is Head of the Brain

Research Institute (BRI) of RIKEN FRONTIER INSTITUTE in Wako, Japan. If you examine Fig. 2. from Ito's paper on long-term depression (LTD),[25] I think you can begin to see the complexity I am talking about. It seems that synaptic phenomena are not only complex, they are probably more complex than most of us can even imagine!

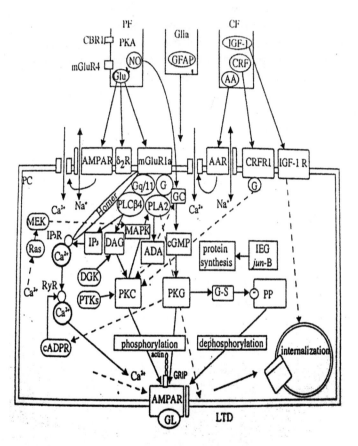

Fig. 2. GA/CF conjunctive stimulation of Purkinje cells. Reprinted from Ito (2001) with permission of the author. Parallel fibers (PF, extension of granule cell axon, GA); climbing fiber (CF), AMPA receptor (AMPAR); yet-unidentified amino acid (AAR), arachidonic acid (ADA); G-substrate (G-S); immediate early gene (IEG); ryanodine receptor (RyR); nitric oxide (NO); metabotropic glutamate receptor 4 (mGluR4). For other abbreviations see current text, or refer to Ito (2001 for details).

Let me explain Fig. 2. It will help to consider the following points:

1. Ito was early to demonstrate LTD, the experience-based down regulation of neuronal firing (i.e. the opposite of LTP). The required trigger for LTD in the CB is when Purkinje cells are simultaneously fired off by numbers of granule cell axons (GA, also abbreviated as PF for parallel fibers), and by single climbing fibers (CF). This is so-called "conjunctive stimulation'. It is then that the AMPA receptors (AMPAR) of Purkinje cells demonstrate LTD induction. This is illustrated in Fig. 2. (By the way, Purkinje cells are the primary output neurons of the CB.)

2. The GA carry the stimuli from basket cells (BC) which carry input from two potential sources, either spinal cord and brain stem, or from the cerebellar flocculus. The CFs contain input from the inferior olive or the retina.

3. When the input is from the floccus and retina, the CB is able to provide the vestibular ocular reflex (VOR), which compensates for head movements by eye movements to keep retinal targets stable. Ito has done much to understand the basis for the VOR, which obviously involves learning.

4. In Fig. 2 the upper part of the diagram shows the simultaneous input from PF (i.e. GA), and CF, along with glial input. At the bottom the rectangle stands for the PC, with its AMPAR. Within the rectangle Ito diagrams many subprocesses, for example: (a) the initial processes of signal transduction (including the now familiar first messengers, receptors, ion channels, G proteins, and phospholipases), (b) processes of the transduction itself (including ion concentrations, second messengers, protein kinases and protein phosphatases, activation of the AMPA receptor, and the chemical network for LTD), and, (c) the roles of various other complex factors.

5. It is important that unlike LTP, in the case of LTD "there is no evidence indicating that adenyl cyclase, cAMP, or PKA have any role in [LTD] induction" (Ito, p. 1155).

At this point I think you can better appreciate how my initial assertion that CKs effect memory and learning, stated as it was without immediate further qualification, came dangerously close to inviting a grossly oversimplified view of the synaptic changes behind memory and learning. Obviously, on the one hand, one needs to be very careful in making a judgment about the nature and degree of CK effects, that is, CKs do not operate in isolation. And yet on the other hand, CK-induced gene activation clearly plays a significant role in synaptic plasticity, especially as regards the establishment of neural networks and LTM.[26] What remains for neuroscience to determine is the exact involvement of CKs in various types of changes in synaptic plasticity, and the factors which control these changes, as, for example, Ito has provided par excellence for the CB and LTD.

Before leaving this section let me distill more clearly the significance of Ito's article, as I see it: Ito is postulating that the detailed memory mechanisms which he has worked out for the CB and motor learning in particular might very well apply equally to all implicit learning. As he puts it, there are "functional roles of the CB in implicit memory and learning in general" (Ito, 2001, p. 1182). His second important conclusion is that the "*investigation of gene regulatory mechanisms for LTD will be of essential importance* [italics added]. A possibility [also] exists that LTD as functional depression is consolidated as a structural change in synaptic contacts and spines" although he adds "as yet there is no [concrete] evidence ... showing morphological changes correlated with LTD" (p. 1182). Obviously, it will be important to examine each of the elements in the implicit memory system and see which are actionable via gene activation and which by other means.

One additional comment on Ito: having known him personally for a long time I want to remind you if you don't already know it that Ito was the researcher who realized that the CB moves ideas, not just limbs, and is thus deeply involved with learning generally, and not just motor learning. I have often used this idea of his in my own analytic work, especially in the sense of paying attention to the patient's movements or lack thereof, thinking this can sometimes provide important clues to what the patient is feeling, but not otherwise communicating except in a kind of pantomime.

I further imagine, that if Loren Eiseley were in treatment with me he would communicate a lot in such pantomime, and it might well be my place to comment upon it, that is, if I could find a non-intrusive way of doing so. This might conjure up in his mind recollections of his interaction with his deaf mother, who was undoubtedly communicating with him in sign language and via gestures and facial expressions, a very special kind of communication that was once quite embarrassing for deaf people to use in public, and for their hearing children as well, although nowadays this situation has greatly improved as sign language has achieved the status of a formal language, on a par with any other. Importantly, if I used my knowledge of sign language to communicate with Eiseley, at the right time, he might respond to me very differently, that is, with more emotional associations than if the same message were communicated by other means with less personal associations for him. Of course, this would be still another clue that memory is affectively organized and primable.

VI. AMPA and NMDA receptors

Summarizing to this point, there are no less than six possible molecular mechanisms that are candidates for explaining the stable synaptic changes we associate with LTM (see Lisman & Fallon, 1999; Bhalla & Iyengar, 1999): (1) a second messenger switch (in which MAPK activates PKC via PLA2, and where a reverse feedback effect can also occur in which PKC activates MAPK via RAS or RAF); (2) a kinase switch (in which CAMKII, i.e. CAM-kinase II, autophosphorylates itself once activated by an increase in Calcium ion, a process reversible via phosphatase); (3) a transcriptional switch (such as our mention of CK altering gene expression or undoing it); (4) a translational switch (starting from mRNA which would give rise to a protein and then to a second messenger, where the latter would stabilize a translational switch in the synapse); (5) a structural unit change associated with turnover within the synapse (such as hinted at in Ito's article); or (6) a structural unit change without turnover (an example being the action of agrin within the neuromuscular junction, a subject, however, peripheral to the present discussion).

We need also to remind ourselves that just as is the case for synapses, AMPA receptors, and other receptors as well, are creatable on emotional demand. That is, receptors "are … synthesized in the endoplasmic reticulum, processed in the Golgi apparatus, and transported to the cell surface in membrane vesicles … to dendrites" as they are needed (Nakagawa & Sheng, 2000, p. 2270). The key to their effectiveness in terms of excitatory synaptic transmission effectively relates to the number of such AMPA receptors that are produced, their rate of production and their exact distribution postsynaptically (Nakagawa & Sheng, op. cit.; Shi, 2001, p. 1851). Using recombinant AMPA receptors Shi has been able to cleverly prove that AMPA receptors are in fact delivered to synapses exactly in relation to LTP induction (Shi, op. cit.). As noted earlier, this decisively proves that there must be a method for communication from the postsynaptic membrane to the presynaptic side, otherwise, how could the presynaptic membrane prepare and deliver receptors in such a timely way?

The NMDA receptor is also a key player in synaptic plasticity (Ghosh, 2002, p. 449). Ghosh, reviewing the work of Takasu, Dalva, Zigmond, and Greenberg (2002) points out that post-synaptic NMDA Calcium ion flux is itself dependent on Eph receptors. Eph receptors are a large family of receptor tyrosine kinases that regulate various developmental events", a reference to the cytokines EphA and EphB (Ghosh, 2002; Takasu et al. 2002). Obviously, CK are ubiquitous players in the synaptic activation drama.

Takasu et al. summarize their related findings in the following way: The EphB receptor tyrosine kinases are localized at the NMDA synapses and their role is to effect activity-dependent and activity-independent development and remodeling of synaptic connections (p. 491). The importance of such changes in NMDA synaptic reinforcement is that such modifications in the synapses becomes the basis for changes in the hippocampal CA1 region, which is crucial for converting new memories into LTM in the explicit memory system (Shimizu, Tang, Rampon, & Tsien, 2000).

VII. *LTM*

The possible nexus of events starting with emotional attention and culminating in neural network formation and LTM.

The combined effects of the CK induced cascade of events results in structural changes in the synapse, in changes within the nuclei of neurons, and ultimately the establishment of LTM which grows from larger numbers of such neurons undergoing related changes and operating as parts of neural networks (i.e. ultimately, as flexible databases of mind/brain).

Regarding the creation of LTM, we can summarize again how this likely comes about, based upon knowledge of those specific brain structures most connected with and affected by emotion and how they are activated. Obviously, CKs play a role. I have already described the specific CK involvement, and at least some of the factors that stimulate CK activity. And as noted above, one key is emotional attention, that is, the changes (chemical, physiological and psychological) which accompany the activity of neural systems and which provide emotional attention, especially the ventral part of the anterior cingulate cortex (ventACC).[27] Obviously, the ventACC is a critical component in the system being described.

> It will help to briefly review where we have been. As described earlier, LTM "results from the translocation of PKA and mitogen-activated protein kinase (MAPK) to the nucleus of the sensory neurons where these kinases activate CREB1 and derepress CREB2, leading to the induction of a set of immediate or early response genes and ultimately resulting in the growth of new synaptic connections" (Albright et al. 2000, p. S13, citing the work of Bartsch et al. 1995, 1998).

Ibelgauft, writing under the rubric of CRE (for cyclic AMP-response element), describes the process as follows:

> "Cyclic AMP-response element second messenger pathways provide a chief means by which cellular growth, differentiation, and function can be influenced by extracellular signals ... an inducible enhancer of genes that can be transcribed in response to the increase in cAMP levels" (Ibelgauft, section of CRE, p. 1).

This means that cAMP levels need to be activated as part of the basic pathway leading to the growth of new synapses and the changing of synaptic weights (up as in LTP or down as in LTD). So the question then becomes: What more can we say about those factors which elevate cAMP in a timely way, since after all, this step within the system is what leads to a cascade ending in immediate response genes (IEG, also called ERG for early response genes) and new synaptic production?

Clearly, cAMP can come from a number of sources. If we consider ATP as the source of the cAMP level, then one obvious endocrine initiator, as noted in the early article I cited by Floyd Bloom, would have to be NE[28] which is known, along with epinephrine, both to break down ATP into 3',5'-cAMP and pyrophosphate, and which also is itself released in response to significant emotional stimulations. In addition, as I noted in discussing the immune part of NIN, sympathetic neurons are sources of NE, and we know that NE is of course also a central neurotransmitter.

One question remaining is thus: Have we correctly tied in NE release to affective attention and LTM formation? The answer seems not hard to guess. The original affective signal leading to NE release would most likely be received by the ventral division of the anterior cingulate, along with the amygdalar, hippocampal (CA1 cells), and hypothalamic cells in response to emotional activity deeper in the brain's core (e.g. the PAG). It may help to remind our selves that this ventral (affective) division of the anterior cingulate "is connected to the amygdala, PAG, nucleus acumbens, hypothalamus, anterior insula, hippocampus, and orbitofrontal cortex, and has outflow to autonomic [sympathetic], visceromotor and endocrine systems" (Bush, Luu, & Posner, 2000, p. 216). Once the NE concentration would rise in association with ventral anterior cingulate activation, and sufficient cAMP would be made available thereby, we would expect the cascade of PKA, MAPK, CREB1 activation and CREB2 derepression (i.e. in response to shifts in cAMP which effect the kinases, phosphorylation mechanisms, and protein protein interactions of great complexity),[29] and finally ERG and its effects on new synapse formation.

Regarding immediate or early response genes (ERG), it should be noted that aside from hormones, cAMP signals and cytokines, ERG is triggered by many factors: cytokines of course, but also antigens, neurotransmitters, leukotrienes, prostaglandins, eicosanoids, protein synthesis inhibitors, calcium signals, cellular adhesion molecules, osmotic pressure changes, and stress, to name but a few (Ibelgauft, op. cit., ERG section, p. 1). From this it should be obvious that many other pathways might also play a role in ERG activation in addition the ones mentioned (namely, via cAMP and NE effects) and thus create the final stimulus pathway towards formation of LTM. Whatever the contributing factors, however, clearly the brain is designed to provide LTM on demand by many known mechanisms, such as I have been describing.

From the psychoanalytic perspective,[30] the formation of new LTM in association with learning obviously occurs under a variety of circumstances that relate to emotional and attentive processes, including psychoanalytic interventions. By the way, I believe Loren Eiseley would have been most interested in the relationship between the affects and ideas generated in his imaginary psychoanalysis, and in their associated specific chemical and anatomical changes in his brain. Remember, as a physical anthropologist he often lived mentally at the intersection between the technical chemical and anatomical findings from human artifacts and the history of human stressful experience.

VIII. *Interdisciplinary Research*

I have just presented some mind/brain details connecting the psychoanalytic and the neuroscientific understanding of learning and memory, at least as this involves learning within the psychoanalytic situation. In spite of my effort, however, I suggest that it still remains very difficult to align these two perspectives; to date only a small handful of reliable mind/brain correlations and linkages have been generally accepted as valid.[31] Only time will tell about the acceptance of the correspondences I noted today. Where then does hope come from for further bridging between mind and brain?

My answer is that our principal hope comes from collaboration among specialists across disciplinary boundaries, and employing various philosophical approaches; only then do we move bit by bit closer to deeper and specific bridgeable understandings within neuroscience and psychoanalysis.

I noted two influential approaches at the beginning: Pragmatism, and what I called thinking things through deeply and creatively. Regarding the former, Stanley Fish states (cited by Arnold Goldberg, 2002, p. 249) that "Pragmatism is the philosophy not of grand ambitions but of little steps; and while it cannot help us to take those steps or tell us what they are, it can offer the reassurance that they are possible and more than occasionally." But we also need to respect the creative search for truths independently of what is practical. This seems to me a complementary area where psychoanalysis excels.

One could summarize by stating that interdisciplinary efforts to understand learning and memory are likely an expression of four developments: (1) the current historical trend for collaboration across disciplinary boundaries (itself a product of man's interest in comprehending the organizational levels called mind and brain); (2) our urgent need to get a better fix on the essentials of psychoanalysis and, of course, at the same time those of neuroscience; that is, we are facing many more questions about the formation of mental associations in memory and their modifications than we can possibly answer now; (3) the growth of the application of philosophy to psychoanalysis, including Pragmatism and thinking things through creatively. By Pragmatism I especially mean how to break complex problems into parts which can be reasonably addressed piecemeal (see Goldberg, 2002, p. 248), and by truth seeking I intend how we expand our knowledge by patiently searching for in depth solutions, rather than jumping to practical approaches prematurely (obviously science involves combining these two methods creatively); and (4) the discovery of and attempt to understand the deeper emotional strata of self (especially in those brain areas not so visualizable in man). I believe the core emotional systems of our species are integrated into intermediate and higher levels (i.e. upper brainstem and cortex develop their own unique take on feeling states most fully expressed in the systems influenced by the PAG and related deeper structures).

When we recognize the limitations of our current knowledge, and the obvious benefits of collaborating across disciplinary boundaries, both personally and professionally, we gain in strength, and slowly expand our horizons about such phenomena as memory, emotions, and learning. Therefore, even though we cannot be sure exactly in what way emotional signals emanate from the mind/brain and serve as a critical trigger for the creation of new hope and useful knowledge, we cannot afford to give up our efforts towards eventually discovering their complete technical details. These details obviously lie in our describing more clearly as many as possible of our current unclarities (die "Unklarheiten"), which I hope you will agree I have succeeded in presenting to you. Only then does Night become brighter, as when in analysis we do our best to connect with a fellow sufferer in a compassionate way, and hope this helps him or her also better connect with their self.

Notes

1. The author wishes to thank Jean Carney, Todd Davis, Nancy Desert, John Gedo, Eric Gillett, Stanley Palombo, Michael Posner, and Arnold Wilson for their useful suggestions, while he personally takes full responsibility for the final product, and inevitable mistakes.

2. An earlier version of this chapter was presented November 23, 2002 to the Austrian Academy of Sciences meeting on Psychoanalysis as an Empirical Disciplinary Science, Vienna, Austria, and published in Giampieri-Deutsch (2004).

3. On the dust jacket of Eiseley's (1971) book, Ray Bradbury sees Eiseley's writings as likely to "linger for the next century".

4. The reader should not confuse my speculations about the imaginary Eiseley, later in this text, with the real man I introduce on pages 1 and 2. As noted, they are merely imaginative speculations to illustrate various points about psychoanalysis, and any similarity to the real Eiseley is purely coincidental.

5. If one asks how it matters for our understanding of psychodynamics that the mechanisms discussed in this chapter and not others are operating, the answer is as follows: reliable treatments, like reliable prediction in any science, rest on accurate understandings, and these can only be discovered by clinical and laboratory experimentation. Proper scientific technique and related theory are based upon various kinds of hard evidence, and many generations of such observations and correlations are often required for real progress to occur.

6. This is not meant to depreciate interpretations within analysis, but rather to elevate the role of analytic associative learning (conditioning) that can profoundly alter mind/brain organization and personal adaptive functioning.

7. Thanks to John Gedo for this observation (personal communication).

8. From 2001 for several years meetings were help at the Austrian Academy of Sciences, under Drs. Gianpieri-Deutsch, to share ideas on neuro-psychoanalysis both inside and outside Europe. These lead eventually to arrangements for a Ph.D. program in Psychoanalysis to be created at the University of Vienna, from which there is an expectation of further collaboration between psychoanalysts and experts in other specialties. Such interdisciplinary collaboration is the stuff progress is made of.

9. Incidentally, since my reference to Pragmatism may confuse some readers, let me briefly expand on what I intend here. I am especially thinking of Charles Sanders Pierce's original thinking about Pragmatism, that is, that sees the basis of truth determination in acts of experi-

mental results, and I am much less inclined towards William James' and others later modification of Pierce's viewpoint in the direction of seeing pragmatism as mere efficacy (see Rescher, 1995). I also intend the idea that scientists make critical practical decisions in the discovery phase of any investigation, which involves deciding, for example, how to divide complex problems into subproblems that will yield more easily to experimental study.

10. The precise meanings of the technical terms "transcription", "translation", and "copying" within genetics are not obvious, but may be distinguished from each other as follows: *transcription* refers to the copying of DNA into messenger RNA (mRNA); *translation* refers to the copying of RNA code into related proteins (which then express gene functions); *copying* refers to the creation of new forms of RNA from other RNA (something that occurs under the influence of RNA-dependent RNA polymerase) (Ahlquist, 2002, p. 1270).

11. Within the promotor region are docking components where the many transcription factors attach to each other and the DNA, which enables RNA polymerase to align next to the gene which is to be replicated.

12. One complication of the learning picture presented to this point is that although previously thought impossible, it is now known that new neurons can appear in the brain in various locations. Primate research has shown, for example, that prefrontal, inferior temporal, and posterior parietal cortex is important for cognitive functions, and these three zones demonstrate new neurons that originate in the subventricular zone and migrate through the white matter to the neocortex, where they extend axons. This apparently can continue throughout adulthood (see Gould, Reeves, Graziano, & Gross, 1999).

13. Another major complication of this simplified picture is that evidence is accumulating that there are also retrograde messengers informing the presynaptic membrane of events in the postsynaptic membrane, thus controlling or influencing presynaptic membrane neurotransmitter vesicle formation and release. Nitric oxide may play a role here, and arachidonic acid as well (Bliss, p. 88; see also Linden & Routtenberg, 1989, especially Fig. 2, p. 289). In addition, endogenous cannabinoids can function as retrograde messengers activating CB1 receptors on the presynaptic side, suppressing neurotransmitter release. CB1 receptors are "one of the most abundant ... in the brain" expressed at high levels in the hippocampus, cortex, cerebellum, and basal ganglia, accounting for the striking effects of cannabinoids on memory and cognition (Wilson & Nicoll, 2002, p. 678). Also, another

retrograde signaling pathway involves EphB receptor-Ephrin B ligand interaction in hippocampal mossy fiber-CA3 synapses (Contractor, et al. 2002).

14. (Jean Carney, personal communication).

15. Squire divides memory into declarative (explicit) and non-declarative (implicit); the latter also being called procedural. Explicit involves memory for facts and events; implicit involves memory for skills, priming, simple classical conditioning, and non-associative learning (Squire, 1998, p. 62).

16. NMDA and AMPA receptors are two glutamate receptor families, glutamate (glutamic acid) being the major excitatory neurotransmitter of the brain (Bliss, 1998, p. 88-89).

17. Like any generalization, my comment about the number of passes required for new implicit memory formation is only relative to explicit memories. Implicit memory formation also requires repetition. Moreover, given our limited present knowledge, it is probably wise not to insist that there are only two major types of memory without overlap; it will also be important to delineate how explicit and implicit memory systems operate together (see the later chapters of this book). Recent studies of perceptual learning have further shown clear evidence of V1 modification as a result of training, and it would be surprising that such modification would not occur in many other networks (personal communication, Michael Posner).

18. For additional information on priming see Schacter and Buckner, 1998.

19. Bliss states that arguing that LTP is not the basis for LTM brings to mind Mark Twain's remark about those who assert that Homer may not have been the author of the Iliad: "If it wasn't Homer, then it must have been another old blind Greek poet of the same name [!]" (Bliss, p. 91).

20. A further complication touched upon is that something needs to turn off LTP once it has been induced (Bliss, p. 89). This is one aspect of long-term depression (LTD) described most extensively by Ito (2001).

21. It would seem that the preceding paragraph accurately summarizes most of what is known about synapses, at least so far as signal transduction leading towards long-term memory is concerned. However, this is of course an illusion. The real complexity, for example, also would need to include many other subjects, such as lipid rafts. Sphingolipid- and cholesterol-rich domains in the plasma membrane of cells are known as lipid rafts. Within this subcellular domain or compartment, proteins (CKs) are sequestered, and this "increases the specificity and efficiency of signal transduction" (Zacharias, Violin, Newton, & Tsien,

2002, p. 913). Also, within these spaces protein-protein interactions "maintain many signaling complexes" (Zacharias et al., op. cit., p. 913). We are only gradually learning about the nature of lipid rafts and their controls.

22. The time course of neurotransmitter (CK) induced activation of genes makes clear what leads to what: first neurotransmitter binds to receptor, then very quickly (within a few minutes) this is followed by the curve of cAMP response, followed by the curve representing the activation of Protein Kinase, then activation of CREB, the activation of ERG and the protein synthesis it leads to (e.g. Fos or Jun) in sequence (Stahl, 2000, p. 8, see especially Fig. 2). Curves for late-gene mRNA synthesis, late-gene protein synthesis, and long-term effects of late-gene products all follow the previous cascade, in order, as one would expect (i.e. the effects of early genes produce products which can activate late genes starting within 60 minutes or so).

23. It has been known that glial cells increase the ability of neurons to form and maintain synapses, by as much as a factor of 7, but prior to this study, it was not clear how this effect was obtained (Helmuth, 2001). A second synapse-promoting signal is apparently the release of cholesterol from glial cells (the work of Mauch et al. 2001). Mauch et al. in turn credit Pfrieger and Barres for their work in 1997 on retinal ganglion cells.

24. M. Beattie (personal communication, 2002) agrees "the effects of TNF alpha on gene expression are very interesting and could be important in the long term regulation of glutamate receptor sensitivity. In the work reported, though, the effects on AMPA receptor surface localization take place within minutes. The previous data from the Malenk/ Stanford group and others suggest that there is considerable regulation by modulation of AMPA receptor recycling without (necessarily) the induction of changes in gene expression. Whether longer term effects may be mediated by transcriptional/translational effects remains to be seen."

25. Originally Figure 5, p. 1151 of Ito's paper, reprinted with his publisher's kind permission. Although I will not go into great detail here, it should be understood that in cerebellar LTD even the synapses are chemically and functionally different from those of the rest of the brain.

26. In particular, although Ito does not discuss CKs as a separate topic in his paper, he does include no less than four of this "species" within his map of synaptic activity: IGF-I (Insulin-like Growth Factor- I), IEG (immediate early gene/ERG), MAPK (MAP kinases; also called Mitogen-

activated protein kinases, or ERK for extracellular signal-regulated kinases), and BDNF (for brain derived neurotrophic factor).

27. By emotions I am referring not merely to the cortical systems, and of course the limbic system, but also to the deep structures of the brainstem or core, as pointed out by Panksepp (2000, 2001), including the periaqueductal gray (PAG), hypothalamus, etc.

28. This statement is based on the classical work on Hodgkins, Huxley, and Katz (1952), and a minor bit of personal research (Levin, 1962) demonstrating that the effects of epinephrine on liver essentially are identical with those induced by 3'5'-AMP (cAMP), which epinephrine produces by catalyzing ATP into cAMP and P-P. NE follows this pattern (Bloom, op. cit.).

29. "At least ten different CREB protein genes have been cloned, including CREB, CREB1, CREB2, CREBP1, ATF2 , ATF (activating transcription factor), ATF43, ATF1, TREB 36. The CREB1 gene maps to human chromosome 2q32.3-q34. The human CREB2 gene maps to 2q24.1-q32, a site very close to that of the CREB1 gene. CREB proteins are activated by phosphorylation by cAMP-dependent protein kinase A" (Ibelgauft, op. cit., CRE section, p. 1).

30. See Olds (2006) for a thorough review of the general relevance to psychoanalysis of interdisciplinary studies.

31. In my opinion, credit for the most important mind/brain correlations is particularly due Jaak Panksepp (1998, 2000, 2001), and to Mark and Karen Kaplan Solms, some of which appears in the latter's book (2000) or in the pages of Neuro-Psychoanalysis (for example, in M. Solms, 1999).

CHAPTER SIX

Recent neuroscience discoveries, and protein cellular pathways: their possible interdisciplinary significance[1]

Fred M. Levin

Précis: This chapter primarily reviews articles published in the journal Science. The subjects presented seem to me to have some potential relevance for psychoanalysis, by helping us better bridge mind/brain perspectives. The focus shifts throughout from cognitive controls, to emotional systems, or to the fact that cognitive and emotional systems of mind/brain are more closely interconnected than we often realize, just as the two memory systems called implicit and explicit are likely connected in complex, interesting ways, even if these connections sometimes elude us. In this chapter I begin with research on corollary discharge. Next I take up reports on important revisions of the neuron doctrine. I then add a discussion of some innovative neuroscientific conceptions of what controls development, citing recent work in molecular biology on protein pathways. Some of these efforts to bridge mind/brain may seem far fetched, and perhaps they are; others, however, say those connecting corollary discharge with brain mechanisms for transferences and their recognition, may seem more useful. At each step, however, a sincere effort is being made to plumb our understanding of things in fundamental terms. This effort especially concerns the phenomenon of emotion, which we generally take for granted, yet to understand it better we may require a more novel definition of emotion to really make sense of what emotion represents to our species.

I. Of Crickets and Men

A recent article by Poulet and Hedwig (2006), clarifies an older neurological concept called "corollary discharge", in a way that may help us better understand a key aspect of brain organization and mental life. Amazingly, these researchers wired the nervous systems of singing crickets sufficiently to anatomically determine "a single, multisegmental interneuron [that] is responsible for the pre- and postsynaptic inhibition of auditory neurons... Therefore, this neuron represents a corollary discharge interneuron that provides a neuronal basis for the central control of sensory responses" (p. 518). The core idea, in a nutshell, is that the cricket's "ears" (located in their feet) modify its hearing based upon information[2] forwarded from motor areas to sensory areas about motor plans (e.g. intentions for action, such as the instruction to flap the cricket's wings, an action that could well add to the cricket's auditory input). Let me elaborate.

Kolb and Winshaw (1980) define corollary discharge as "transmission by one area of the brain to another, informing the latter area of the former [area's] actions [or intentions to act]. Commonly [this is] used more specifically for a signal from the motor system to the sensory systems [announcing] that a particular movement is being produced" (p. 476). For example, in the case of the cricket experiments, at the time the motor system begins to execute a signal to flap the cricket's wings, a signal ("corollary discharge") is sent to the sensory system informing it of this incipient action, thus allowing the cricket to factor in the effects of the increased sound of the wings, as the cricket is listening to other signals and trying to carefully identify them for various purposes, including the need to discriminate self-generated sounds from those outside sounds that might indicate danger. If this mechanism helps avoid errors in discriminating internally generated from externally generated sounds, it would obviously have clear adaptive value for the cricket.

It seems clear from this example that the mind/brain is organized to protect its owner, whether cricket or man, and that the long hypothesized corollary discharges experimentally demonstrated in the cricket experiments (sometimes also called "efference copies" (Poulet & Hedwig, p. 518; see also Blakemore, Frith, & Wolpert, 2001) are indeed critical for the creation of a solid basis for safety.

Now let me relate the above comments on corollary discharge to work in psychoanalysis. Although it will at first seem a huge leap, it is not unreasonable to consider the possibility that corollary discharges might well occur in man where they could play a role as they do in the cricket experiment, namely, to help the sensory systems of the human brain know quickly of some intended action plans, such as the impending development of a psychoanalytic transference. As in the case of the cricket, this would have profound significance in keeping sensory areas alerted to make a more refined distinction between inside/outside (self vs. other) as a source of the complex blend of sensory experience that results in and from transference interactions. Presumably, this input would not necessarily enter into consciousness, but could nevertheless serve as an internal signal, with a number of possible roles:

(1) it could assist our ability, outside awareness, to identify "events" as following from our own intentionality, better differentiating them from those with external sources, and

(2) it could help in our making use of this knowledge (outside of our awareness) and

(3) it could guide our responses within the transference interaction in subtle ways, making use of our "knowledge without awareness".

Considering all this, we owe a debt to Poulet and Hedwig, for reminding us that much is going on inside our nervous systems that facilitates not only our ability to exploit sensory phenomena (which we are here considering transference to be one variety of); but it may also improve our conceptualization of how we might learn from such a process. Put differently, if we take corollary discharge seriously, and apply it to transference phenomena, our refined ability to detect transferences and learn from them may involve an intuition or insight that is itself grounded in internal efference copies or corollary discharge from motor systems to sensory systems within our brains, all occurring without conscious awareness.

Thus, the internal communication between brain systems is critical for the recognition of our personal involvement in complex social interactions, such as transference. And in this way it will become easier for us to accept the consequences of our actions.

II. *Revision of the Neuron Doctrine*

Originally, the so-called neuron doctrine, a creation often credited to Ramon y Cajal, the Spanish anatomist and Nobel Prize winner, held that "a neuron is an anatomically and functionally distinct cellular unit that arises through differentiation of a precursor neuroblast cell. The neuron was thus postulated to be a commensurable unit that could be arranged geometrically, and whose resulting functions could be calculated more or less mathematically" (Bullock et al. 2005, p. 791).

It was also assumed that inter-neuronal communication was limited to neurotransmitter-related electrical activity at the synapses. However, things have gotten much more complex over the years. For example, Bullock et al. (2005) describe the modern view as follows: "…The neuron… [is now seen] as a discrete cell that processes information in [many] more ways than originally envisaged: Intercellular communications by gap junctions,[3] slow electrical potentials, action potentials initiated in dendrites, neuromodulatory effects, extrasynaptic release of neurotransmitters, and information flow between neurons and glia, all [of which] contribute to information processing" (p. 791). The neuron doctrine is thus no longer the same, and although synapses are still important, they are by no means the exclusive basis for neuronal networking.

As is well known, there is reason to believe that Freud, early on (1895), understood the existence and importance of synapses. Thus for him there were essentially two ways neurons affected one another: (1) they transfer quantity, quality and exciting effect; and (2) each of these elements ultimately leads to one consequence: the transfer of information. In its focusing on information transfer, Freud's perspective was actually very much in tune with the revised version of neuron doctrine.

The synapse (synaptic cleft) was first seen by electron microscope in 1954. Hodgkin and Huxley (1952) won a Nobel Prize for defining the action potential and its chemistry (classically, an all or nothing response, passing on down the neuron in the form of a depolarization wave, contingent upon the movement of electrolytes such as sodium ions, mostly outside the cell, which move inside, and potassium ions, mostly inside the cell, which move outside the neuron to create the electrical depolarization wave). By 1959, however, we also knew that rather than being all or nothing, electrical discharge in neurons is graded, and furthermore, it decays over distance (Bullock et al. 2005, p. 791).

Let's consider neuronal *gap junctions* or *gap junction channels*, which are "a type of junction between two cells through which ions and small molecules can pass. Gap junction-mediated intercellular communication allows synchronized cellular responses to a variety of intercellular signals by regulating the direct passage of low-molecular-weight metabolites (<1000 daltons) and ions between the cytoplasm of adjacent cells" (Bullock et al. Ibid.).

In other words, gap junctions are protein pores in cell membranes that are small aqueous channels [for example, they can serve as potassium or sodium channels, which are themselves influenced by calcium], and these are widespread in mammalian nervous system neurons, just as synapses are widely distributed. Moreover, these gap junctions can "synchronize neuronal firing" (Bullock et al. p. 791) just as synapses can. Moreover, we now know that these gap junctions do not fire off all the time, but are instead modulated by transmission from chemical synapses of the same "presynaptic" neuron (Bullock et al., p. 792). And to make things even more complicated, unexpectedly, gap junctions exist between neurons and glial cells, not just between neurons. This latter finding was not anticipated but is now fully documented. It introduces the modern serious study of glial cells, which is too complicated a subject to be included in this review, though it is noted elsewhere in this book.

Still another complexity involves neuromodulation and neuromodulatory substances (for example, amines and neuropeptides). The time scale of their effects on neurons can extend reactions to minutes or hours, rather than the thousandths of a second timeframe for classical synaptic events. Behavior, learning, and memory are clearly influenced by the effects of neuromodulators on neurons.

Marcel Mesulam (2000) at Northwestern University Feinberg School of Medicine (formerly of Harvard) has contributed to this area of knowledge by demonstrating that such neurotransmitters released and *diffusing broadly* within the brainstem, for example, (rather than via synapses) can have broad impact. Obviously, this makes tracing neurotransmitter pathways within the brain dramatically more difficult than merely following patterns of synaptic connectivity. Thus we have glial cells and neurons communicating with each other in complex ways, and employing what will appear to some of us as unusual methods rather than generating simple depolarizations and neurotransmitter release only at localized synapses, as has been taught at universities for years.

Moreover, there is a new understanding in the past decade that action potentials sometimes actually travel backward from the axon into the soma of the neuron and then into the dendrites (that is, in the opposite of the usual direction)! Obviously, this complicates how the dendrites respond to input from other neurons. The types, densities, and properties of the newly recognized voltage-gated ion channels are obviously very diverse (Bullock et al., p. 792).

And we have not exhausted the subject of neuronic/glial relations (richly deserving a special review). An example of significant findings in this area is that glial cells provide various supplies to neurons, and thus enable neurons to fulfill their functions, such that without glial support neurons could not do what they ordinarily accomplish. This naturally undermines our theory that neurons are the leading edge of neuronic transmission of critical information, as opposed to our reconceptualizing the brain as a complex system in which neurons and glial cells work together by various means to keep each neuron functioning optimally, and to provide the hypercomplex functions we associate with minds and brains. Moreover, we know now that glia can give birth to new neurons (Bullock et al., p. 792), affecting, for example, the hippocampal areas in each temporal lobes, the olfactory nerves, and no doubt other areas as well.

One additional surprising complication is the discovery that the so-called "Dfrizzled2 surface receptor" at the neuromuscular junction, when bound by a particular ligand, releases a fragment that travels to the nucleus of the cell and signals synapse formation (Mathew et al. 2005)! Thus the neuromuscular junction also plays a previously unknown role in synaptic activity.

There are of course many implications for psychoanalysis that flow from this totally new understanding of intercellular communication within the brain. One obvious conclusion is that we need to consider those neural systems that operate over longer time frames in the production of various mental functions. This means, for example, paying more attention to such structures as the periaqueductal gray (PAG), which has so much to do with managing human affectivity, but which operates on much slower time scales than higher centers. It also is beginning to give us a much greater appreciation of what happens in dreaming, the royal road not only to the Freudian unconscious, but also to appreciating memory consolidation mechanisms and their impact on our affects, goals, and psychological development. It should be noted that, obviously, the brainstem and subcortical structures within the brain have more to do with our mental life than previously imagined.

III. *Protein Cellular Pathways: A neuropsychoanalytic perspective*

A. *Background*

Clearly, the human brain is influenced by various levels of control at the level of genes, transcription factors, and various proteins; at the cellular synaptic and gap junction levels involving neurons and glia (astroglia and oligodendroglia); and at the level of other neurocellular networks and functional systems. How the information in our genes gets transferred from DNA to RNA, and is expressed, stored, or destroyed in various protein (polypeptide) systems or so-called pathways that control the complex chemistry of cells is a most important matter of study that has rarely been summarized and examined for a psychoanalytic purpose.

A major problem for neuro-psychoanalysis is the challenge of correctly identifying what is relevant and to distinguish it from what is not. A subsidiary issue is dealing correctly with complexity in the organization of the mind and brain, and not oversimplifying our theories. In an earlier review of such matters (Levin, 2002) I presented background on CKs and their abilities to turn genes on and off, reporting especially on the work of Eric Kandel et al., among others. I explained how the brain and the immune system are currently considered to be one system (the Neuro Immune Network, or NIN) with multiple aspects. Importantly, the NIN plays a role in memory such that emotional attention activates new synapse formation (Levin, 2003).

Here I briefly summarize work on P-Bodies, on the various kinds of RNA. This includes mRNA (messenger RNA), miRNA (micro RNA), rRNA (ribosomal RNA), tRNA (transfer RNA), RNAi (interference RNA). The reasons for mRNA degradation are also discussed. Regarding the latter I describe Dicer, RISC, and Argonaute, elements in a complex system that regulates mRNA. This should help us better appreciate the importance of proteins in the form of systems (pathways) involving cofactors, CKs, gene activators and in-activators (those CKs also known as transcription factors), all of which ultimately have a powerful bearing on the final outcome of the processing of important cognitive and emotional information, and generally upon feelings and behavior in our species. Apoptotic (self destructive) cellular pathways also are noted along with the subject of endonucleases for their relevance for cancer as well as for development in particular, and more generally for what they tell us about gene functioning. Increasingly, the comprehensive understanding of human behavior and experience psychoanalytically will involve applying detailed genetic information with interacting environmental information, where the genetic-environmental interaction occurs at multiple levels within mind and brain (see especially the article of Victor Ambrose [2006], Professor of genetics at Dartmouth Medical School, and winner of the 2006 Genetics Society of America Medal for his work on the role of miRNA on development and behavior).

P-Bodies (also known as GW or Dcp bodies) are the tiny speckles discovered 10 years ago (Caponigro & Parker, 1995) at the U. of Arizona, involving work on yeast cells; P-Bodies are the sites of both RNA storage and degradation, and are considered "the heart of the cell's machinery for regulating protein synthesis" (Marx, 2005, p. 764). It may help to review the steps in protein synthesis as follows: (1) the reading of genes to create messenger RNAs (mRNAs) from DNA; this step, of course, takes place in the cell nucleus where the DNA in the form of chromosomes is located; (2) messenger RNAs are made of a large and a small ribosomal subunit, along with the initiating transfer RNAs (tRNAs), which assemble onto the mRNA (Freeman, 2000/2002, p. 1); (3) the ribosome (located in the cell cytoplasm) is then correctly positioned at the initiation codon by two RNA elements (A and P). Just upstream of the initiation codon is what scientists call a Shine-Dalgarno sequence, which pares with the 3' end of 16S ribosomal RNA (rRNA) (Freeman, 2000/2002, p. 2); (4) the next step is called "translation elongation" and it involves several steps; first, with the initiator tRNA placed at the P site of the ribosome, aminoacytl-tRNA enters the ribosome at the A site (Freeman, p. 3); (5) next, the amino acid at the P site is transferred to the tRNA at the A site (n.b. the tRNA is constructed of a short backbone with three bases on the other side, coding for a particular amino acid; the tRNA's come in units this way, specifying one amino acid at a time, until all such amino acids are lined up in series and connected to each other, thus forming the correct protein [polypeptide] representing the instruction set of a particular gene; the ribosome moves one codon farther along the mRNA, releasing the empty tRNA (Freeman, p. 4); the cycle is repeated as the ribosome travels along the mRNA, resulting in a growing polypeptide chain (Freeman, p. 5); the next stage is called translational termination; this is triggered by a stop codon in the mRNA. Stop codons are recognized by release factors, which help release the fully synthesized polypeptide chain from the ribosome (Freeman, p. 6); and finally (6) translation then ends with dissociation of the ribosomal subunits (Freeman, p. 7).

In other words, the chromosomes in the nucleus of the cell are copied by mRNA that leaves the nucleus and joins the ribosomes in the cytoplasm (also called the "cytosol"). Proteins are produced at the ribosome, basically one for each gene, and these are capable of building cell structures and also functioning as enzymes (i.e. catalysts) for various cellular processes. They are basically long chains of small molecules called amino acids. Different proteins are coded by using different sequences of amino acids. As noted above the four key base pairs (abbreviated A, T, G, C) appearing in the DNA are the code, in the form of triplets, and larger stretches of this code are called genes. They are called pairs because A always matches T and G always matches C. Once produced on the ribosome, such peptides (proteins) can travel through the endoplasmic reticulum to reach other sites within the cell.

So what is going on in P-Bodies? From the above, we can conclude that P-Bodies can operate as mRNA "chop shops". But the question then becomes: What is accomplished by the demolition of mRNA? One answer seems to be that it can help in the fight against disease (e.g. cancer, autoimmune disease, or viral invasion) or excessive heat. In the case of autoimmune illness, in at least one patient studied carefully, antibodies seemed sequestered in the patient's P-Bodies (Marx, 2005, p. 765, the work of Edward Chan at the University of Florida in Gainesville and Marvin Fritzler at the Univ. of Calgary in Canada). Betrand Seraphin at the CNRS of the Center for Molecular Genetics at Gif sur Yvette, France et al. have also shown that P-Bodies contain a protein called RCK that may help drive cancer development. That is, microRNA seems implicated in various human cancers. "The storage of mRNA in P-bodies could [also] help regulate embryonic development" (Marx, 2005, p. 765).

Importantly, sometimes mRNA is not destroyed but merely inactivated, allowing for the RNA to be reactivated again at a later time. This inactivation can also be brought about by a still different mechanism, namely, a type of RNA called RNAi, which stands for interference RNA. This type of RNA was discovered about 10 to 15 years ago by researchers studying how certain known genetic characteristics of flowers were not penetrating as expected.

Further, Roy Parker, working with Gregory Hannon at Cold Spring Harbor Lab on NY's Long Island, together with George Sen and Helen Blau at Stanford Univ. Med. School, found that mRNA degradation occurs in P-Bodies, and that the proteins Argonaut 1 and 2, which are the key components of the RNAi machinery (known as RISC) are concentrated in these same P-Bodies (Marx, p. 765). Based upon the work of the Parker-Hannon team, and that of Witold Filipowicz at the Miescher Institute in Basel, Switzerland, there is also a miRNA (or microRNA), which represses the translation of mRNA into proteins, without degrading it. This is apparently accomplished by means of the so-called RISC machinery that is active in P-Bodies. It seems that RISC proteins direct mRNAs to the P-Bodies. The picture is one in which mRNA moves into and out of P-Bodies. Thus, these P-Bodies are not dead ends, but part of a dynamic system for translation, repression, degradation, and storage. One final note here: Parker and Jeff Coller (also at Arizona), have shown that cells lacking two P-Body proteins (Dhh1 p and Pat 1) can no longer turn off protein translation. This, and other details suggest that within the P-Body there is a balance between translation at the polysome for protein synthesis and repression of protein synthesis in favor of storage of mRNA. The importance of the vicissitudes of the various kinds of RNA for psychoanalysis should become clearer in the next two sections. I apologize for the complexity of the narrative, but suggest it represents my personal effort to present brain science without simplifying it, so we can bring our knowledge up to par with specialists in other areas, better appreciate how specialists outside psychoanalysis are reaching out to us in trying to piece together their findings at a microscopic level with our findings at a clinical level, and reach across to each other in an interdisciplinary collaboration where each side is informed about the other's domain.

B. *Complex role of riRNA and Apoptotic pathways (Apoptosis)*

What follows owes a considerable debt to two review articles in *Science* (Couzin, 2005; Denicourt & Dowdy, 2005) on the role of microRNAs (miRNAs) in cancer and other areas. For example, interference RNA (RNAi) and miRNAs silence gene expression, and in doing so can help provide an antiviral mechanism in plants and animals (Wang, et al. 2006). The story begins when Frank Slack, a biological researcher on worms made an important discovery in 1997. He managed to delete one of the 120 known worm miRNAs in experimental worms and as a result 1/2 of them died. Replacing the miRNA keeps such worms intact. Slack investigated and discovered that the particular miRNA deleted was let-7, and its deletion prompted the overexpression of Ras, a gene strongly associated with cancer. So clearly the miRNA let-7 can blunt the effect of Ras.

A recent paper in the *New England Journal of Medicine* (NEJM) reports 13 miRNAs that form a "signature" associated with a particular prognosis and disease progression in chronic lymphocytic leukemia (CLL). Phillip Sharp at MIT and Joshua Mendell at Johns Hopkins have been extensively exploring the miRNA and cancer connection. They both have identified a cluster of 6 miRNAs that are associated with c-Myc, a proto-oncogene. That is, when the proto-oncogene is expressed, the cluster of six miRNAs is activated. They believe these miRNAs control the balance between cell death (apoptosis) and cell proliferation for the particular blood elements in CLL. Hammond and Mendell et al. (as noted above) conducted an experiment in which they forced the over-expression in mice of six miRNAs associated with lymphoma. After 100 days, all experimental mice and none of the controls developed lymphoma! This was the first direct vs. indirect proof of the role of miRNAs in cancer. Shortly afterward, Carlo Croce of Ohio State University in Columbus reported in two patients with CLL that the loss of two miRNAs boosts the expression of a gene promoting cell survival, thus tipping development towards leukemia. Theoretically, defects in transcription factors could also be playing a role, confirmed by Nikolaus Rajewsky at NYU, Michael McManus at the University of California in San Francisco, and Tyler Jacks, at MIT's Center for Cancer Research. Another recent article by Croce et al. in the New England Journal of Medicine (NEJM) indicates that two patients with CLL were recently found to have miRNA mutations, confirming the suspicion that mutation is indeed a major pathway to cancer, and produces the flawed expression of specific miRNA.

Denicourt and Dowdy (2005) report on two novel ways to stop cancer: the method involves using new (so-called mimetic) molecules that activate the apoptotic programs in tumor cells. This research was done by Walensky et al. (2004) and Li et al. (2004). The drugs they have developed mimic key interactions that belong to either the receptor-dependent (extrinsic) or mitochondrial-dependent (intrinsic) apoptotic pathways of normal cells. The extrinsic pathway is associated with the cell membrane, and the intrinsic pathway centers within the organelles we mentioned above, for example, the mitochondria in the cytosol.

The mimetic compounds are SMAC compound 3 and SAHB (BH3). The first anticancer drug (which mimics SMAC) attacks XIAP (an inhibitor of apoptosis), which is an element downrange from the membrane-related TNI receptor superfamily called death receptors (TNFR1, IAI, and TRAIL). Proteins such as FDD are recruited, and influence DISC (death inducing signaling complex), which leads to the activation of caspace 8 (Casp-8), which cleaves and activates Casp-3, the executioner enzyme.

The second anticancer drug (which mimics BH3) heads for the mitochondria where the pro-apoptotic BCL2 family members BAX and BAK translocate, along with BID. BID activates BAX and BAK which itself mediates the release of cytochrome c in the cytosol, which triggers the assembly of the aptosome (APF1 and casp-9), followed by activation of casp-3 and other caspaces.

The next section of this review will be needed to pull our discussion together more completely by explaining Argonaut, RISC, and gene silencing. Briefly, the study of cancer growth is useful not only for its emphasis on treatment, but for understanding normal development. And development is something we need to understand to better appreciate the changes in mind/brain that occur over the human life-cycle, which are genetically controlled, yet highly influenced by environmental factors, and carried out via protein-protein pathways expressing the interaction between specific genes and specific environmental input.

C. What about Argonaute, RISC, and gene silencing?

Erik J. Sontheimer and Richard W. Carthew (2005) report on Argonaute and RISC. Specifically, they credit Liu et al. (2004) and Song et al. (2004) for finding the catalytic subunit that executes RNAi, that is, that provides the "slicer" function. According to these reviewers, slicer "has been staring us in the face for years" (Sontheimer & Carthew, 2005, p. 1409), but we didn't see it, just as in Sophocles play Oedipus Rex the killer of Laius (Oedipus' father) was not appreciated at first to be Oedipus himself!

In the case of most eukaryotes (organisms with cells having nuclei) RNAi (RNA interference) is one method of silencing double stranded RNA (dsRNA) by chopping it up into strands of 21- to 23-nucleotide long siRNA fragments. These fragments then associate with a large protein assembly called the RNA-induced silencing complex (RISC). A siRNA within RISC recognizes specific mRNAs by means of base-pairing, and in this way guides RISC to the appropriate targets. The RISC complex harbors a catalytic activity that specifically cleaves the bound mRNA without affecting the guide siRNA. RISC has been known for over 4 years having been discovered by Hammond, Bernstein, Beach, and Hannon (2000); but the catalytic subunit "slicer" (the protein) has only just been identified.

Argonaut2 was the first protein subunit found in RISC. There are a number of other proteins, which form a family characterized by the presence of so-called PAZ and PIWI "domains". PAZ helps the step of binding to siRNA that which is to be cleaved. Hannon and Joshua-Tor have now shown more of the details of the functions of Argonaut proteins within RISC. In particular, *they have proven that Argonaut2 is "slicer"*. The PIWI domain is the precise harbor where "slicer" resides. In other words, the PIWI domain "act[s] as an endonuclease (scissors) that cleaves the mRNA strand within the siRNA/mRNA "duplex". Other nucleases complete the process. Argonaut2 deficient mice show its importance for development; the result is defective formation of the neural tube, heart, and other organs. There is still much left to be understood about the roles of Argonaut 2 in early developmental events.

Liu et al., in their abstract, summarize the situation as follows: Gene silencing through RNAi is carried out by RISC, the RNA-induced silencing complex. RISC contains two signature components, small interfering RNAs (siRNAs) and Argonaute family proteins. The multiple Argonaute proteins present in mammals are both biologically and biochemically distinct, with a single mammalian family member, Argonaute2, being responsible for messenger RNA cleavage activity. This protein is essential for mouse development, and presumably for human development as well.

Their goal has been to understand the role of "slicer activity"; I believe that as we understand more about RISC and Argonaute2 we may better understand development generally, including our own. For example, Lien et al. (2006) have shown that the hedgehog pathway plays a decisive role in regulating the size of our developing cerebral cortex (both the number and size of cells) during development, based upon input from so-called adherens junctions between cells, that provide a critical negative feedback loop).

If we are to understand development, we need to appreciate not only the important psychological/ethological releasing factors for its various steps; we also need to appreciate the multiple biological "grundlagen" (critical elements or structures) upon which the various releasers act, which for all the mammals critically involves the protein pathways described in this review.

Let me add one additional comment. It may be of interest to those interested in cancer, that a few years ago some research emerged on the subject of telomerase. This enzyme is produced at the ends of chromosomes, and helps them potentially repair the damage that occurs when chromosomes enter meiosis (duplication). Basically, each time the chromosomes duplicate, they shorten a tiny bit. Junk DNA at the end of the chromosome prevents things from unraveling right away, but eventually, when the chromosome is too short (multiplied too many times), it has a choice of either going into apoptosis, or, of becoming immortal (cancerous). The later step occurs under the influence of telomerase (it repairs the end of the gene, known as a telomere), and this can begin the process of unlimited growth we call cancer.

It should be apparent from the protein pathways described that much is understood about growth, development, and behavior at the microbiological protein pathway gene-activation level. What is exciting is the collaboration of neuroscientists, geneticists, and other biologists, with psychoanalysts of every persuasion. As Eric Kandel has asserted, this is our future, on the research side, to integrate knowledge at every level. "[We need to make psychoanalysis] ... a more rigorous, biologically based science ... [We need]...to make a serious effort to verify its concepts and show which aspects of therapy work, under what conditions, for what patients and with which therapists... If we can we will revolutionize the field. After all, Freud always said that one day in the future we will need to bring psychoanalysis and the biology of the mind together" (Kandel, 2006; see also Kandel, 1998, 1999).

The protein pathways carry out all cellular processes. They turn genes on and off, generate energy for the cell, control communication, provide defenses against viruses for plants and animals, generate growth and development, and control life and death. We are deeply emerged, via neuro-psychoanalysis, in the careful, stepwise, integration of biology and psychology as regards mind and brain. We are arriving at a critical cross road where we can either stay ignorant of other disciplines studying some of the same things we in psychoanalysis are studying, or we can learn about these disciplines, become cross-trained, and carry out interdisciplinary research together. By opening ourselves up in the latter way, we are beginning to see what theories of mechanisms of recovery in psychotherapy or analysis make sense when examined from the perspective of complex multiple frames of reference. So far, psychoanalysis is holding its own, which should give us all more confidence. In this sense, our understanding of brain chemistry such as Argonaut2 is not limited to knowing that it is slicer, the RISC-related component for gene silencing; but in Argonaut2 we have nothing less than a symbolization in concrete terms of our determination to travel together like the Argonauts of Old into some of the great mysteries of life, and emerge with precious new insights applicable to the amelioration of human suffering. The argument is simply this: we can better get there by combining the insights of psychoanalysis and of neuroscience, along the way learning about the details of how things work from the perspective of multiple interdigitating points of view. Emotions are then understandable as a result from biological and psychological cascades within the mind and brain, which closely correlate with each other.

Notes

1.   An earlier version of this chapter appeared as an article in *Psychoanalytic Quarterly*, November 2006.
2.   As stated in Blakemore, Frith, and Wolpert (2001, p. 1883) so-called efference copies are important for accurately predicting self-produced sensations, based upon error detection (see p. 155 of this book for elaboration regarding the CB role in predicting the sensory consequences of action).
3.   See also Sohl, Maxeiner, and Willecke (2005).

CHAPTER SEVEN

Introduction to the cerebellum (CB): Ito Masao's controller-regulator model of the brain, and some implications for psychodynamic psychiatry and psychoanalysis (including how we understand the conscious/unconscious distinction, and the role of feelings in the formation and expression of the self)[1]

Fred M. Levin

Précis: This chapter reviews some research on the CB and then weaves it into our conceptualization of what the CB might be doing psycho-dynamically. What is difficult in this is how best to tie together the many details of CB activity that we have been touching upon throughout this book, and how to help the reader best understand the reasoning behind our theorizing. We hope that we have already established a sufficient basis, however, in our earlier writings, and in the earlier chapters of this book, to make our case that the CB plays a number of critical roles in mental life. We are fully aware, however, that only future experimentation can determine how

correct we are regarding to the role of the CB in mind/brain. Interdiscipli-
nary insights aim to improve our neuroscientific explanations of Freud's
psychodynamic ideas about consciousness, our core self, and our deep
unconscious motivations. It seems that under particular circumstances of
modeling other brain systems, the CB essentially connects the explicit and
the implicit memory systems. This connectedness of the two great memory
systems (explicit and implicit), would thus be a product of the CB, to some
significant degree. Of course, there may well be other connections between
the explicit and implicit systems. In the earlier model of Ito dealing with
the controller-regulator function of the brain, Ito assumed four regulators:
(1) the CB, (2) basal ganglia, (3) limbic system, and (4) sleep centers. These
regulatory centers are seen as accounting for the four different aspects of
the ucs mind, as follows: (1) the CB provides internal models for other con-
trollers; (2) basal ganglia provide selection and stabilization; (3) the limbic
system provides the emotional input, and the SEEKING system attends to
our drive states; and (4) sleep centers provide for the switching on and off
of wakefulness and the different forms of sleep, which we have covered in
the first two chapters in this book, and of course, during sleep, other centers
produce dreaming. We are asserting that the CB helps all five controllers (for
reflexes, compound movements, innate behavior, sensori-motor functions,
and association-cortical functioning). Innate behavior is an expression of
psychobiological emotional systems, and in this sense, the CB is related to
the behavioral expression of emotion. However, (and this is an important
caveat) although we suspect that the CB provides an important internal
model for emotion, since we do not yet possess complete knowledge of all the
systems that pertain to emotion, therefore, we believe it makes sense to be
careful in assessing how exactly to weigh this particular CB contribution to
the emotion and cognitive systems.

I. *Introduction*

We have previously described the contributions of the cerebellum (Levin, Gedo, Ito, & Trevarthen, 2003a, 2003b)
and readers interested in the details should examine our
earlier writing in this area. In this chapter we intend to clarify more
details about the CB, because in our opinion the CB plays a decisive
role in the mind/brain. It most likely is the locus of the experiential
or core self, functional from before birth, and it undoubtedly plays a

major role in cs/ucs relations, and in the realm of human feelings, in learning, and in prioritizing various kinds of decision making.

In our earlier work we introduce our subject by reviewing a number of "durable" problems in contemporary science regarding the conscious/unconscious nosology. One issue is understanding the conflict among philosophers, on the one hand, and neuroscientists and/or psychoanalysts on the other, over what is strictly knowable in a Kantian/Freudian sense (vs. that which is merely inferable), and what is causally connected (vs. what is merely correlated); as well as sorting out the complex relationships between consciousness, perception, emotion and memory. Another is explaining the limited-capacity paradox, viz. the observation that consciousness is limited to a relatively small number of items, whereas the non-conscious seems virtually without limit. A third involves explaining consciousness as a necessary design feature of mind and brain. A forth concerns understanding the relative roles of consciousness and subliminal perception. Some of these issues have already been discussed in earlier chapters of this book, others will be covered in this and remaining chapters, and some cannot be covered because we do not yet have anything like agreed upon answers.

It will help for us to begin with Ito's controller-regulator model of the brain, which elaborates the McLean classic Triune model of the brain. Chapter Eight will include still more details for our thinking about exactly how the CB plays a critical role in our mental life. One role, that the CB is capable of is making copies of various systems of the brain, either a part acting as a controlled object (forward model) or a part acting as a controller (inverse model). By this mechanism the CB may then replace by itself (that is, independently of these areas of the brain) a significant part of the cerebral cortical functions that are operated consciously by cerebellar processes that undergo unconsciously the management of ideas and drive states (read this also to include how to create action plans and execute them in ways that take into account complex considerations from various simultaneous perspectives; for example, that of the ego, superego, and the id, and how various feelings and decisions are related). In what follows we stick to the outline of our earlier publications in this area (Levin, Gedo, Ito, & Trevarthen, 2003a, 2003b, as noted above) but add our latest insights.

II. *Controller-regulator model of the brain:*
Building mind/brain in steps

This model starts from *three core brain control systems*: (1) reflexes (of the spinal cord), (2) compound movements (spread from the spinal cord to medulla oblongata and midbrain), and (3) innate behavior (involving the hypothalamus and other structures in the rostral end of the brainstem). To this core are added four regulatory structures. The first is (a) the limbic system (an older part of the cerebrum, from an evolutionary perspective), whose primary role is the modification of innate behaviors by positive or negative reinforcement. The second addition is (b) the basal ganglia, which serve to settle conflicts between simultaneously operating controllers in the brainstem and the spinal cord by suppressing or selecting desired functions. The third addition is (c) the CB, a critical learning element driven by error signals and a unique type of plasticity, discovered by Ito, known as LTD for long-term depression. LTD is in contrast to LTP (long-term potentiation) in which the more a nervous network is stimulated, the easier it is to subsequently fire off. LTD is the opposite, namely, the increasing difficulty in the firing of a nervous network in response to previous stimulation. In this way, the CB is able to provide specific novel rather than routine responses to stimuli. In essense, the CB works out non-error command signals. And the fourth regulatory structures added are (d) the brainstem sleep-wakefulness centers, which enable switching between these two states for rest, recovery, and for off-line processing.

The three controller systems (1-3) act with the four regulatory structures (a-d) to produce all possible lower vertebrate behavior (from fish to reptile).

To round out the model, we need several more steps. One is the addition of sensorimotor and perisensorimotor areas of the neocortex and the underlying thalamus, and with these additions we see the stage of development in lower mammals, that is, rats, cats, and dogs.

The next step occurs in primates, and involves the appearance of the association cortex, which enables us to generate images, values, concepts, and ideas from what will be called parietotemporal cortical areas (which are surrounded by the sensory cortex), and these mental experiences will also be stored away in memory. This association cortex also includes the prefrontal cortex which acts as an executive cortex sending command signals to the parietotemporal cortex, to act upon mental representations in the latter.

One key would appear to be that *the prefrontal and parietotemporal cortices form a loop*, so that arguably these connections "represent the process of thought" (Ito, 1998, p. 193). It is also important that since feedback is built-in to any such thinking process, it helps account for what we appreciate psychologically as the dialectical quality of some thought; in other words, thought involves output, yet this output becomes input to the same system, and thus feedback alters (refines) further output (here the reader may recall the mind/brain model presented in Chapter Four, which we are building upon). It seems likely that the latest system to evolve (i.e. the associative cortex) also comes under the influence of the regulatory structures noted above. By regulatory structures we intend, as well the idea of feedback, since functions such as consciousness obviously involve the re-presentation of selective material to the experiencing subject for reconsideration or modification, as Olds (1992, 1994) has clarified. This re-presentation, or as Olds puts it, this "sign function", is what gives us the capacity to adjust our thinking and actions in real time, and/or, to at least feel that we have some information about what is likely to happen next in areas of concern to us; without it, our higher mental functioning (symbolic processing) would be more subject to errors and undue delays in thinking, and it would be harder for us to orient our self to our place in the overall process.

Regarding the subject of consciousness alluded to in the previous paragraph, a number of complicated issues need to be attended to. As Ito points out, if we examine carefully how the choroid plexus provides an essential link in the brain pathway that leads to sleep induction (Urade et al. 1993), although there is a lot of research on this subject, it becomes obvious that no one yet definitively knows what turns sleep on or off in the brainstem, or, for this matter, exactly what controls attention. Hence we need to be cautious in making conclusions on what controls sleep, and consequently dreaming (as we indicate in Chapters One and Two). Secondly, regarding consciousness as selective awareness, its prime target is the external world; however, we would like to add here that, of course, the mind is also necessarily attentive to internally generated thoughts. Put differently, conscious attention, from our perspective, seems most important when it is in the service of adjusting, i.e. changing the current register of databases of the nonconscious mind. We like using the word "learning" for this kind of mind/brain activity. Thirdly, to have a theory of mind/brain mechanisms as regards something as complex as consciousness, we need to understand what Crick and Koch (1992) call "binding", that is, how the various aspects of an experience are unified into a composite image, at least potentially available for self scrutiny (see also Rubinstein, 1997).

Ito makes two technical suggestions for explaining "binding": *resonance* (that is, some frequency of oscillation that connects—in other words, that synchronizes cells into a time-controlled system) or *a convergence of anatomical pathways*. Ito then raises another consideration: Is self-consciousness essentially the same or different from self-monitoring pure and simple? (2003a). We will return to this difficult question shortly.

III. *Bridging to Freud*

One complication is that it is not clear which of the many Freudian models are appropriate to employ in any such bridging. For example, the structural model of Freud currently is primarily helpful within psychoanalysis for explaining the narrow issues that relate to (neurotic) conflict, but its epistemological shortcomings[2] become obvious when dealing with anything beyond that. In fact, Ito's phylogenetic approach to CNS organization actually clarifies the difficulty of thinking of consciousness as anything other than a set of synergistic functions that are more usefully studied separately. What we are asserting is that "... *the psychoanalytic unconscious is centrally affective and motivational [in nature] and...this is what psychoanalysis has to teach ... cognitive [and neuro-] scientists*" (Weinberger & Weiss, 1997, cited in Barry, 1998, p. 9. italics added). Another way of thinking of this would be to consider that the unconscious (in the Freudian sense) is a system of mentation from which a well-developed capacity of higher-order consciousness has been withheld, for defensive (adaptive) reasons. Therefore, before such a capacity develops and comes "on-line" for individuals (i.e. before symbolization has sufficiently developed) there is only one system: non-consciousness. And our educated guess has been that the non-conscious operates on the basis of a symbolic system largely characteristic of either the right brain (i.e. the limbic system) in other words, on the basis of the CB, which is also what Freud called "primary process" more or less (Levin, 2003).

Before returning to the significance of Ito's comments on "binding", we wish to make a few additional points on the matter of cs/ucs relationship, and the CB. Here it may help to simply quote from our previous paper (Levin, Gedo, Ito, & Trevarthen, 2003a) as follows:

> We know that self-awareness does *not* depend on wakefulness (for dreamers may be fully aware that they are dreaming); that there are various degrees of wakefulness (from the hypnoid states already noted by Breuer, through hypnogogic and hypnopompic conditions, the states of people under hypnosis, and so on); that sleep may even heighten awareness of the emotional world and that a state of hyper-alertness (say in the face of external threats) may actually shut off self-awareness; etc. We also have observations which show that perceptual awareness of the external world has to pass through an associative filter to become available for symbolic processing (viz. negative hallucination; denial of reality; disavowal of meaning; isolation of affect). Such anxiety-producing data often receive attention only in the form of traumatic dreams (2003a).

> Ito is particularly illuminating about the (nonrepressive) operations that Hartmann (1939) called "automatization". Ito's postulation of cerebellar maps, which permit adaptive behavior without explicit awareness, gives support to his cerebellum-based model of self-in-the-world, i.e. that *non-symbolic self-organization is the probable core of human personality* [i.e. the self] (Ito cited in Levin, 1991, and in Levin & Vuckovich, 1983, 1987; also see Gedo, 1991a, 1991b, 1996a, 1996b, 1997). A developmental neurophysiology that spells out the evolution of this module of the CNS would provide the necessary foundation for a biologically valid psychoanalytic model of the mind (2003a).[3]

Now to one final comment on whether self-monitoring and self-consciousness are the same or different phenomena. We believe this to be important because it would appear from what we have said with regard to the CB that both self-monitoring and self-consciousness would be involved with its functioning; that is, the two mental activities logically go together. Remember, when we cited the work of Olds earlier, we were focused then first upon consciousness (re-presenting), and then, secondarily, its relationship to that monitoring action which involves using our re-presenting something to the self for the purpose of making adjustments, corrections, and so forth. So what is important here? What is important is Ito's insight that imbedded in the concept of "binding" is some means of connection between various systems, so that if we wish to discover how the CB might accomplish this, Ito is postulating it is either by some anatomical convergence, or some frequency of oscillation that creates a time-controlled (CB) system. Based upon the speculation we are making in the next section, it may well be that both aspects are involved, by means of the CB operating independently by using a model (its own creation) of other systems (say the SEEKING system, and/or the limbic or other systems), rather than merely input to the limbic system, or the SEEKING system, or any other system that the CB participates with as part of an extended neural network. But one then needs to clarify what the contingencies are that result in the one (independent modeling) vs. the other (cooperation of the CB within multiple extended neural networks or systems).

IV. *The Cerebellum (CB)*

As noted in Ito's model of brain evolution, there is reflex control (which involves a reflex center acting as a controller upon a control object such as the skeleto-muscular system), more complicated compound movements (which require a function generator, e.g. a rhythm generator) as well as innate behaviors (still more complex patterns that require an internal program). We believe the CB is involved in all three levels of function, although the evidence is less clear for innate behavior.

As we stated earlier, cerebellar control does not require external feedback; rather feedforward control is accomplished in two ways. First, when the CB provides an internal model of the controlled objects, the controller may replace the external feedback with it (forward model). Second, whenever the CB has dynamics inversely equal to the dynamics of its control object it can replace the controller (inverse model). Another way Ito puts this is to say that there might be "... two stages of motor learning: first, the control is made feedforward [for example] using a cerebellar forward model of the skeletalmuscular system, and second, *it is performed [non-consciously] by passing the motor cortex through the cerebellar inverse model"* (italics added, Ito, 1998, p. 195).[4] Since evidence for an inverse model for eyeball has been obtained in Purkinje cell activity (ventral paraflocculus) during eye movements, the CB must contain inverse dynamics for such movements (Levin, Gedo, Ito, & Trevarthen, 2003a).

As regards the forth and fifth functional systems (i.e. the cortex— both sensorimotor and associative, and the thalamus as well) the CB can provide internal models.[5] This is important enough to elaborate upon. Essentially, the CB copies some other system by receiving input from the system to be copied, and uses error signals (discrepancies between its early model and the actual system as modeled) to self-organize its neural network until the signal transfer characteristics of the CB unit (read here as "model") is a perfect copy. In practical terms, such modeling, in the case of the motor system, results from the loop existing between the motor area and the paravermal cortex (i.e. cortex and CB). The command signals for voluntary movement, in this example, are essentially sent to a model of the musculoskeletal system in the CB, the output of which is returned to the motor cortex. This loop is most interesting in that it allows the performance of movements without using external sensory feedback, instead relying upon internal feedback through the model being used at the moment within the CB.

In this scheme, the CB replaces the motor apparatus as a controlled object, or the cortex as controller: presently both possibilities are maintained. Any voluntary movements operated by a CB (forward model), will be performed without concerns about the actual results, and those operated by a CB inverse model will be performed "without conscious efforts to operate the motor cortex" (Ito, op. cit., p. 195). In other words, it will flow from non-conscious CB models of self-in-the-world, as noted in earlier chapters. This also helps to explain the well-known research finding that mental imagery of movement is fully equivalent to actual movements in its effects on learning (see Roland & Friberg, 1985, cited in Levin, 1991; see also Roland, 1981). One additional important point made by Ito (op. cit., p. 195): motivation is a factor even with regard to the activities of the motor system since in that case the supplementary motor area receives input from the sensory association areas and cingulate gyrus. That is, sources of emotion are integrated with this sensory input and ultimately provide instruction signals to the motor area for the onset of voluntary movement.

Ito intends to explain the above schemes of motor control with forward and inverse models for movements to problems of mental control of thought. Because, in the thought, we move mental representations in the cerebral cortex (images, ideas, and concepts), the same control principles may apply to both movement and thought. Based on the formal analogy, it will be possible that, after repeated trials, thought becomes automatically and unconsciously performed just as a movement becomes so. Movements and thoughts are very different in their nature, physical and mental, but once these are represented in a neuronal circuit, these may be dealt with by similar information processing principles. While a representation in the cerebral cortex is formed in cerebral cortical networks by the process of associative learning, its copy in the cerebral cortex will be formed in the process of error learning. However, computational exercises have yet to be made on this translation of ideas from the one domain to the other.

In the next section we elaborate more on the systems that the CB might create models of. This will include a significant number of systems,[6] but will be exemplified initially by a discussion of the CB's possible use of models of the SEEKING system and Limbic system. If this would be the case, then this would help us understand more precisely how emotional systems related to human drives (and unconscious motivations) might be expressed by the mind/brain, namely, under CB control.[7] It should be stated that here we are not stating a position of Ito, since it is our impression that he would not come to such a conclusion about this possibility at this time. This is therefore merely the speculation of the author of this chapter, independently, for the purpose of seeing where it might go.

V. The SEEKING system and Limbic system

In Chapter Two we have described the work of Jaak Panksepp on the SEEKING system, a critical dopaminergic system that deals with human drive states, that helps us make decisions about meeting both biological and psychological needs.

The reader will already be familiar with the limbic system, which includes the amygdala (aggression and fear), cingulate gyrus (heart rate, blood pressure, and attention, that is, for executive control), the fornicate gyrus (includes the region that encompasses the cingulate, hippocampus, and parahippocampal gyrus), hippocampus (decisions about long-term memory storage and retrieval), hypothalamus (autonomic nervous system, hormones, blood pressure, heart rate, hunger, thirst, sexual arousal, sleep/wake cycle), mammilary body (formation of memory), nucleus accumbens (reward, pleasure, addiction), orbitofrontal cortex (decision making), and parahippocampal gyrus (formation of spatial memory). These are the structures of the human brain that are involved with emotion. Those interested in more details of these systems should consult Wikipedia (2006), along with Levin (1991, 2003).

Basically, these systems will provide other unconsciously operated subcortical systems, in addition to the CB. Dopaminergic systems operate with the enforced learning principle, as contrasted to error-related learning in the CB. If the unconscious would be at least in part, modeled within the CB, and controlled by it, then, quite speculatively, there would be reason to wonder if the integration of emotions, and the proper attention to unconscious/non-conscious drive states (biological and psychological needs) would be attended to in a most efficient way.

VI. *Summary*

We have presented Ito's controller-regulator model of the brain. In the process have reviewed some important perspectives on the CB, which we believe contributes to both conscious mental experience and to the Freudian dynamic unconscious. Freud's critical contribution to understanding human psychology was the concept of drive theory and the idea of a dynamic unconscious, that is, the creation of emotions as a mechanism for the communication to self and to others of our biological and psychological needs. Jaak Panksepp's concept of the SEEKING system goes a long way towards grounding Freud's contribution in terms of modern neuroscience research. Whether neuroscientists accept Freud's theorizing in this area is a different matter, but probably much less relevant than the fact that

Freud's theory seems to have a solid base both within psychoanalysis and neuroscience. And the fact that the details of the function of the CB involves the critical capacity to model other controller parts of the brain, not just the motor system, but likely also the neocortex. The SEEKING system and the limbic system constitute the emotional system and, begins to provide scholars, researchers, and clinicians with a means to advance their understanding of emotion as a unique subcortical system. In essence, we are attempting to establish a basis for a psychodynamics by studying the CB, basal ganglia, and the emotional systems as neural substrate of the unconscious domain of the mind. The next chapter will carry these ideas further along, and try to identify at least some of their implications for NP.

Notes

1. Earlier versions of Chapters 7, 8, 9., and 10 were presented November 27, 2006 to the Brain Science Institute of RIKEN, under Ito Masao, in Wako, Japan, and December 3, 2006, to the Japanese Psychoanalytic Society, in Tokyo. The author thanks Professor Ito for his generous input.

2. The reader will appreciate, however, that we are not excluding the structural model of Freud, in fact, far from it. This will become clear when we consider which models the CB models, and how this might determine its mode of operation: id, ego, or superego.

3. In the meantime, however, it is possible to construct proto-neurophysiological models (Rubinstein, 1997) to accommodate the clinical data of psychoanalysis.

4. Later in this essay we will elaborate on our idea that the conscious system helps the unconscious system make necessary changes in memory that constitute learning. This contribution of consciousness to the interpretation of nonsymbolic self-organization might also be conceptualized as a two-step process, more or less following Ito's suggestions for learning within the skeletomuscular system.

5. Here we are referring to Ito's "self-in-the-world model" without exactly using this terminology, to keep it more general (see Levin, 1991 for many related citations of Ito's pioneering work).

6. For example, the sensory-motor system (when the CB would be in "ego" mode) and the associative cortex (when the CB would be in "superego mode". This will be elaborated upon later in this book).

7. There is now some supportive evidence that the microsaccades within
    eye movements (Martinez-Conde & Macknik, 2007) communicate sub-
    conscious desires to some extent, as when a subject looks one way, while
    the microsaccades move another, where the latter tract a women attrac-
    tive to the viewing subject. Such saccadic eye movements are of course
    largely under CB control.

PART IV

THE CEREBELLUM, ADVANCED CONSIDERATIONS: THE ROLE OF RECALIBRATION, AND MODELING OF ONE PART OF THE BRAIN BY ANOTHER

When might the CB be involved in modeling the Limbic System, the SEEKING system, or other systems?

Fred M. Levin

Précis: This chapter continues our discussion in Chapter Seven on CB modeling of other parts of the brain, and asks what the implications are of this known fact. Evidence is introduced to support the probability of various CB models, including the probability that copies are likely made in the CB of the limbic system, the SEEKING system, and others We are extending what is known, and asking reasonable questions, stating when we are speculating and when we are standing on firm ground.

I. *Introduction*

I n reviewing the subject of conscious/unconscious relations in Chapters One and Two, we (Levin, Gedo, Ito, & Trevarthen, 2003a, 2003b) came to number conclusions about the role of the CB in mental life. We have presented some of our ideas on this subject in Chapter Seven. The most important is the fact that the CB can create models of other systems of our brain. Once it would have created such a model, say of the premotor system, it could then use error signals (discrepancies between its early model and the actual system as modeled) to self-organize its neural network until the signal transfer characteristics of the cerebellar unit (read here as "model") are a more or less perfect copy.[1]

As stated in Chapter Seven, we believe, reasoning by analogy, that it is likely that the CB could copy the limbic system, the SEEKING system, or a variety of other systems, since it is known to be able to copy the cortex that ordinarily controls the motor system, and carry out motor activities without the premotor cortical system needing to be actively initiating anything. If the CB would be able to emulate the limbic system, this might provide the brain with a means of rapidly "recalibrating" many details of our emotional life. If it could model the SEEKING system, there are implications for its ability to manage our biological drives of various kinds, say for sexuality or aggression. Such "recalibration" by the CB is known to occur in the case of the vistibulo-ocular reflex (VOR) within the visual system. The VOR keeps the visual image focused on one spot of the retina in spite of shifts in the position of the object in space, or, of any movements of our head or neck. This kind of activity obviously plays an important part in protecting the accuracy of our vision, one of the oldest sensory systems we have.[2]

We need to wonder, therefore, what extensive CB modeling of other systems of the brain might accomplish. Would it not be better, so to speak, for the limbic system (or any other system of the brain) to operate as a member of an extended neural network) which is what it does most all of the time? Or, to put it differently, why should the CB chose to operate any system that it could just as well provide input to as a member of its extended neural network?

A correct answer is not as easy as it might seem (although we do attempt a more comprehensive answer in Chapter Nine). Our short response here, however, would be that the limbic system, for example, might be able to perform many of its functions on its own much of the time, but not necessarily all of the time: that is, it might not be the best contributor of its input when unexpected speed would be required, nor, when unusually complicated events are occurring that would require time-consuming toll-taking among the various limbic components over extended neural space (and via connections at a distance). Put differently, sometimes the CB might do a better job modeling the limbic system than the limbic system could do with the CB as mere input to its usual neural network activity. Is there any evidence to support such conclusions? We believe there is.

A recent article by Bruno and Sakmann (2006, see also Alonso, 2006) is a good place to start. These authors have studied carefully *how sensory stimuli from the thalamus reach the dendrites of neurons in Layer 4 of the cortex.* It would seem that such neurotransmission is not difficult; however, if (in rat experiments, for example) one measures the specific strength of these thalamic relays, the thalamocortical synapses show extremely "low efficacy" (p. 1622)! Apparently, the major reason the relay works at all, according to these authors, is that the thalamic neurons are able to become synchronously active, and by this means "thalamic input alone [becomes able to] drive the cortex" in this instance.

We believe it is possible that the situation that exists between the thalamus and cortex layer 4 may not be unusual within the brain.[3] If we are correct in this speculation, this means that some brain systems with a significant number of far-flung components probably normally require synchrony of discharge, or some equivalent mechanism, in order to overcome a relatively low efficiency of connectivity. And this would be part of our basis for assuming that one way the brain may work around such an endemic problem (in individuals, and in a species) would be to create a subsystem within the brain, in this case the CB, that could intermittently create a model of other systems, and then, when needed, emulate the other system to increase efficiency, including energy efficiency. The efficiency would come from having a compact system like the CB contain all relevant subsystems within itself in the form of usable models, thus eliminating any disadvantage growing from the far-flung nature of some neural networks.

But this is not the only basis for our thinking in terms of enormous adaptive value for a CB contribution via the use of models. Our second basis for assuming the brain might benefit from the CB's copying systems, such as the limbic system, the SEEKING system, or any other system, and then operating it without the usual controller(s) is that the CB would be operating an updated copy of the system emulated, and such updates could be easily created upon demand (Ito, 1998; Levin, Gedo, Ito, and Trevarthen, 2003a). A third point worth making is that the CB is also specialized in coordinating both movements and ideas, yet coordinating ideas would be unlikely to succeed if thoughts were manipulated in isolation from the affects that give them meaning. In other words, as we have pointed out repeatedly in this book, meaning grows from context, and one of the decisive contexts for ideas and thoughts is the emotion associated with them. From this perspective, modeling the limbic system would give the CB a way of actively participating in emotion and extending this information extensively beyond the CB and in real time.

Moreover, a fourth consideration in support of our speculation about the utility of CB modeling is that, as cited in Chapter Seven, we are already familiar with experimental evidence that mental imagery of movement is fully equivalent to actual movement in its effects on learning (Roland & Friberg, 1985, cited in Levin, 1991; Roland, 1981, cited in Ito, 1998). Thus, the CB, because it is already a specialist in learning within the context of a virtual reality, would likely be able to improve upon learning if it would emulate the limbic system because this would provide the CB with considerable information about particularized emotional meanings for the subjects involved.

Still another line of reasoning supports the probability that the CB has a special relationship with emotion anyway: we know that from birth onwards, long before the cortex is ready to function, the CB is clearly already functioning (and it probably starts its activities even before birth). On this basis the core self is felt to be part of the CB, and it could be expected to contain a repository of personal memories relating to the self from the beginning of life formed significantly before the cerebral cortex provides any such functioning. The first emotions and the earliest rhythms of movement, sound, and life itself, one might expect to be exclusively recorded in the CB. This would seem to give the CB a privileged status among the various brain systems relating to emotion (see Levin, 1991, 2003).

A further consideration supporting a linkage between the CB and emotion is research on the connection(s) between music and emotion. One of the finest articles on this subject that this author is aware of is one by Stein (2004) reviewing Roman Polansky's movie *The Pianist*. This movie portrays the real life experience of the pianist Wladyslaw Szpilman, originally written as an unpublished memoir "Death of a City" in 1946. This manuscript was eventually discovered by his teenage son, then translated into English and published in 1999, after which it was made into the movie. The devastation of the Warsaw

Ghetto, and the killing of most of the Jews in that city (and country) is a public record. The movie portrays in great detail exactly what Szpilman lived through, as he descends from being a famous pianist of Poland, especially an interpreter of Chopin, to being on the run for his life. Stein's essay makes a serious effort to explain how music and emotion are connected in a number of non-trivial ways. From the perspective of our thinking about the CB, however, it seems highly probable that there is a close connection between the CB and music, since the CB's activities are often concerned with critical rhythms, the control of movements, and the calibration and recalibration of reflexive timing.

There is in Stein's essay, for example, a focus (1) on the influence of music on the experience of time and memory in the face of trauma, (2) the role of music for the self-identity of the traumatized musician, and (3) on the potential for music to express our inner life "as a symbolic, extra-narrative [procedural] language" with psychologically healing power (Stein, 2004, p. 756). Let us consider each of these statements (or categories) separately. In support of the first assertion, we have Szpilman's capacity, when first attacked, to adaptively immerse himself in his memories of music (which he could no longer play publicly or privately, lest he be found and exported to the death camps) to help him deal with the enormous trauma he endured during the Nazi persecution in Warsaw. Thus there are scenes in the movie in which he is, for example, living in hiding, sitting at a piano, and quietly moving his hands over its keys (but not touching them), in order not to let any note be heard. No one must know he is there; so he lives at these times only via the memory of his music.

Lastly, we have his making further use of his identity as a musician. In this case he identifies with Chopin who over his own lifetime rewrites some of his own music, especially his famous C# minor nocturne, incorporating "periodic revisions ... [as] incomplete self-quotations, into his later works" (Stein, op. cit., p. 760). Here Stein feels, citing S. Feder (2003), that "the sound or memory of music [can serve an adaptive, defensive function as] a simulacrum, an analogue of the totality of mental life", a special capacity to lose one's self in the face of trauma, [and] as a [general] way of coping (p. 758). And, of course, we have the training of musicians, the long hours of practice, and their resultant ability to delay gratification for those precious moments after sufficient study has made the music production into something of a class by itself. As Stein puts it: musicians develop "idiosyncratic ways of registering, synthesizing, and psychologically metabolizing life events" (p. 757). He also cites Carole Pratt (1952) in this regard: music she says is "a pre-encoded narrative...isomorphically concordant with the listener's emotions", or, in other words, "music sounds the way emotion feels" (p. 758). And the CB, one can argue, communicates to other brain systems what is coded both emotionally and "musically".

II. *Some further comments on CB modeling*

We hope that the above examples, stimulated in part by the movie *The Pianist*, and related to the realm of music, will help us begin to connect more affectively with the relationship of emotion to sensory experience and motor expression, that is, something not merely limited to the playing of a piano as a defense against massive trauma. Nonverbal communication is another way of reflecting on the mind/ brain's near infinite repertoire for expressing how we feel. One of us (FML) learned about this during the time he was active in working with individuals who were hearing impaired (read this as "deaf"), in a free psychiatric clinic created at Michael Reese Hospital in the early 1970's. Eugene Mindel, McKay Vernon, Laszlo Stein, and Teresa Jabeley were instrumental in getting this program off the ground. But what was obvious was how much emotion these deaf patients communicated using not only American Sign Language, but the most amazing gestures, facial expressions, and novel movements.

Over the years since, Levin has also slowly developed the useful but surprising illusion that he can sometimes imagine what system of a patient's brain might be leading the patient's commentary at any given moment in psychoanalysis. Some of this work has already been reported on earlier, but it is worth mentioning as we try to reconstruct what the CB is doing that is interesting both neuroscientifically and psychologically (i.e. emotionally). In Levin (1980) there were times when he felt he was listening in on a conversation between the cortical associative areas for speech, vision, and touch, as they attempted to integrate an experience cross-modally (that is, in some way integrating the modalities, or generalizing upon what these different perspectives shared in common). Along with this Levin also felt there was a resultant "aha" reaction with deep emotional insight associated with what he designated the use of transference-related "metaphors" in his analytic comments or interpretations. Levin and Vuckovich (1983) further believed that some patients made their analyst feel he or she was helping one hemisphere translate itself (or not) for the other hemisphere, for the purpose of assisting psychological defenses; here repression and disavowal seemed to be functional interhemispheric communication blocks in exactly opposite directions. Thus Levin and Vuckovich (1987) suggested that analysts sometimes felt "as though" in particular situations with analysands that they were watching the patient's CB facilitate a complex integration across time and space, resulting in significant learning on the patient's part, along with expansion of the patient's ability to move themselves and their ideas more gracefully. Naturally, such insights about metaphorical transference interpretations deeply impressed Levin and Vuckovich during this early period of NP speculations, especially when informed by the contribution of Ito on the subject of what Ito then called the "self-in-the world model" (see Levin, 1991). Thus, the model presented in the later research of Levin and Vuckovich seemed a possible key to understanding how adult patients under stress solve complex problems by using the CB to separate emotions from the meaningful memories they are associated with. In this phase, Levin and Vuckovich (1983) defined defenses such as repression and disavowal as interhemispheric communication blocks in different direction, the purpose of which was to separate emotion and its immediate causal connections (associations) in memory.

A final piece of evidence presented by Levin and Vuckovich (1983, 1987) was that Levin experienced in his own scientific writing, especially as the final phases of manuscript editing occurred, a tendency, towards recreating the postures and concrete sensory experiences associated with the time when he first learned or mastered critical aspects of writing and editing. Prior to this point, he could edit the document on the computer; at this point onward, however, he needed real paper and pen in his hands to do the most difficult level of the editing job. This also seemed to reflect an aspect of the CB control in using procedural memory via sensory priming of his personal self-in-the-world model (see Ito, 1984).

Reexamining these various insights from over the years, it seems easier to see the CB role as one of carefully monitoring various brain systems, creating models to make their "calibration" more accurate, and then perfecting these models for the self over longer periods of time. When we are operating in "CB mode", there would thus appear to be a natural increase in our abilities to create, to assemble, disassemble, and reassemble ideas in novel ways.

III. *Introduction to a review of neuroscience literature on CB*

Up until now we have not thoroughly reviewed for the reader the full gamut of the technical literature on the CB. For various reasons it seemed better to proceed with those novel neuro-psychoanalytic observations that have built to this point into a theory of the CB that includes its important relationship to emotion, learning, and to the probable role of CB in modeling of other parts of the brain. However, at this point it seems appropriate to proceed with a more comprehensive literature review to see how modern neuroscientific perspectives fit with the perspectives we have discussed over the course of this book.

We start with a review of those diseases that are associated with some significant CB pathology. Along the way, however, there will be some necessary "intrusions" that relate to the two other perspectives which have been applied throughout this book, namely, psychodynamics and the viewpoints of NP. Psychopathology is still another term, primarily psychiatric in nature, for the names that identify certain diseases or syndromic categories. The latter nosology will appear in standard diagnostic references books, for example, the *Diagnostic and Statistical Manual, Edition 4* (DSM-4), or the ICD-9 coding system, or the like. In contrast to diagnostics, psychodynamics refers, of course, to a psychoanalytic perspective in which the world is seen according to its so-called "mental contents", "complexes", or "psychic structures" (obviously, there are many words that are used to describe those parts of mind in conflict or resonance with each other) which interact in ways that become understandable to psychoanalysts and their patients. For example, consider someone who hates his mother based upon a complex history of growing up with that person. The history of his mother relationship can then shed some light on this person's difficulties in relationship to other woman in his life, and possibly, as well, with the feminine side of himself.

Obviously, past experience can influence the present, and vice versa (i.e. present insights can invite us to reinterpret the past, just as we noted in the earlier chapters of this book when we considered phenomena such as the phenomena such as "nachtraglichkeit").

IV. Some further details from neuroscience

Geschwind (1999) noted that the striking expansion of the lateral CB hemispheres and dentate nucleus that occurred during primate evolution, along with the corresponding expansion of the cerebral cortex, reaching a peak in humans, clearly supports the notion that the CB was expanding its capacity to manage non-motor functions. Ito (1981, 1984) has been cited repeatedly by his neuroscience peers, as well as by those in other specialties (Levin & Vuckovich, 1983, 1987; Levin, 1991), as a pioneer in recognizing the details of this expanded perspective, including the role of the CB in procedural learning generally, and in cognition in particular, not just as regards motor learning.[4] Vogel (2005) notes how "we have gone from thinking of the CB as primarily devoted to movement, coordination, and motor learning, to considering the CB role in language, executive functions, and special cognition, but interestingly, leaves out any mention of learning!"

There is general agreement, however, that the CB is involved in **autism** (Gowen & Miall, 2005; Murakami, Courchesne, Press, Yeung-Chourchesne, & Hesselink, 1989; Fatemi et al. 2000; Allen, Müller, & Courchesne, 2004), **ADHD** (Anderson, Polcari, Lowen, Renshaw, & Teicher, 2002; Courchesne, 2001, 2003; Saskia, Palmen, van Engeland, Hoff, & Schmitz, 2004); Townsend, Courchesne, & Egaas, 1996), **mood disorders** (Davies, Lloyd, Jones, Barnes & Pilowsky, 2003; Bremner, Vythilingam, Vermetten, Vaccarino & Charney, 2004; Panksepp, 2005; Schmahmann, 1996, 2004), **cognitive disorders** (Andreasen et al. 1993; Geschwind, 1999; Simon et al. 2005; Rae et al. 1998), and **schizophrenia** (Varambally et al. 2006; Vogel, 2005; Ende et al. 2005; James, James, Smith & Jovaloyes, 2004; Venkatasubramanian et al. 2003; Okugawa, Sedvall, & Ågartz, 2003; Volkow et al. 1998; Jacobson et al. 1997; Schmahmann, 1996; Snider, 1982).

Schmahmann (2004, Table 1) comprehensively reviews CB diseases under the following schema of categories:

- develolpmental problems (Nonprogressive CB ataxia; Chiari malformation, Dandy Walker cyst, Agenesis and partial agenesis, Joubert Syndrome, and Pontocerebellar hypoplasia),
- toxicity (mercury and other heavy metals, including lead and thallium, hyperthermia; organic solvents such as toluene, benzene, carbon disulfide; phencyclidine, heroin leukoencephalopathy),
- autoimmune/inflammatory problems (multiple sclerosis (MS), paraneoplastic CB degeneration, postinfectious cerebellitis, Celiac Disease, Behçet's Disease),
- Vascular disease (infarction as in giant cell arteritis or polyarteritis nodosa; hemorrhage, Von Hippel Lindau Disease; superficial siderosis),
- metabolic illness[5] (Vitamin B12 deficiency, Thiamine deficiency as in Wernicke's encephalopathy),
- infectious disease Abscess; encephalitis; human immunodeficiency disease: progressive multifocal leukoencephalopathy; Creutzfeldt Jakob Disease; Lyme Disease),
- iatrogenic illness (anticonvulsants, chemotherapy, lithium, amiodarone, cyclosporine, bismuth, bromides),
- traumatic injury (penetrating closed head injuries),
- degenerative/hereditary disease (Spinocerebellar Ataxias [SCAs], Friedreich's ataxia, [Huntington's Disease], Ataxia telangiectasia, ataxia with oculomotor apraxia, Spastic ataxia of Charlevoix-Saguenay, and various other "inborn errors of metabolism" with CB features, etc.)

In support of a CB role in cognition, Schmahmann indicates, for example, that in SCAs quite a variety of deficits occur, incuding short-term memory problems, impaired executive functioning, generally poor memory, concentration difficulty, conceptual processing problems, verbal fluency problems, etc. In SCA 13, which involves chromosome 19, there is moderate mental retardation (IQ 62-76). In SCA 17 there is dementia, psychosis, seizures, and extrapyramidal symptoms. In SCA 21, linked to chromosome 7, there is akinesia and hyporeflexia, rigidity, and also cognitive impairment. In contrast to the other ataxia's, however, in Friedreich's ataxia we see that the major pathology lies outside the CB, and patients tend to remain cognitively intact, obviously supporting a role for the CB in cognition. (The inherited illnesses are caused by autosomal recessive or dominant traits, some are X-linked or mitochondrial disorders, and some degenerative illnesses noted by the author are listed as sporadic.)

Schmahmann includes a detailed history of the development of thinking diagnostically about CB functioning, including a very appropriate reference to the pioneering work of Frick (1982), which we have discussed in detail elsewhere (Levin and Vuckovich, 1983, 1987; Levin, 1991). The point is that Frick early on realized the importance of the CB for hypercomplex functioning (i.e. higher level cognitive and affective processing, including learning).

What exactly, however, can we learn about the CB from studying its impact on disease? The answer lies in our closer examination of individual case material. For example, Leroi, O'hearn, Marsh, et al. (2002), examined and compared 31 patients with degenerative CB disease, with 21 Huntington's cases and 29 healthy controls, and showed that psychiatric disorders occurred without cognitive symptoms in 77% of the CB degenerative cases, 81% of the Huntington's cases, and only 41% of the controls. Mood disorders were 68%, 43%, and 19% of the same three groups. The authors thus reasoned from the positive response to psychiatric interventions, that *the CB must play a significant role in modulating both emotion and cognition* (see also Margolis, 2001), and we completely agree.

Schahmann does not include psychiatric disorders in his diagnostic listing, but any general list would certainly include depressions and grief reactions (although the latter might be considered under his category of "traumatic injury"; however, this is obviously not his intention). Nevertheless, there have been scientific studies of grief which indicate increased activity in posterior brain regions, including the CB, posterior brainstem, posterior temporoparietal and occipital areas; also, there is evidence that in such studies decreased activity was more prominent anteriorly and on the left hemisphere (Najib, Lorberbaum, Kose, et al. 2004).

If we examine more carefully Schmahmann's work (2004), he regards the CB problem in autism as an expression of the reduction of lobules VI through VII of the cerebellar vermis (which he describes as limbic CB). Citing Le, Pardo, and Hu (1998), he takes seriously these authors research on non-spatial shifting of selective attention in normal subjects, showing that the lateral cerebellar hemisphere was significantly activated ipsilateral to the finger used for the responding task. And for the principal comparison of interest, there was a contrast between the condition of shifting vs. sustained attention as follows: the latter produced significant activation in the lateral CB hemisphere, folium, posterior superior parietal lobule, as well as the cuneus and precuneus bilaterally. Schmahmann (op. cit.) considers the lateral hemisphere of the posterior CB to be involved in cognitive processing, and, as noted above, the CB vermis to be limbic cerebellum[6]; that is, *the CB is for him undeniably associated with affectivity*. In fact, he states that CB pathology may be associated with difficulty in mental functions, at least as much as with poor motor performance.

Ende, Hubrich, Walter, et al. (2005) studied the CB and pons of 14 patients with schizophrenia using proton magnetic resonance spectroscopic imaging, and compared to normal controls, these patients showed lower N-acetylaspartate concentrations in the CB cortex and vermis. They believe this supports the theory of schizophrenia as an illness in which the corticocerebellar-thalamic circuits are dysfunctional.

Anderson, Polcari, Loven, et al. (2002) studied the effects in boys with ADHD of methylphenidate [treatment] on the CB (especially the vermis) using fMRI; their results supported a role for the vermis in this disease. The vermis would seem to be a critical modulator of forebrain dopamine outflow, and stimulation of the vermis seems to correct dopamine availability. Also the direction and magnitude of the changes were dependent upon the subject's basal level of hyperactivity (i.e. the ability of the subject to sit still). This also confirmed the work of Andreasen, O'Leary, Cizadlo, et al. (1996).

In particular, Schmahmann (2004) addresses a syndrome he names cerebellar cognitive affective syndrome (CCAS), characterized by disturbance in executive functions, verbal fluency, spatial cognition, visual-spatial organization, visual-spatial memory, and linguistic difficulties (agrammatism and mild anomia, inlcuding dysprosodia), in association with "personality difficulties", which sound to us related extensively to emotion (affect flattening or blunting, and disinhibited or inappropriate behavior). Lesions in these cases involve the posterior lobes in the territory of the posterior inferior cerebellar hemisphere, with progressive cerebellar degeneration(s).

Schmahmann is struck, even puzzled, by the manifold higher order brain functions apparently facilitated by the CB. These he seems to explain by noting, as others have done, the bidirectional pathways linking the CB with autonomic, limbic, and associative regions of the cerebral cortex. The function he refers to, of maintaining a homeostatic baseline, he calls "the universal cerebellar transform".[7] However, we would like to suggest that in addition to the CB forming a circuit with other executive control areas, including those for emotion (e.g. the limbic system) and drive states generally (e.g. the SEEKING system), that there is the other probability we have been supporting through much of this book, namely, that the CB makes models of critical other areas and can thus modulate the brain, and emulate the other systems, more or less on its own.

If we would examine Gordon, Panksepp, Dennis, and McSweeny (2005), work that builds on Panksepp's earlier work (1998a, 1998b), then we would conclude that the neurodynamics of the basic emotional systems of the brain and affective experience are more or less isomorphic. But this does not necessarily mean that there is any general agreement yet on such a matter as what the CB is doing specifically regarding emotion. But there is less likely to be an argument, so far as we can see, that under ordinary non-threatening circumstances (meaning non-complicated states, where there are no compelling risks), that a system made up of the CB through its important linkages (circuits) to other areas relating to executive/affective and cognitive functioning (for example, the SEEKING system, the somatosensory and dorsolateral prefrontal cortex, the limbic system including the PAG, and amygdala, and the anterior cingulate) are likely to serve a coordinating/regulatory role for mind/brain. Panksepp (1998a) has stated that the CB has long been known to be involved with attentional and emotional process (p. 204).

There is also the interesting research of Calarge, Andreasen, and O'Leary (2003), studying "theory of mind" (TOM) with PET scanning. In this case, two experimental subjects were compared, one making up a story about the mental state of a stranger who they imagined running into on a park bench (the TOM group), while the other subjects were reading a story out loud requiring no mental attribution of mental state. The results: only the theory of mind (TOM) or "mentalizing" task group showed an active network including the medial frontal cortex, superior frontal cortex, anterior and retrosplenial cingulate, and anterior temporal pole, with most activations in the left hemisphere, and the largest activation in the contralateral right CB and the anterior vermis. The other group showed no such activations. Obviously, this experiment demonstrates *the CB role in thinking and feeling about others and self in relationship to each other*, which would seem to be a key element in what the CB accomplishes.[8]

Shifting back to Panksepp, for a moment, he makes clear in his discussion of emotion, that we are not talking about something that is unitary, but respecting that many feelings can be involved in mind/brain, each with their characteristic signature of patterns: "there are sites in the most ancient part of the cerebellum (in the deep cerebellar nuclei, such as the *fastigial* and *interpositus*), where one can elicit aggressive tendencies with ESB" (Panksepp, op. cit.). On the basis of the work out of Andreasen's lab, and Panksepp's lab, and all of the other research we have been discussing in this chapter, we believe no sophisticated researcher is ruling out the possibility that the CB can become a (or possibly, *the*) *superordinate executive controlling system of the brain*, at least on some periodic as-needed basis. Nor could they at the present time rule out our hypothesis of more widespread modeling on the part of the CB. So this is where we have come from all our hypothesizing, and all our studies of the CB in disease, and in health, especially using the latest radiological technologies of visualizing mind/brain.

Summarizing, Schmahmann (1998, from the abstract to his article) notes as follows, and we agree: "(1) The associative and paralimbic [cortical] incorporation into the cerebellar circuit is the anatomic underpinning of the cerebellar contribution to cognition and emotion. (2) There is topographic organization of cognitive and behavioral functions within the cerebellum. The archicerebellum, vermis, and fastigial nucleus are principally concerned with affective and autonomic regulation and emotionally relevant memory. The cerebellar hemispheres and dentate nucleus are concerned with executive, visual-spatial, language, and other mnemonic functions. (3) The convergence of inputs from multiple associative cerebral regions to common areas within the cerebellum facilitates ... regulation of supramodal functions. (4) The cerebellar contribution to cognition is one of modulation rather than generation. Dysmetria of ... thought and emotion are the clinical manifestations of a cerebellar lesion in the cognitive domain. (5) [And finally,] the cerebellum performs the same computations for associative and paralimbic functions as it does for the sensorimotor system (p. 74)."

Notes

1. If compared to our comment on p. 129 on the importance generally of corollary discharge and efference copies, as demonstrated in the work of Blakemore, Frith, and Wolpert (2001), one is reminded that information about motor commands and the discrepancies between these and actual outcomes (as picked up by error detection mechanisms, for example, within the CB) can help detect the sensory consequences of movement (see below).

2. There is evidence that vision was originally acquired by living organisms on earth more than 540 million years ago (Fortey, 2000).

3. Canolty, Edwards, et al. (2006) suggest that transient coupling between low- and high-frequency brain rhythms helps "provide a mechanism for effective communication [between brain subsystems] during cognitive processing" (p. 1626).

4. See Akshoomoff and Courchesne (1992), and Akshoomoff, Courchesne, and Townsend, J. (1997).

5. No mention was made for normal metabolic differences, for example, between the sexes, with women showing higher metabolism in the CB (Volkow, Gur, Wang, Fowler, et al. 1998), but the significance of these findings was not discussed. Also, schizophrenic patients have shown low CB metabolism.

6. "The CB vermis is connected to limbic structures, including the hippocampus and amygdala" (Jacobson et al. 1997, p. 1663).

7. According the Margolis (2001, p. 230) "The cerebellum can be divided into distinct regions based primarily on its structure and projections. The key to the cerebellum, however, is the presence of a microcircuit found in nearly identical form throughout the cerebellar cortex. The central player is the Purkinje cell, the primary source of output signals from the cerebellar cortex. The connections between the Purkinje cells and the other cells…form a processing unit that transforms input signals…but the net effect…remains controversial". Ito's work on LTD clarifies much of this.

8. It also reminds us that the so-called emotional and the cognitive systems of the brain are most often not clearly demarcated but more or less imbedded with each other.

CHAPTER NINE

The CB contribution to affect and the affect contribution to the CB. How emotions are calibrated within a virtual reality (of thought and dreaming) for the purpose of making complex decisions about the future, with minimal error

Fred M. Levin

Précis: This chapter attempts to further tie together how ideas presented in earlier chapters on the CB and affect, and the research literature from neuroscience on the CB, including diseases involving CB pathology, might best be understood in relation to each other. Central to this integration are the seminal ideas of Susanne Langer, who anticipated where we were going long before many of us knew it, and did so with lucid style, philosophical insight, and amazing grace.

I. *Introduction*

As Ito stated:

> During the present century, one of the most fundamental questions to arise in the emergent field of neuroscience is how an assembly of neurons becomes a functioning brain. During the 1950s and 1960s interest centered on the way in which neurons behaved and communicated with each other. During the 1970s the focus shifted to the problem of how heterogeneous groups of neurons act together in an intricate neuronal network... [While] during the 1980s the time [was] ripe for asking how local neuronal networks are assembled to constitute large-scale neuronal systems... [Ito, 1984, p. 465]

Later Ito added, in his review of this important history of CB research (Ito, 2002), that the 1980s included the discovery of long-term depression (LTD) in his laboratory, where many more details were worked out regarding the VOR adaptation, adaptive locomotion, eye blink conditioning, and the detailed neural-chemical and neuroanatomical mechanisms of CB functioning.

In the 1990s, according to Ito (2002), questions were focused upon how the CB provides control over complex functions, including its role in learning and its newly discovered ability to make copies of various brain systems. During this period Ito also worked out many details regarding complex signal transduction processes, "towards a fusion of knowledge of the CB at molecular and cellular levels and those [details] in systems and computation" (p. 273), thus pursuing LTD and many aspects of the innate [implicit] memory system. Since the millennium, interest within neuroscience also seems to be taking into account in an increasingly serious way the need to integrate into neuroscience the findings of sister sciences. And there has been a revolution in cognitive psychology, and a new openness within psychoanalysis to neurobiology.

Having presented in Chapters Seven and Eight some of our ideas on the CB role for affect, and having reviewed some more of the neuroscientific literature bearing on our speculations, we wish to continue to describe further details of what we believe the CB is called upon to perform for the brain as a whole. In a sense, however, this will be familiar to the reader, because we are in some ways returning to the first two chapters of this book, which, from our perspective, takes us full circle to where our journey began.

As you will recall, the issues in Chapters One and Two concern how we are to understand dreaming, which in turn hinged on how we understand the human predicament from a psychoanalytic perspective, namely, from the meanings of our experience of our emotions generally, and the experience of our dreams more particularly. Dreaming, we concluded, consolidates memory for our waking insights, especially for the purpose of sorting out important decisions, based primarily upon analyzing deferred action plans that we know about partly consciously, but partly as an expression of the activity of our dynamic (Freudian) unconscious. Our memory, whether conscious or unconscious, helps us remember, but what seems most critical is appreciating more exactly how memory helps us plan our future.

It should be clear that just as Freud enunciated many years ago, and as every psychoanalyst knows full well, there is a dynamically unconscious mind, and paying attention to it can pay off generously if our goal is to follow the inner life we all have, and learn about our self, relationships, drives, frustrations, conflicts, etc. But to do so we need to be comfortable with our emotions and what they imply. The Freudian unconscious, in other words, is approachable in most every dream we experience with emotion, whether we take the time to analyze these dreams or not, and this is true even if we do not fully comprehend what these feelings are nor what they are about, at the time of our dreaming.

In this book's first two chapters we concentrated upon explaining how the dreaming process occurs, and what it appears to be really about. It is essentially about emotion in the sense of feelings that relate to our drives, for sex, aggression, stimulation, attention, empathy, food, social relations, insights, etc. And one thing dreams accomplish is they use the information in emotional registers (the limbic system) and in the drive/need system (the SEEKING system of Panksepp), and they feed these into a practical problem resolving system which asks a number of decisive questions, an important one being: How can my needs be meet in ways that are safe, that is, that respect my values, self-esteem, circumstances, relationships, and so forth? What then happens is that our dreams become a virtual private theater in which we imagine acting out our wishes, testing out various details before ever acting on our wishes in waking life. As we indicated in that discussion, a complicated system becomes involved, particularly when one is dealing with potentially risky business, but in essense, the result can be adaptive for both our self and our species to the extent that our dreaming helps us learn about problems we face in meeting critical needs, and make decisions about how to "render" them safely and in a form that accomplishes complex goals. Remember as well that the CB has as one of its goals the anticipation of events, which obviously provides us with a sense of protection, at least so long as these predictions are accurate.

But the one problem about employing the complex systems of our mind/brain is that a lot of energy must go into keeping these mind/brain systems functional, which means our mind/brain must find the most efficient way to run its self. This is accomplished by a management or executive control system in which it appears that the CB apparently takes over, more or less, when the anticipated outcome of particular decisions is unusually important for the self, just as we saw this principle at work in dreams. In terms of neurophysiology, the CB would have to have a special important reason for making a copy of the limbic, SEEKING, or any other combination of systems of the brain, and using them to model (emulate) those parts of the brain without their actually needing to be involved directly. And it would seem, following the logic of our previous reasoning, that the CB also updates these models at will. Of course, this does not prevent the CB from behaving very differently in the case of situations it judges to be non-dangerous, or more or less routine; in such cases we believe that the CB is able to follow a more routine, low priority method in which the usual mind/brain systems participate directly, and the CB is just one "player" among many others in various extended neural networks.

One additional important development is the discovery of "mirror neurons" by Rizzolatti, Fogassi, and Gallese (2006) about a decade ago, and the elaboration on this work by Ramachandran and Oberman (2006). The mirror neuron system (which includes the CB) allows us to identify the intentions of others because as we watch their actions identical neurons are activated in us as are active in them during the period of observation. This activation of mirror neurons becomes one of the critical steps in our capacity for empathy, and thus we appreciate why autistic individuals have trouble correctly knowing the intentions of others: they lack mirror neurons from birth. Important for us, however, is that the mirror neuron network involves a number of structures that, as noted above, includes the CB. The other parts of the mirror neuron system are the anterior cingulate gyrus (ACC) (for regulation of empathy and other emotions), the inferior frontal gyrus (IFG) (for guidance of movement and also the assessment of intentions), the Insula (I) (for pain and disgust responses) and the Angular Gyrus (AG) (for comprehension of word meanings, and combining sensory information) (Ramachandran & Oberman, 2006). Obviously, the CB is here involved once more in activities that create meaning, or, perhaps we should say "emotional (empathic) meaning".

But the question remains, have we fully understood all that we can about how the CB gets involved with the higher cortical functions, especially, how the CB makes use of emotion, or, speculating further, if not only making use of emotion, how and for what reason the CB may play a role, at times, in even generating (via its modeling activities) at least some of the emotions we experience? To answer such speculations it may help to move on to the next section, which deals with the contributions to affect theory by Susanne Langer a generation ago.

II. *Susanne Langer on emotion*

Browning (2006) has written a most informative and lucid essay on the subject of the contributions to affect theory of Susanne Langer. Her scholarly article reminds us of an amazingly gifted theoretician of the previous generation, the philosopher Langer, and her unique approach in combining interpretive and biological approaches towards understanding human emotion. Without any doubt, Langer anticipated our new field of NP. One way examining Langer's approach may help our current subject, understanding the CB and its relationship to emotion, is that on the one hand we know that the CB is involved in language and communication, while on the other hand, we have Langer's strong intuition that *the transformation of emotion into language is a decisive contribution* to the human endeavor (Browning, op. cit., p. 3).[1]

To quote Browning: "Carrying on Cassirer's integrative tradition of philosophy, some of whose work she has translated, Langer carves a middle philosophical ground between the logical positivism of the

Vienna Circle and the ontological/existential work of Heidegger. Langer works within the objective sciences of evolution, but finds a way to properly locate human subjectivity as the essential topic of her investigation. As a philosopher originally of the arts, she does her homework in the sciences, thus putting herself in a unique position to bridge both scientific and artistic domains. [Since she worked in the 1950s and thereafter] some of her science is [obviously] out-of-date, but this does not diminish the usefulness of her philosophical framework for understanding the human mind from both perspectives within a single continuum. Langer's scaffolding for examining the human mind is not presented for scientific testing, but for conceptual serviceability. Her poetic use of language for building this scaffolding may be distracting to some, but it enhances the novel integrative model [Langer] builds" (pp. 6–7).

Browning's elucidation of Langer begins with two central ideas: (1) that there are two aspects of the human mind which operate more or less simultaneously, and then become seamlessly integrated with our behavior. These aspects are first the mind's unique symbolic capacity, and second "our pre-symbolic animal nature" (p. 7). And (2) the next central idea that follows from the first is that Langer defines feelings as something we do rather than something we have, that is, as an activity that equates with consciousness.

As one might expect, the way this comes together with Freud's work on drives and the unconscious, is that, as Browning summarizes Langer's position, "our animal feelings [read here as our drives, are what] constantly broker[s] between the pre-symbolic and symbolic in our uniquely human mind" (p. 8). In other words, our capacity to feel is imbedded in both our experience of objective/empirical perspectives and our subjective/interpretive perspectives, Or, if one prefers, one could imagine that Langer is possibly discussing something similar to the two kinds of memory, which some scientists feel are really not so separate after all: explicit/declarative vs. implicit/procedural.

To quote Browning again: "Neuroscientists still do not appreciate fully the *qualitatively* different nature of human consciousness when it is transformed by imagination and symbolic activity. While they make many distinctions in levels of consciousness, they do not understand symbolic activity well enough to appreciate the radical shift it produces in conscious experience. Langer's unique contribution is to recognize and elaborate upon the qualitative difference in the symbolizing mind without entirely leaving the realm of biology. *From her philosophical perspective she makes a place in natural history for the human project of meaning[-]making.* In other words, Langer provides a novel philosophical framework to bridge neuroscience and psychoanalysis" (Italics added, pp. 9–10).

Three additional ideas are important for a fuller appreciation of Langer's position on emotion: (1) the so-called "qualia" we feel are essentially derivatives of our sensory experience, and they derive from *feelings of impact*; (2) In contrast, *feelings of autogenic action* is the expression Langer uses to cover our experience of the subjective world (or possibly, the self-in-the world, to use Ito's terminology); and (3) imagination is critical because "to imagine is to feel spontaneously" (Browning, p. 12). To further elaborate on Browning's insights on Langer: "Imagination can function *involuntarily*, as it does in dream consciousness, or *voluntarily*, as it does when we speak.[2] To speak is to symbolically render the world and our selves into a 'new key' through our imagination. It is the capacity to voluntarily control our imagination that is the basis of our symbolic activity and that produces our pursuit of meaning" (p. 12). Browning states Langer saw our symbolic capacity as purposeful in the sense of giving us self-expression, not so much for conferring an evolutionary advantage thereby, although it clearly does. Obviously, this last point is one where one could differ with Langer, though we do not think it is a critical position for either her theory or our own. Obviously, much more important are Langer's position statements on the relationship between human symbolizing activity, the imagination, and the search for meaning. Arguing about some of the nuances here, in the case of this most original scholar who was so far ahead of her time, would be a bit like quibbling over how Jascha Heifetz played Bach's Chaconne.

By the way, regarding Langer's idea about imagination, we feel her formulation also supports our way of conceptualizing the CB role in cognition and affect. From our perspective, imagination involves creating novel ideas, and to our mind this involves putting ideas together which may not be in exactly the usual way, and then further being free to decompose and recompose them so as to improve upon them. Such "movements" of ideas is a well-known and accepted function of the CB.

One conclusion that seems obvious from what we have just presented is that Langer's position on the human mind can be used to further bridge mind and brain. There are many points which dovetail with our previously stated perspectives, that involve how sensory input gets ideas going, which stimulate feelings of all kinds, and which lead to the assignment of meaning, and the expression in language behavior, both symbolic and pre-symbolic, and in other kinds of behavior as well. Langer's keen anticipation of some of the distinctions in memory provides one with a sense that through her, we are capable of listening in a new way to the many data points that make up our theory of executive functioning within the context of human meaning, consciousness, self expression, and drive (i.e. unconscious) psychology. We are living in an age that can contain all the wisdom of Langer, Freud, and the psychoanalysts, and still not need to throw out much, if any, of Panksepp, Damasio, or Solms, as exemplars of the neuroscientists. We can have our unconscious and our conscious too. And we can collaborate with each other and watch the ideas we share grow into a strong new music that can move our respective fields both emotionally, physically, and intellectually.

Two final clarifications seem in order. What we are asserting is that at times, the CB is able to model systems, and operate them on its own, independent of the usual "machinery" required (of extended neural networks). The CB does this when it is operating on the basis of an internal cerebellar model of the limbic system, the SEEKING system, or other systems of the brain, and utilizing emotions related to these systems. In this sense, it is showing us that at least sometimes emotions are, exactly as Langer told us, something we *do* rather than something we *have*. But in this case, what the CB is doing may also include creatively modeling some feelings in order to better comprehend some details of our life, that is, to help us with what the CB has determined might well be a very important step on our part, one it wants us to solve without undue risk to us, and one in which it intuits that the states being modeled have a close relationship to a particular (cognitive) solution it is seeking. This, of course, is another way of describing a critical aspect of the motivational schema of the Freudian psychodynamic unconscious system.

We would also like to remind the reader of a comment in Chapter Three where we noted that as part of the executive control network, and as an important participant in the utilization of psychological defenses (such as repression and disavowal) (Levin and Vuckovich, 1983, 1987) the CB is capable of carrying out defensive measures that have the effect of altering the emotional world in which we live. By using older models of our past experience, the CB obviously helps us avoid the pain of difficult relationships, losses of loved ones whom we might chose not to mourn but rather pretend are still around, and in various other ways control our progress or lack of progress in dealing with at least potentially painful realities. To the extent that all of us sometimes need encouragement to move on with life emotionally, psychoanalysis specifically aids our working through such difficult aspects of life. But here we need to stay mindful of the role of the CB in the defensive processes themselves, since these contribute to all of us, to some degree, living in two worlds, one real, and the other wishful. This is an important consideration for any book on the psychodyamics of the CB.

Notes

1. Obviously, Langer also was a very early contributor to our understanding of the role of language development as the critical "speciation event" in human evolution, after which we and the other descendents of our great ape ancestors parted company.
2. This would seem to be a reference to the Freudian unconscious, which acts outside of our conscious mind.

PART V

WHERE WE HAVE BEEN

CHAPTER TEN

Review, summary, and conclusions

Fred M. Levin

I. *General Overview*

I n Parts I. and II. of this book we covered some important topics within NP. We began with a review of sleep and dreaming research, then moved on to the role of emotion for mind/brain. The journal NP itself began with target articles by Solms and Nersessian, the editors of NP until recently, on the core of Freud's contribution in terms of emotion and the dynamic unconscious (i.e. drive theory). The commentary on these target articles by noted neuroscientific and psychoanalytic scholars demonstrated how complex the field of NP was at its beginning, and it has not become much simpler since then, though it has created many insights bridging mind and brain!

In Part III. we examined details of relating learning to gene activation, spontaneity, and the priming of memory. These topics naturally reflect the importance of emotion for psychoanalysis as a clinical discipline where learning is critical to recovery. We also considered the changing landscape for psychoanalysis, which now requires anyone who is serious about scholarship in the field to pay attention to what is being learned about memory and learning within neuroscience so that these insights can be utilized in creating an optimal learning environment for a psychoanalysis to occur. Making interpretations is not sufficient in itself any more, if it ever was; the modern psychoanalyst is expected to be a scientist of both psychoanalysis and a number of related disciplines, including neuroscience. But neither neuroscience nor psychoanalysis seem exempt from the passage of time. Each field has shifted over time in its understanding of emotion, and emotion cannot be studied comprehensively scientifically without taking into account what psychoanalysts and neuroscientists have been learning from a very large number of perspectives! We also began to review the importance of the CB for various psychodynamics, including its place in the evolution of brains, culminating in the brain of mammals, and, of course, the human brain. This lead us to consider still more details about the role of emotion in the formation, and the development of our sense of self, the core part of which may well be the CB.

In Part IV. a much more specific focus was brought to bear on the CB. We reiterated our sense, as well, of the importance of the limbic system, and the SEEKING system of Panksepp, but we especially considered, and then extended the idea that the CB is importantly involved in modeling other parts of the brain. But the CB doesn't just passively model other brain systems; when modeling, the CB is actively operating various mind/brain systems on its own, more or less. With this perspective in mind, we especially considered the following question: What if the CB would model various specific systems? Those included were the limbic system and the SEEKING system, the sensory motor cortical system, or the associative cortical system. This naturally raises quite a number of questions that we attempted to address in the two chapters of Part IV. We reviewed the scientific literature on the CB, at least that relevant to our main topic. And we ended up suggesting, echoing our conclusions from Chapters One and Two, that by modeling the limbic and/or SEEKING system, and other systems, the CB becomes capable of generating actions or action plans related to emotions, of using them to test external and internal situations, and using the results in dreams and waking life to sort out how we might resolve complex problems in living, such as how to satisfy our biological and psychological needs without causing ourselves and others too much pain and suffering, or how to solve various concomitant self-related or ethical problems. We concluded that when modeling the limbic and SEEKING system the CB would be at least part of the operation of Freud's dynamic "unconscious" system; when modeling the sensory-motor cortex the CB would be operating at least part of Freud's so-called "ego", and when the model used would be the associative cortex, the CB would be at least part of operating in the "superego" mode.[1]

II. *Some of the specific insights along the way*

We can now review some of the most important insights as follows, by Section:

Part I. (Chapters One and Two)

(1)   The short answer to the question as to why we dream is that we don't really know for sure. The longer answer is that we dream because we obtain pleasure from "seeing" our unconscious desires acted out in the virtual reality of our dreams during sleep, when we cannot cause any real trouble. But we also accomplish something that is adaptive in an evolutionary sense for our selves by in this way testing out specific "deferred action plans", until we are ready to test them out in the reality of waking life. Such action plans ("images of movements with purpose") are probes for the exact nature of potential dangers, for guiding the learning about their contextual details, and for storing this emotionally critical information in implicit (procedural) memory and explicit (declarative) memory.

(2)   That is, what we learn during dreaming becomes fixed in memory (consolidated or reconsolidated, by various neuro-chemical mechanisms); in other words, the process results in

learning, and this knowledge has an impact on our problem solving whether we realize it or not.

(3)   Extremely important supportive evidence was introduced to buttress conclusions 1. and 2., especially, the work of Mark Solms (2003b), showing that the MVFL and the PTOCJ are necessary but not sufficient for dreaming to occur. What makes them sufficient is when the pons provides the proper neurochemical stimulus to initiate sleep (i.e dreaming usually requires a sleeping subject). The reason this is critical is that the decisive roles of the MVFL (for emotionally meaningful content of dreams) and the PTOCJ (for the proper visualization and sensory experience of dreams) greatly helps address the criticism of some neuroscientists who previously believed there was no real evidence proving that Freud was right, that is, that dreams are emotionally significant and deeply meaningful events. Now, given Solms research, these critics of Freud can no longer support any such conclusion; this is because the MVFL which is so needed for dreaming is a part of the brain everyone agrees is involved in emotion, psychological thinking, and the attachment of meaning to personal experience.

(4)   There is thus an abundant source of information about Freud's unconscious (his "dynamic unconscious") from the research on dreaming. Here we reviewed extensive research by Shevrin, Bond, Brakel and Williams (1996), Opatow (1999), Westen (1999), Revonsuo (2000), Mishkin and Appenzeller (1987), and others.

(5)   We introduced Revonsuo's work (2000) on ˇTSTˇ theory because it was not known to us when we first discovered the adaptiveness of dreaming; thus the work in Finland has supported the findings in the U.S. on the idea that dreams have an evolutionary and not just an individual adaptive effect.

(6)   We suggested a number of specific experiments that could be used to confirm REM consolidation of the learning during dreams (first discovered by Pearlman, 1973; Greenberg & Pearlman, 1974). But our consensus position was that REM allows the basic emotional circuits of the brain to be accessed in a systematic way (Panksepp, 1998).

(7)   As part of our discussion of memory we presented current research results that demonstrate that memory is not stable;

whether we use it (and it deteriorates thereby), or whether we don't use it (and it still deteriorates), the only way to stabilize it temporarily is to reconsolidate it (with Zif/268), or consolidate it (with BDNF), otherwise memory "extinction" occurs.

(8) The adaptive reason for the turnover of memories is multiple: (a) it reduces the need for using large amounts of energy from the body for maintaining memories in the brain (20% of our energy is used for this purpose); (b) it can allow for memories of fear relating to the amygdala to disappear over time; (c) it provides a basis for the continuous rebuilding of memories into a more and more updated database with multiple utility.

(9) We discuss the role of emotional attention in the activation of the genes for new memory formation; this statement illustrates the relation between "mental" and "biological" events in relation to this vital function. In Figure 1 of Chapter One we diagram the two different related "cascades" involved and their relationship with each other. In Figure 2 of the same Chapter we portray schematically the larger system in which the ucs and cs systems are related to the variables we have been discussing, thus connecting dreaming, transference, same-difference analysis, the priming of memory, and the role of spontaneity (the latter activates working memory for what we are thinking about, thus enabling our current subject of interest to be learned more easily).

(10) The SEEKING system of Panksepp is important to dreaming and the ucs, since it involves the effects largely but not exclusively of dopamine-related neural systems on the creation of predictive error signals, and the assignment of incentive salience (a state of both wanting something, and figuring out at the same time how best to get it) (Hyman, 2005).

(11) Besides the VMFL and PTOCJ, other areas of importance for dreaming are the ACC, PAG, CNT, CB, HT, ITC, NA, and various basal ganglia and upper brainstem structures, along with the amygdala.

(12) Regarding the SEEKING system, pleasure occurs in anticipation (and as the specific effect of dopamine [DA]) on using perceptual information to motivate behaviors to obtain what we want and/or need (Panksepp, 1998, 2005a, 2005b; Hyman, 2005).

(13) DA enables us to have human aspirations, and the chemis-
tries involved in the SEEKING system enable us to explore
our environment energetically for resources. Panksepp docu-
ments that this system is a basic emotional system, innate,
and not dependent on higher brain functions. He makes
the strong point that this system is not a pleasure-triggered
system; rather it fires off an exploratory urge that is built-
in. One can only conclude that dreaming, as described, is an
emotionally meaningful experience and neither random nor
a mere stimulus response.

(14) Explicit memories involve the hippocampus and neocortex,
plus the amygdala and mammilary bodies; implicit memories
depend upon the basal ganglia and CB. Importantly, consciousness is only associated with the former, not the latter
system of memory. However, both can be recovered, though
in different ways. Explicit memories are in consciousness, and
are recovered as such, that is, by conscious intention. Implicit
memories are recovered by a more indirect method. Often the
explicit system is capable of taking "snapshots" of the implicit
system output. When this happens, it is possible to then reconstruct "events" within implicit memory by putting all these
related "snapshots" together, much as crime detectives put
their evidence on bulletin boards, and then tie them to each
other until the crime can be reconstructed. Another way of
looking at the recovery of memory is to examine how else the
two systems, explicit and implicit might be connected to each
other. One critical way they are connected would seem to be
via the CB. This is because the CB can make models of various
brain systems, and run these parts of the brain by itself. But
if we think about this fact, essentially it means that there are
circumstances where the CB which, together with the basal
ganglia, is the implicit system, is running the explicit system
(the models of the rest of the brain that it would be copying
and running)! This means that the two great memory systems,
explicit and implicit can come together at those moments
when the CB is modeling the rest of the brain. To summarize,
there are two ways the explicit and implicit memory systems
come together. The first involves reconstructions, based upon
"snapshots of the implicit system taken by the explicit system.

Of course, this often happens within a psychoanalysis (Levin, 2004c; Mancia, 2003; Talvitie and Ihanus, 2002). And the second method is when the implicit system copies and runs models of the explicit system, thus combining explicit and implicit systems into one supersystem periodically. Finally, to be complete, sometimes implicit memories are primed by other (explicit or implicit) memories or experiences. It should be obvious from the above considerations that these two memory systems are not as separate as they seem, something we have long known, but not exactly had as much of an idea of how they come together until recently.

(15)   Watt (2003) has made some critical points about dreaming and "reentrant architecture". He believes that a large number of functional systems, in the case of dreaming, have access to the computational product. Thus we need to be careful in concluding what system is "in control". He believes evidence suggests that the dreaming contents of REM sleep are actually controlled more by the lateral hypothalamic SEEKING system than by the pontine REM generators. The LH system would seem to be the monitor of both our sleep debt and other homeostatic needs.

(16)   Regarding the ACC, there is evidence that the hippocampus and ACC are needed for the retrieval of memories associated with contextual fear memories. Such retrieval is associated with an increase in Zif/268 and the production of another activity dependent gene, c-fos in the ACC, and in other areas. The conclusion: there are likely many neuronal growth and gene transcription factors playing a role in the large number of protein pathways; clearly the details of these factors and pathways will ultimately need to be factored into any overarching theory of memory we might develop.

(17)   Also, the ACC (especially the vACC) is involved, along with the CB, in handling conflicting streams of information, detecting errors and discrepancies, and in anticipating errors. As such the ACC participates in learning, along with the CB. With regard to dreaming, the cingulate cortex would be a mediator for conflict resolution between one set of automatized solutions and another set that is less automatized (and possibly more creative in its responsiveness).

(18) The PAG plays an important role in making emotion an active motoric process (Watt, 2003; see also later references to Langer's definition of emotion as "something we do"). This involves differentiating the various prototypical emotional states from each other as we experience them, and establishing the rules for their appearance. It apparently links to pontine and brainstem motor systems, and also recruits all kinds of input from the upper brainstem, diencephalic and basal forebrain systems.

(19) In summary, dreaming represents for the psyche the possibility of expressing deep ucs wishes and fears, while allowing the priming of implicit (not just explicit) memories involved ontogenetically and possibly also phylogenetically in critical decision making. While actions are deferred, various action plans can be considered. This allows ucs wishes to be carried into reality to varying degrees, and the testing of reality considerations and matters of safety for self and others, and for relationships.

Part II. (Chapters Three and Four)

(1) The focus here is on the target articles in the inaugural issue of the journal NP (1999), by Solms and Nersessian, and by Panksepp. Commentary by Damasio, Green, LeDoux, Schore, Shevrin, and Yorke is placed in the general context of what is important about emotion, seen from an interdisciplinary perspective.

(2) Solms and Nersessian start with Freud's assertion about the centrality of emotions, and their tie to inner needs (read here as "drives"). The paradox of course is that something in the way of feelings becomes conscious, yet is itself part of the activity of the brain, in complex interactivity with the rest of the body. Since little during Freud's age was known about neurotransmission, and such things as sexual hormones were certainly not known at the time (though they were speculated about by Freud when he suggested they might be behind such things as sexual drive), it then is up to neuroscience to speculate further upon what is essential about Freud's drive theory, that is, on how it is instantiated in us.

We have already covered this in Panksepp's discussion of the SEEKING system.

(3)   So the first assumption that is generalized is that hormones play a distinct role in affect: the hypothalamic-pituitary axis is obviously a good example of such hormone distribution, including the role of sexual hormones and the gonads for sexual feelings.

(4)   Solms and Nersessian appreciate Mesulam's (1985) distinction between "channel" vs. "state" functions of the brain: the former include such things as external perception and the various representational processes derived from them (memory and cognition); the latter involve the emotions themselves together with their internal perception. They see these as two aspects of consciousness mediated by two different anatomical and physiological systems, one modality-specific and discrete (associated with sensory "qualia") and the other modality non-specific and diffuse. Such distinctions are important for them because they are on a quest "to locate putative anatomical and physiological correlates of Freud's affect theory" (p. 8).

(5)   The roadmap that these two authors are pursuing is thus leading them to the conclusion that at least some of what we call affect is experienced consciously, and is associated with core brain nuclei which regulate state dependent functions of the cortex (p. 8); in other words, functions that occur in relation to specific neuro-transmitter systems, for example, serotonin, acetyl choline, norepinephrine, and dopamine. This is their neuroscientific bent.

(6)   But on the other hand, on the psychological side they note that Freud saw thinking as experimental action (cf. our sense of dreaming as related to "deferred action plans"); therefore, one key from this perspective is learning what it is within mind/brain that regulates or "tames affect"? One speculation (Levin and Vuckovich, 1983) suggests that the CB plays a critical role in how the hemispheres are connected or not, for the purpose of psychological defense, sometimes using this strategy to create the specific defenses of "repression" (for left to right hemispheric information blockade) vs. "disavowal" (for right to left blockade). The effect in each case is to keep

the perceptual input and the emotional meaning separated from each other, thus taming the affect or protecting the self from dangerous levels of affective intensity.

(7) Although Panksepp agrees with much of what Solms and Nersessian have to say, he sees problems with bridging the psychoanalytic and neuroscientific perspectives. Perhaps most significant is his view that "the biological values and the affective neural processes via which they are instantiated penetrate all of the cognitive structures of the mammalian mind/brain" (p. 17). I believe this is becoming a consensus, namely, that what is labeled cognitive and what is designated emotional within the brain is not an absolutely clear distinction. So thinking and feeling are either not that different, or their relationship to each other has not yet been properly understood.

(8) Panksepp also agrees that Freud was courageous, and correct when he placed emotion at the center of his theorizing. And he further argues, and I agree, that subcortical contributions to emotion are likely much more important than has been thought in the past, where the cortical contributions have been assigned extra significance. As he puts it: "…all higher forms of consciousness may still be grounded in the most primitive forms of consciousness, which I assume were affective in nature…[so that] rational thought may only be a relatively fragile tip of the iceberg of affective experience" (Ibid., p. 17).

(9) Panksepp feels the core self is most likely grounded in the centromedian areas of the brainstem, areas such as the PAG and nearby collicular and tegmental zones. The MFB and VTA are bidirectional circuits interconnecting the SEEKING system and the limbic system (including the PAG), with the cingulate, frontal, and insular areas. (I suggest, in this book, that the CB should not be excluded as part of the core self.)

(10) An example Panksepp discovered (1998b) of interest to our thinking about emotion, is that young rats, for example, are capable of laughing, that is, of showing their pleasure in play. They have fun. In fact, in some circumstances they would rather be tickled than fed, even when they are significantly hungry. This demonstrates that our basic emotions are linked to "instinctual readiness systems" in our brains, which is another way of referring to Freud's drive theory.

(11) We will continue now with insights from those who formally commented on the target articles (in NP's inaugural issue) by Solms and Nersessian, and by Panksepp. The first will be the comments of Antonio Damasio. He states his belief that Freud's ideas on emotion are in line with the latest neuroscientific findings. He has serious questions about bridging mind and brain.

(12) André Green, a psychoanalyst, is in favor of collaboration between analysts and neuroscientists, but shares with Damasio some skepticism about bridging these domains. His contributions to the debate include a belief that psychoanalysis is just as scientific as neuroscience. He further criticizes neuroscientists, including Solms and Nersessian, for portraying Freud incorrectly. Green sees a key to Freud's affect theory in basing it on perceptions and their associated feeling states, and not on representational processes. He feels that Solms and Nersessian, along with Panksepp, are essentially trivializing the importance of sexuality and destructiveness in particular, and drives in general. From Green's perspective, such drives are always active in disguised forms, and we have not yet fully comprehended the Freudian unconscious, although analysts are doing a passing job at that task.

(13) Joseph LeDoux is an experimentalist, and his work on the amygdala is original and helpful to the present discussion of emotion. He sees working memory as the staging area for consciousness. The amygdala can detect danger and signals when this happens It is not, from LeDoux's perspective, directly responsible for conscious feelings (of fear); rather fear is [only] felt consciously "when working memory is occupied with the fact that the amygdala has detected and begun to respond to danger" (LeDoux, 1966) (p. 45).

(14) Reviewing his work on split brain patients, LeDoux concludes that "emotion" is merely a label for a category of mental activity (on a par with the categories of perception and memory); he does not see emotion as a function, and believes there is no single area dedicated to emotion (generally), but rather multiple subsystems of the brain that focus upon specific classes of emotion, such as anger, sexuality, etc. (LeDoux, 1996, p. 16; cf. Panksepp, 1998a). In his

opinion "there might be some affective compartmentalization in working memory that could constitute something like
a modality for affective consciousness" (Ibid.). The prefrontal
cortex, from his perspective, "is critically involved in working
memory" and thus the likely target of talking therapies.

(15) Schore's major contribution has involved specifying details
of how the development of the self is critically dependent
upon affects that are reflective of emotion-related brain components that become preferentially connected to the right
hemisphere. Via critical interactions with caretakers, there is
structuralization of the VMFL, the right hemisphere, and this
involves especially limbic connections and the growth of both
emotions and motivations.

(16) Shevrin indicates that in Solms' and Nersessian's target article
"affects cannot be preconscious or unconscious, but are quintessentially conscious..." (pp. 55–56), but he has a problem
with this statement, originally attributed to Freud, and
with the distinction of a difference between the two classes
of affective experience that they highlight, and upon which
their distinction of conscious/unconscious is based. One class
of affective experience of Solms and Nersession is linked to
sensory experiences (which they are asserting *can* become conscious), the other is linked to action readiness systems (which
they assert *cannot become conscious*). Shevrin suggests a way
out of the dilemma he feels that their distinction creates. It
would be best to identify two different classes, namely, those
experiences that are motivated, and those that are [merely]
affective. This would then allow us to speak of unconscious
motivations that can become conscious, and conscious affects
that can become unconscious. As Shevrin puts it: "this alternative allows for a more flexible and varied relationship
between affect and motivation, [and between the] conscious
and unconscious mind, than the view attributed to Freud by
Solms and Nersessian. It also shifts conscious experiences
from pleasure/unpleasure towards gratification vs. frustration" (Ibid., pp. 55–56).

(17) Shevrin further argues "all affects have this purpose. They are
signals, sometimes subtle and unconscious, sometimes gross
and conscious, which indicate the import of the internal battle

for what we must or must not do next" (p. 58). They give us breathing space for making correct decisions about actions (i.e. they are part of the development of "deferred action plans", exactly as we have been using this expression in this book).

(18) Yorke feels that Freud's drive theory has stood the test of time. He agrees with Freud's (1940) perspective: "The id, cut off from the external world, has a world of perceptions of its own. It detects with extraordinary acuteness certain changes in its interior, especially oscillations in the tension of its instinctual needs, and these changes become conscious as feelings in the pleasure-unpleasure series" (cited in York, p. 62). Thus drives and emotions are intimately connected.

Part III. (Chapters Five, Six, and Seven)

(1) Learning is an inherently emotional phenomenon that is important because it satisfies vital needs. Cognitive neuropsychological approaches to learning are not yet sufficient in themselves because they often downplay emotions, which can be hard to quantify, and because they are restricted primarily to surface structures that can be seen on scans, and tend to leave out deeper structures such as the PAG and hypothalamus.

(2) The biology of learning and memory involve macro-, micro-, and submicroscopic levels of brain organization. The psychology of learning and memory within psychoanalysis involves interpretations, conditioning (procedural learning), free association, as well as attention to affect, countertransference and transference, conscious perception and subliminal perception (the latter leading to knowledge without awareness).

(3) Emotional attention (affectively charged selective attention, under the influence of various drives) has a direct relationship to the transcription factor-related activation of the genes for new synapse formation (of the NMDA type). The new memories captured are the biological counterpart to what Freud called the "drive organization of memory".

(4) Transcription factors are examples of the larger group of soluble proteins and peptides that act as humoral regulators and gene activators. They are CKs largely produced from glial cells, neurons, and skin cells.

(5) There are three pathways from the periphery to the brain; two are unidirectional, namely, Pathways A (the autonomic system or ANS), and B (the hypothalamic-pituitary axis, the HPA), and then there is Pathway C, composed of immune cells, which is bidirectional. One arm of Pathway C stimulates sensory paraganglia of the vagus nerve, which in turn carries impulses to the nucleus tractus solitarius (NTS) and the area postrema (AP) in the brainstem. A second arm of Pathway C runs from the vagus to the NTS and AP but ends up in the hippocampus and hypothalamus, where interleukin-1 (IL-1) is generated in brain cells. This IL-1 can act either as a neurotransmitter, an immune molecule (producing a proinflammatory response), or it can become bound to a postsynaptic receptor and induce gene transcription and translation. Transcription is copying DNA into mRNA; translation refers to making copies of RNA code into related proteins, which can then express gene function.

(6) The immunological functions of CK are reviewed in Chapter Five. The bottom line is that the brain and the immune system are considered one system, the neuroimmune network (NIN). In this system CK are involved in the amplification, coordination, and regulation of communication pathways.

(7) Long-term-potentiation (LTP) (Bliss, 1998) is the enhancement or easier neural firing secondary to neuronal use and associativity. This is in contrast to long-term-depression (LTD) which was discovered by Ito and is characteristic of the CB. In LTD the more a neuron is fired the harder it will be to fire off the next time. In the case of LTD, unlike LTP, there is no evidence indicating that adenyl cyclase, or PKA have any role in it's induction (Ito, 2001, p. 1155).

(8) Each form of memory, explicit and implicit are recordable in two phases: short-term memory (STM) and long-term memory (LTM). Importantly, LTM is not just enhanced STM. The major difference is that STM is mediated by the kinases PKA and PKC, and involves the modification of pre-existing proteins (rather than the creation of new proteins as in LTM), effected by these particular kinases. LTM further involves the translocation of the proteins PKA and MAPK from the cytosol into the nucleus of sensory neuronal cells, followed by their

action in the nucleus on CREB1 (to "activate" it) and on CREB2 (to "derepress" it). To continue with the steps of gene activation in the case of new LTM from new synapses, the changes in CREB1 and CREB2 lead automatically and quite quickly to the next step in which immediate early gene (IEG) is activated (sometimes this is called early response gene, ERG), which in turn results in the rapid creation of new synapses of the NMDA type. These synapses can then be used to capture new memories. (Actually, some additional steps in STM formation also need to be mentioned; namely, STM involves the effects of neurotransmitters, for example, serotonin, upon the energy molecule of the cell, ATP, causing ATP to break down into pyrophosphate and 3'5'-cyclic AMP. Once cyclic AMP is generated it s responsible for an immediate increase in PKA, which then, as noted above, plays a key role in STM formation. The Nobel Prize Eric Kandel won included his insights not only about LTM but his critical insights regarding STM. In this he made good use of his creative thinking that what happens in the brain that activates critical processes was likely similar to the mechanisms by which cyclic AMP activated chemical signaling in fat cells, muscle cells, and in the action of hormones, such as adrenaline/norepinephrine).

(9)   The rapid advance in neuroscience has clarified some subjects within neuroscience and complicated our understanding of others. This creates a problem for psychoanalysts wishing to bridge psychoanalysis and neuroscience. Chapter Six presents a number of important developments within neuroscience that analysts need to pay attention to. One involves the work on corollary discharge, an old but useful concept describing how information from the motor system (i.e. action system) is routinely passed on to the sensory system so that the latter can take it into account, that is, distinguish new sensory input that has been altered by the self's motor output. Sensory input represents an independent view of the environment, but it can be confusing to the self's identification of dangers if self-directed activities occur that change sensory input but are not known to the self, so the self cannot factor these effects on environment input into the larger picture. The new research in this area may be useful for our analytic

understanding of phenomena such as transference. Transference has an impact on sensory input, yet it is self-initiated; thus its similarity to sensory input in the instance of corollary discharge, which tells life forms from insects on up to humans that the environment is changing by an increment of self-initiated motor activity, therefore factor this increment in so the systems for identifying (external) dangers can continue to operate properly.

(10)   A second area of importance concerns modern revisions of the neuron doctrine. Originally the neuron was seen to act through its synapses with other neurons more or less exclusively, although there has been understanding that sometimes neurotransmitters can diffuse through areas and cause effects on a broader region of the brain. The new doctrine includes the idea that neurons are capable of communicating via gap junctions (not just via synapses), slow electrical potentials, extrasynaptic release of neurotransmitters (as noted above), and that information flow between neurons and glial cells is important and contributes to information processing. These new discoveries also alter the time scale of some reactions expected in information flow within the brain, from fractions of a second to minutes, hours, or longer periods. This is extremely important for our consideration of the special role of the CB, which, via its use of models of other brain systems, could make some things happen on different time scales than one might expect given the usual mix of intercellular communication within the nervous system.

(11)   In addition, a great deal has been learned about protein cellular pathways. There are now many different kinds of RNA known to exist within cells, and some of these have a decisive effect, under certain conditions, on development and behavior. RNA storage and degradation are considered "the heart of the cell's machinery for regulating protein synthesis" (Marx, 2005, p. 764). So-called RISC machinery active in P-Bodies (including Argonaute) not only can determine which cells live or die, or are blocked (see references to gene silencing) in their normal activities; it is possible that emotions are effected by at least some of these events, or that emotions play a role in them. Since we know that the turning on and off

of genes can be affected by emotions (see references to emotional attention), it becomes important for NP not to ignore this critical aspect of life. The recovery of patients undergoing emotional stress is vulnerable to a host of dangers, which analysts need to become aware of, so proper intervention is made. A trivial example is the introduction of anxiolytic medication for those patients whose anxiety levels are sufficiently elevated that they run the risk of damaging their hippocampal memory systems from their increased blood level or corticosteroids.

(12)   Ito's model of evolution of the brain starts with three core functional systems: reflexes of the spinal cord, compound movements spreading from the spinal cored to medulla oblongata and midbrain, and innate behavior involving the hypothalamus and rostral end of the brainstem. To this are added four additional regulatory structures: the limbic system, the basal ganglia, the CB, and the brainstem sleep-wakefulness centers. These seven functional systems produce all possible lower vertebrate behavior.

(13)   The additional steps are as follows: sensory and perisensory neocortical areas are added, along with the underlying thalamus (represented in the parieto-lateral-occipital lobe) in the first stage, taking us to the stage of development of lower mammals, that is, rats, cats, and dogs.

(14)   The next step takes us to the primate level, and it involves the appearance of association cortex, which enables us to generate images, concepts, and ideas, which can be stored away in memory. Such association cortex also includes the prefrontal cortex that can send command signals to the sensorimotor cortex, affecting attention and altering the parameters of future searches of memory.

(15)   At the primate and human level the prefrontal and parietolateral cortices form a loop, that arguably represents the process of thought (Ito, 1998, p, 193). This thought is considered to have a dialectical quality since it is structured (in the loop) to allow feedback, so output in the form of thought feeds back into the system that produces the thought in the first place. It should be noted, that by definition, the experience of the re-presentation of thought is one way we define consciousness.

Another way is to see consciousness as selective awareness. The selectivity here involves attention to both the so-called "outside world" and the "inner" world of private thoughts, feelings, and intentions.

(16)   Bridging from the neuroscience of consciousness and the dynamic unconscious (i.e. from neuroscience to Freud) is of course complicated, but a very real possibility, given the specific language used in the descriptions of the various phenomena described within the two disciplinary perspectives. We could say, for instance, that the psychodynamic unconscious that psychoanalysis values is the centrally affective (i.e. emotional) and motivational part of thought, which has, like conscious thinking, its own developmental pathway. It further seems correct to argue that this unconscious system of mentation matures and provides a well-developed system that allows for psychological defenses. These will take various forms, but include the capacity for consciousness to be "withheld" at times. Non-consciousness means that events occur, but without our ability to appreciate and experience consciously the complex motivational states and feelings that our behavior entails. This consciousness may merely indicate that the implicit memory system is operating, and it will do so without consciousness as a matter of routine. The Freudian unconscious is somewhat different in that here emotions and motivations are disguised for more complicated reasons. In this case, even if the explicit system is involved, which allows consciousness, an internal decision may be automatically made not to become aware in a conscious sense of what is going on, in order to protect our drive satisfactions.

(17)   Our educated guess is that the non-conscious operates on the basis of a symbolic system largely characteristic of either the right brain, i.e. the limbic system, or, possibly, on the basis of the CB, and this mode would correspond with what Freud called the "primary process" (see Levin, 2003a). Ito's postulation of CB maps, which permit adaptive behavior without explicit awareness (which is what we are discussing right now), gives support to his CB model of self-in-the-world, i.e. that non-symbolic self-organization is the probable core of human personality (Ito, cited in Levin, 1991, and in Levin

& Vuckovich, 1983, 1987; see also Gedo, 1991a, 1991b, 1996a, 1996b, 1997). There is no consensus about this as yet, but it may eventually occur as neuroscientists and psychoanalysts continue to collaborate.

(18)   We cannot emphasize enough the importance of extending consideration to the possibility of the CB emulating various other brain systems, such as, for example, the limbic system and/or the SEEKING system, not just running the brain without the motor system by use of an exact duplicate or model of the CB's creation. This would then allow the CB many possible roles in managing the mind/brain with regard to cognition, emotion, memory, and behavior, and it would especially provide a way for us to better understand the exact mechanisms involved in unconscious and conscious relations (that is, how the CB parses these functions). As noted above, it also enables us to appreciate Freud's parsing mental activities into ego, superego, and id, we would now say, depending upon which subsystems of the brain are undergoing CB emulation: the sensory motor cortex (for ego), the associative cortex (for superego), or the limbic and SEEKING systems (for id).

Part IV. (Chapters Eight and Nine)

(1)   In positing the possibility that the CB creates and uses working models of other parts of the brain, including the limbic and SEEKING systems, we are suggesting certain advantages that might be accomplished by this means. One reason we can think of is based upon some recent research that suggests that some key connections within the brain, such as the sensory stimuli connections from the thalamus to the cortex Layer 4, might require some special "efforts" in order for this to be strong enough to work properly (Bruno & Sakmann, 2006; Alonso, 2006). The "low efficacy" of this connection was found by measuring specific strength of these relays. What enables the connection to work is the synchrony of the discharge of the thalamic cells. Our thinking is that there may be other situations like this within the brain, such that under certain circumstances, the far-flung elements making up

a system might not be able to connect optimally with each other, and this might be the type of circumstance where the CB "decides" to create and use a model instead of merely participating as a member of an external neural network. For once a model would be used, the communication lines are no longer a potentially critical factor; the CB would be communicating within itself as it uses its model(s), and this would eliminate the need for communication within complex neural networks.

(2)   A second reason for CB modeling would be the CB's prior experience in coordinating movements and ideas. We believe that such dual processing is likely to interest the CB over time in bringing together affects and the activities/actions they are naturally connected with. For example, emotion is what gives the impulse towards action meaning, so in its case, it would make sense to bring these brain systems closer together (as in a model) so as to boost their efficiency. Another way of putting this is that learning is involved in CB activity normally; this is one of the CB's major functions, so why wouldn't the CB be interested in bringing together our emotions, actions, and their drive-relationship with each other? In this way it would integrate three critical parts of mental life all in one agency of executive control. It might also allow the CB, which is involved in predicting what will happen next, more control over certain decisions that it considers more critical or sensitive than others.

(3)   There is further evidence (see below) that the CB is involved in language. This suggests to us that movement for the CB has meaning in terms of rhythms with meaning, a kind of body language. Our work with deaf clients using sign language and so-called "total-communication", has lead us to better appreciate the relationship between music and emotion, and this suggests to us that the CB is likely to be the brain system or agency that is most oriented towards using its nonverbal and verbal skills as a way of optimizing its understanding and use of information about the emotional state of the self. Finally, we suspect that the CB is likely to be the core self, since it is active from before the time of our birth, recording our earliest memories of life, even before the cerebral cortex

becomes myelinated. This would give it a major investment in tracking the models of our mental life.

(4) A review of the scientific literature on the CB makes clear that many illnesses are associated with this brain structure, proving beyond a doubt that the CB is deeply involved in motor and non-motor functions. In the latter category we have a consensus about the CB's participation in the brain's handling of cognition, memory, emotion, language, movement, coordination, executive functioning, reality testing, empathy, and last but certainly not least, learning. Autism, ADHD, mood disorders, cognitive disorders, and schizophrenia is the short list of serious problems that have been associated with CB pathology. In addition Schmahmann (2004) lists 9 classes of CB diseases (not counting psychiatric disorders per se). It is hard to find any single brain system more entrenched with who we are, as humans, symbol users with complex relationships with each other. One example of research suggestive of our position on the great importance of CB is a recent study by a distinguished group of researchers on theory of mind (TOM) (see Calarge, Andreasen, and O'Leary, 2003) showing the greatest activations (in subjects reading stories that suggest attributes of mental states the subject can identify with) occurring in the contralateral CB and anterior vermis.

(5) Schmahmann (1998, 2004) considers the lateral hemisphere of the posterior CB to be involved in cognitive processing, the CB vermis to be limbic CB, and for him the CB is undeniably associated with affectivity. He further describes a specific syndrome he designates cerebellar cognitive affective syndrome (CCAS). Panksepp (1998a, p. 204) has long taken the position that the CB is involved in both attentional and emotional process.

(6) The argument is presented that the CB, by copying the SEEKING and limbic systems, and emulating them on its own without these other systems needing to participate, would save energy, which is a critical quantity for the brain, since 20% of the body's energy is used to maintain the brain, especially to maintain memory.

(7) Susanne Langer (1942, 1953, 1967, 1972, 1982, 1988; see also Browning, 2006) contributed greatly to our scientific and phil-

osophical understanding of emotion, but her work has not garnered the current attention because she was a very early pioneer, and her work was done largely before the insights of modern psychoanalysis and neuroscience, and certainly before NP began as a scientific movement.

(8)   Browning's elucidation of Langer begins with two central ideas: (1) is that there are two aspects of the human mind which operate more or less simultaneously, and then become seamlessly integrated with our behavior. These aspects are first the mind's unique symbolic capacity, and second "our pre-symbolic nature" (p. 70. And (2) the next central idea that follows from the first is that Langer defines feelings as something we do rather than something we have, that is, as an activity that equates with consciousness". One can see here the bridging of affect theory and drive theory around the notion of action.

(9)   Thus, as Browning indicates (op. cit., pp. 9–10) "Langer provides a novel philosophical framework to bridge neuro-science and psychoanalysis" by focusing upon the symboliz-ing mind and its use of emotion to create meanings and fulfill drives. From this "Langerian" perspective we can integrate the work on differing kinds of memory, the levels of con-sciousness seen within dreaming and wakefulness, and the thread of emotion running through the activities of the mind and the adaptive plans and behavior of people.

III. *Concluding Statement*

To state it succinctly, our important conclusion is that CB models tie together explicit and implicit memory systems, creating a unique set of capabilities ranging from CB contributions via multiple distrib-uted neural networks to high priority highly exact problem solving in id, ego, and superego domains, and activities in other modes as well.

To elaborate briefly, this synthesis of much material about the CB suggests that the CB at times follows one of two modes of activity. In the first mode, which we call CB mode #1, its thinking is more "cog-nitive", its memory is of the "explicit" type, and its behavioral inclination is towards "action" in the here and the now. We will say, in a kind of shorthand, that mode #1 is essentially a "conscious mode" of varying depth. Our guess would be that this first mode is the mode of CB activity when relatively low level contingency planning is being employed to solve problems that can be dealt with entirely by routine measures. We further argue that what is distinctive about mode #1 is that in this case the CB is participating in a multitude of extended neural networks of the brain, along with a number of other brain system components, such as the limbic or the SEEKING systems, but where the CB is not so much controlling these overall networks as merely contributing input to them.

CB mode #2, however, is quite different from mode #1. In the unique CB mode #2, the CB's style is more "emotional", its memory operations would be a combination of "explicit" and "implicit",[2] and its behavioral orientation is towards "fantasy", careful "action planning", that is, "reflection before taking action", making sure to take into account the feedback from subtle practicing during dreams, and subtle actions remembered from waking life. We believe that in the case of CB mode #2 the CB is dealing with matters judged to be of high priority or great sensitivity that require the highest level of skill and planning and a low tolerance for errors. And it is important that in CB mode #2 the CB is not operating as part of an extended network, but rather using its personal copies of the limbic system, the SEEKING system (or any other systems it has updated copies of) to model various parts of the brain on its own, and thus make decisions more or less independently (i.e independent of its more usual neural networking).

We wish to highlight, as well, that in our opinion, in mode #2 the CB would have simultaneous access to both kinds of memory, that is explicit and implicit: explicit memory because this is the memory system that would be built into many of the copies made of the extended neural networks, which are mostly explicit; and implicit memory would be available as well, because implicit memory is provided uniquely by the normal activity of the CB operating, of course, in concert with the basal ganglia.

In the above description of CB mode #1 and CB mode #2 we are clearly taking umbridge, that is, we completely disagree with the usual argument that because the implicit memory system involves "fast, frugal, and implicit mechanism[s]" (Ross and Martin, 2006,

p. 1652; see also David Geary, 2004), it is needed mostly for adaptation to environments that are considered largely invariant and repetitive, whereas when the environment is variable, this kind of information requires greater cognitive resources of an explicit nature, which are seen as "slow, effortful, complex, and explicit/conscious mechanisms" (Geary, cited in Ross & Martin, Ibid.).

First of all, the view described by the researchers cited in the previous paragraph does not even mention the CB, nor the issue of CB modeling, which we believe uniquely alters any consideration of what memory system is best for which contingencies. Obviously, we believe that a CB-dominated system offers highly flexible cognitive shifting (between CB modes #1 and #2). Moreover, we further argue our belief that in the situation where the CB is modeling other significant mind/brain systems (in mode #2), that since (as stated above) the CB would be involved in combing both explicit and implicit mechanisms since the CB (with the basal ganglia) *is* itself the implicit memory system, and the systems modeled by the CB *are* largely the various explicit systems, therefore, it should be obvious that by combining implicit and explicit systems into a unified system, the CB can provide greater flexibility and power than when the mind/brain would be using either of these memory systems separately.

One further qualification makes sense to us regarding the capacity of the CB to operate in two (or more) distinctly different modes. It seems best to associate the CB mode #1, of distributed processing, to what Freud called the "conscious mind". In mode #2, however, where the CB operates compactly (that is, within and by itself, as through the use of models) the result is obviously closest to what Freud called operating in either an ego, superego, or "dynamic unconscious" ("id") mode. In this latter mode (#2) the CB is primarily using different models to accomplish effort of great intensity: (1) in the ego mode we believe the CB would be modeling the sensory motor cortical system; (2) in the superego mode it is operating with models of the associative memory cortical system; and in the "id" mode it is operating models of the limbic and SEEKING systems on its own, i.e. in isolation of the networks with which the CB usually participates. In this way the CB could help make decisions in situations of significant complexity in ways that offer the greatest safety, and insure a sufficiently high level of success in satisfying important ego concerns, superego concerns, or concerns about various psychobiological needs, without undue risk taking. It seems reasonable to further speculate that when it is operating in mode #2 the CB is likely capable of becoming, in a way, the practical source of guidance to a number of regulatory systems as noted in Chapter Seven (for reflexes, compound movements, innate behavior, sensorimotor functioning, and association-cortical functioning). One might further speculate that the CB is likely involved in deciding independently what emotion to employ for which purpose, using its internal model(s) of affective experience as its guide. It should be obvious, however, from the many observations of CB functioning, such as we have considered throughout our book, that the CB is extremely important for learning, communication, prediction, error detection, movements, human thinking (cognition) and problem solving, affect regulation, planning, executive control, the core self system, regulating and modeling systems that are deeply involved in our emotional life, and modeling various systems of the brain. In other words, studying the CB should be a high priority item, if we are to appreciate the details of how these various complex activities are integrated in such a compact brain system, and how they contribute to overall decision-making.

As stated at this book's beginning, it is hoped that what emerges is a clearer picture of adaptive behavior and learning within the mind/brain from the perspective of NP, a perspective that now takes into account the special role of the CB in integrating within and across systems that deal with so-called cognitive and affective activities, implicit and explicit memory, unconscious and conscious mind/brain, past experience and future planning. It is our belief that the theorizing presented is credible, and could be most serviceable in furthering the study of the CB's contributions. Creating a "psychodynamics of the cerebellum" is also a specific way of further integrating mind and brain perspectives. Although we remain a long way from having a complete insight into every aspect of mind/brain, it certainly does appear that paying careful attention to the CB helps move us closer to many of our long-term goals of understanding mind and brain with detailed, specific, and novel correlations. This can only help our work with our patients, who deserve the best that we have to offer.

Notes

1. Here, obviously, reference is made to Freud's structural model of ego, id, and superego. This is in contrast to Freud's topographic model of conscious, unconscious, and preconscious.
2. Such a unique combination of explicit and implicit memory system activity would be a good example of how these two systems can cooperate with each other closely (that is, to be connected), rather than be competing (and isolated), just as Posner has suggested. According to Levin (2004c), it is as though the explicit system can take "snapshots" of (or prime) the implicit system, and (just as in psychoanalytic reconstructions) these are then rearrangeable into new hybrid memories over time, that are capable of becoming conscious.

Abel, T., & Lattal, K. M. (2001). Molecular mechanisms of memory acquisition, consolidation and retrieval. *Current Opinion Neurobiology*, *11*(2): 180–187.

Abel, T., Martin, K. C., Bartsch, D., & Kandel, E. R. (1998). Memory suppressor genes: Inhibitory constraints on the storage of long-term memory. *Science*, *279*: 338–341.

Agnihotri, N. T., Hawkins, R. D., Kandel, E. R., & Kentros, C. (2004). The long-term stability of new hippocampal place fields requires new protein synthesis. *Proc. Natl., Acad. Sci.* (USA), *101*(10): 3656–3661.

Ahlquist, P. (2002). RNA-dependent RNA polymerase, viruses, and RNA silencing. *Science*, *296*(5571): 1270–1273.

Akshoomoff, N. A., & Courchesne, E. (1992). A new role for the cerebellum in cognitive operations. *Behavioural Neuroscience*, *106*: 731–738.

Akshoomoff, N. A., Courchesne, E., & Townsend, J. (1997). Attention coordination and anticipatory control. In: J. D. Schmahmann (Ed.), *The Cerebellum and Cognition*. (pp. 575–598). San Diego, CA.: Academic Press.

Alberini, C. M. (2005). Mechanisms of memory stabilization: are consolidation and reconsolidation similar or distinct processes? *Trends in Neuroscience*, *28*: 51–56.

215

Albright, T. D., Jessell, T.M., Kandel, E. R., & Posner, M. I. (2000). Neural Science: A century of progress and the mysteries that remain. *Cell*, *10*: S1–S55.

Allen, G., Müller, R.-A., & Courchesne, E. (2004). Cerebellar function in autism: Functional magnetic resonance image activation during a simple motor task. *Biological Psychiatry*, *56*(4): 269–278.

Alonso, J.-M. (2006). Neurons find strength through synchrony in the brain. *Science*, *312*: 1604–1605.

Ambrose, V. (2006). http://www.dartmouth.edu/~mcb/faculty/ambros.html

Anderson, C. M., Ochsner, K. N., Kuhl, B., Cooper, J., Robertson, E., Gabrieli, S. W., Clover, G. H., & Babrieli, J. D. E. (2004). Neural systems underlying the suppression of unwanted memories. *Science*, *303*: 232–235.

Anderson, C. M., Polcari, A., Lowen, S. B., Renshaw, P. F., & Teicher, M. H. (2002). Effects of methylphenidate on functional magnetic resonance relaxometry of the cerebellar vermis in boys with ADHD. *American Journal of Psychiatry*, *159*: 1322–1328.

Andreasen, N. C., O'Leary, D. S., Cizadlo, T., Arndt, S., Rezai, K., Boles-Ponto, L. L., Watkins, G. L., & Hichwa, R. D. (1996). Schizophrenia and cognitive dysmetria: a positron-emission tomography study of dysfunctional prefrontal-thalamic-cerebellar circuitry. *Proc. Natl. Acad. Sci. USA*, *93*: 9985–9990.

Andreasen, N.C., Flaum, M., Swayze, V., O'Leary, D.S., Alliger, R., Cohen, G., Ehrhardt, J., & Yuh, W. T. (1993). Intelligence and brain structure in normal individuals. *American Journal of Psychiatry*, *150*: 130–134.

Anokhin, K., Zaraiskaya, I., Alexandrova, E., Efimova, O., & Lazutkin, A. (2003). Awakening of cognitive plasticity: development of experience-dependent gene expression after birth. *European Journal of Biochemistry*, Abstract number S5.2-02, Supplement, 1 July 2003, cited on the web.

Askenasy, J. J. M. (2002). Sleep: expectations from the human genome. *Neurobiology of Sleep-Wakefulness Cycle*, *2*(2): 40–44.

Atienza, M., Cantero, J. L., & Stickgold, R. J. (2004). Posttraining sleep enhances automaticity in perceptual discrimination. *Journal of Cognitive Neurosciences*, *16*(1): 53–64.

Bahar, A., Dorfman, N., & Dudai, Y. (2004). Amygdalar circuits for either consolidation or extinction of taste aversion memory are not required for reconsolidation. *European Journal of Neuroscience*, *19*(4): 1115–1118.

Barry, V. C. (1998). Review of *Cognitive Science and the Unconscious* (1997), D. J. Stein (Ed.), Washington, D.C. and London: American Psychiatric Press. In: *The Bulletin of the Institute for Psychoanalysis*, Chicago, 7(1): 9–10.

Basch, F. M. (1983). The perception of reality and the disavowal of meaning. *The Annual of Psychoanalysis*, 11: 125–154. NY: International Universities Press.

Bartsch, D., Ghirardi, M., Skehel, P. A., Karl, K. A., Herder, S. P., Chen, M., Bailey, C. H., & Kandel, E. R. (1995). Aplysia CREB2 represses long-term facilitation: relief of repression converts transient facilitation into long-term functional and structural change, *Cell, 83*: 979–992.

Beattie, E. C., Stellwagen, D., Morishita, W., Breshahan, J. C., Ha, B. K., Von Zastrow, M., Beattie, M. S., & Malenka, R. C. (2002). Control of synaptic strength by glial TNFalpha. *Science, 295*: 2282–2285.

Bednar, J. A. (2003). Internally-generated activity, non-episodic memory, and emotional salience in sleep. In: E. F. Pace-Schott, M. Solms, M. Blagrove, & S. Harnad (Eds.), *Sleep and Dreaming: Scientific Advances and Reconsiderations*. Cambridge, UK: Cambridge University Press.

Bench, C. J., Friston, K. J., Brown, R. G., Scott, L. C., Frackowiak, R. S. J., & Dolan, R. J. (1992). The anatomy of melancholia focal abnormalities of cerebral blood flow in major depression. *Psychol. Med., 22*: 607–615.

Beutel, M., Dietrich, S., Stark, R., Brendel, G., & Silbersweig, D. (2004). Pursuit of the emerging dialogue between psychoanalysis and neuroscience: clinical and research perspectives. *International Journal of Psychoanalysis, 85*:1493–1496.

Biedenkapp, J. C., & Rudy, J. W. (2004). Context memories and reactivation: constraints on the reconsolidation hypothesis. *Behav. Neuroscience, 118*(5): 956–964.

Bhalla, U. S., & Lyengar, R. (1999). Emergent properties of networks of biological signaling systems. *Science, 283*(5400): 283–381.

Birksted-Breen, D. (2003). Time and the après-coup. *International Journal of Psychoanalysis, 84*: 1501–1515.

Bish, J. P., Pendyal, A., Ding, L., Ferrante, H., Nguyen, V., McDonald-McGinn, D., Zackal, E., & Simon T. J., (2006). Specific cerebellar reductions in children with chromosome 22q11.2 deletion syndrome. *Neuroscience Letter* (March 2).

Blakemore, S.-J., Frith, C. D., & Wolpert, D. M. (2001). The cerebellum is involved in predicting the sensory consequences of action. *Brain Imaging, NeuroReport, 2*: 879–884, Lippincott Williams and Wilkins.

Bliss, T. (1998). The physiological basis of memory (chapter 5). In: S. Rose (Ed.), *From Brains to Consciousness?: Essays on the New Sciences of the Mind* (pp. 73–93). Princeton NJ: Princeton University Press.

Bloom, F. E. (1985). CNS plasticity: A survey of opportunities. In: A. Bignami, A. Adolyne, F. E. Bloom, & C. L. Bolis (Eds.), *Central Nervous System Plasticity and Repair* (pp. 3–51). NY: Raven Press.

Bonner, J. (December 22, 1999). RU researchers find that waking experiences influence the brain's gene expression during REM sleep. http://www.runews@rockvax.rockerfuller.du

Boring, E. G. (1950). *A History of Experimental Psychology*. NY: Appleton-Century-Crofts.

Bornstein, R. F., & Pittman, T. S. (Eds.) (1992). *Perception without Awareness: Cognitive, Clincal and Social Perspectives*. NY and London: The Guilford Press.

Botvinick, M., Braver, T., Barch, D., Carter, C. S., & Cohen, J. D. (1998). Evaluating the demand for control: anterior cingulate cortex and crosstalk memory. Center for the Neural Basis of Cognition, Pittsburgh, PA, *Technical Report* 98.1. [See also article by same authors (1999), Conflict monitoring versus selection-for-action in anterior cingulate cortex. *Nature, 402*: 179–181.]

Botvinick, M., Nystrom, L. E., Fissell, K., Carter, C. S., & Cohen, J. D. (1999). Conflict monitoring versus selection-for-action in anterior cingulate cortex. *Nature, 402*(6758): 179–181.

Botvinick, M., Cohen, J. D., & Carter, C. S. (2004). Conflict monitoring anterior cingulate cortex: an update. *Trends in Cognitive Sciences, 8*(12): 539–546.

Bozon, B., Davis, S., & Laroche, S. (2003). A requirement for the immediate early gene Zif268 in reconsolidation of recognition memory after retrieval. *Neuron, 40*(4): 695–701.

Bremner, J. D., Vythilingam, M., Vermetten, E., Vaccarino, V., & Charney, D. S. (2004). Deficits in hippocampal and anterior cingulate functioning during verbal declarative memory encoding in midlife major depression. *American Journal of Psychiatry, 161*: 637–645.

Brendel, G., Goldstein, M., Pan, H., Beutel, M. E., Kernberg, O., Clarkin, J., Levy, K., Posner, M., Thomas, K., L. Stern, E., & Silbersweig, D. (2004). Abnormal fronto-limbic activity in BPD (Borderline-personality disorder): An emotional/behavioral inhibition fMRI study, presented to the 43rd Congress of the IPA in New Orleans, 13 March 2004.

Brown, J. W., & Braver, T. S. (2005). Learned predictions of error likelihood in the anterior cingulate cortex, *Science, 307*: 1118–1121.

Browning, M. (2006). Neuroscience and imagination: Sussane Langer's relevance to psychoanalytic theory, *Psa. Q.* (In Press).

Bruno, R. M., & Sakmann, B. (2006). Cortex is driven by weak but synchronously active thalamocortical synapses. *Science, 312*: 1622–1627.

Bullock, T. H., Bennett, M. V. L., Johnston, D., Josephson, R., Marder, E., & Fields, R. D. (2005). Neurosciences: The neuron doctrine. *Science, 310*: 791–793.

Bush, G., Luu, P., & Posner, M. I. (2000). Cognitive and emotional influences in the anterior cingulate cortex. *Trends in Cognitive Sciences, 4*(6): 215–222.

Calarge, C., Andreasen, N. C., & O'Leary, D. S. (2003). Visualizing how one brain understands another: A PET study of theory of mind. *American Journal of Psychiatry, 160*: 1954–1964.

Canolty, R. T., Edwards, E., Dalal, S. S., Soltani, M., Nagarajan, S. S., Kirsch, H. E., Berger, M. S., Barbaro, N. M., & Knight, R. T. (2006). High gamma power is phase-locked to theta oscillations in human neocortex. *Science, 313*: 1626–1628.

Caponigro, G., & Parker, R. (1995). Multiple functions for the poly(A) binding protein in mRNA decapping and deadenylation in yeast. *Genes and Dev., 9*: 2421–2432.

Cirelli, C., & Tononi, G. (2000). Gene expression in the brain across the sleep-waking cycle. *Brain Research, 885*: 303–321.

Cirelli, C., Gutierrez, C. M., & Tononi, G. (2004). Locus coeruleus control of state dependent gene expression. *Journal of Neuroscience, 24*(23): 5410–5419.

Contractor, A., Rogers, C., Maron, C., Henkemeyer, M., Swanson, G. T., & Heinemann, S. F. (2002). Trans–synaptic Eph Receptor-Ephrin signaling in hippocampal mossy fiber LTP. *Science, 296*: 1864–1869.

Courchesne, E. (2001). Attention function and dysfunction in autism. *Front Biosci, 6*: D105–D119.

Couzin, J. (2005). Cancer biology: A new cancer player takes stage. *Science, 310*: 766–767.

Crick, F., & Koch, C. (1992). The problem of consciousness. *Scientific American, 267*: 125–136.

Csikszentmihalyi, M. (1975). *Beyond Boredom and Anxiety: The Experience of Play in Work and Games.* San Francisco: Jossey-Bank.

Damasio, A. R. (1994). *Descartes' Error: Emotion, Reason, and the Human Brain.* NY: G. P. Putnam.

Damasio, A. R. (1995). Towards a neurobiology of emotion and feeling: operational concepts and hypotheses. *The Neuroscientists, 1*: 19–25.

Damasio, A. R. (1999a). Commentary on Target Articles. *Neuro-Psychoanalysis 1*(1): 38–39.

Damasio, A. R. (1999b). *The Feeling of What Happens: Body and Emotion in the Making of Consciousness.* NY: Harcourt, Brace.

Darwin, C. (1858). On the perpetuation of varieties and species by natural means of selection. [Presented to the Linnean Society of London].

Darwin, C. (1871). *The Descent of Man, and Selection in Relation to Sex.* London: John Murray.

Darwin, C. (1862/1899). *The Expression of the Emotions in Man and Animals.* NY: Appleton and Co.

Davies, J., Lloyd, K. R., Jones, I. K., Barnes, A., & Pilowsky, L. S. (2003). Changes in regional cerebral blood flow with venlafaxine in the treatment of major depression. *American Journal of Psychiatry, 160*: 374–376.

Debiec, J., & LeDoux, J. E. (2004). Disruption of reconsolidation but not consolidation of auditory fear conditioning by noradrenergic blockade in the amygdala. *Neuroscience, 129*(2): 267–272.

Debiec, J., LeDoux, J. E., & Nader, K. (2002). Cellular and systems reconsolidation in the hippocampus. *Neuron, 36*(3): 340–343.

Delamont, R. S., Julu, P. O., & Jamal, G. A. (1999). Periodicity of a noninvasive measure of cardiac vagal tone during on-rapid eye movement sleep in non-sleep deprived and sleep-deprived normal subjects. *Journal of Clinical Neurophysiology, 16*(2): 146–153.

Denicourt, C., & Dowdy, S. F. (2005). Medicine: Targeting apoptotic pathways in cancer cells. *Science, 305*: 1409–1410.

Donald, M. (1991). *Origins of the Modern Mind.* Cambridge, MA: Harvard University Press.

Donald, M. (2001). *A Mind So Rare: The Evolution of Human Consciousness.* NY: W. W. Norton.

Dudai, Y., & Eisenberg, M. (2004). Rites of passage of the engram: reconsolidation and the lingering consolidation hypothesis. *Neuron, 44*(1): 93–100.

Eiseley, L. (1971). *The Night Country.* NY: Charles Scribner's Sons/ Macmillan Publ. Co.

Ende, G., Hubrich, P., Walter, S., Weber-Fahr, W., Kämmerer, N., Braus, D. F., & Henn, F. A. (2005). Further evidence for altered cerebellar neuronal integrity in schizophrenia. *American Journal of Psychiatry, 162*: 790–792.

Erdelyi, M. H. (1996). *The Recovery of Unconscious Memories: Hypermnesia and Reminiscence.* Chicago: University of Chicago Press.

Erdelyi, M. H. (2004). Subliminal perception and its cognates: Theory, indeterminacy, and time. *Consciousness and Cognition, 13*: 73–91.

Erdelyi, M. H. (2006), (In Press). The unified theory of repression. *The Behavioral and Brain Sciences.*

Fatemi, S. H., Halt, A. R., Earle, J., Realmuto, G., Kist, D. A., Thuras, P. D., & Merz, A. (2000). Purkinje cell size is reduced in cerebellum of patients with autism. *Cellular and Molecular Neurobiology, 22*(2): 171–175.

Feder, S. (2003). Music as a simulacrum of mental life. Presented at the International meeting of the Neuro-Psychoanalytic Association, in New York, 2003.

Fields, R. D., & Stevens-Graham, B. (2002). New insights into neuron-glia communication. *Science, 298*: 556–562.

Fonagy, P. (1998). Moments of change in psychoanalytic theory: Discussions of a new theory of psychic change. *Infant Mental Health Journal, 19*(3), 346–353.

Fortey, R. (2000). *Trilobite: Eyewitness to Evolution.* NY: Vintage Books/ Random House.

Fosse, M. J., Fosse, R., Hobson, J. A., & Stickgold, R. J. (2003). Dreaming and episodic memory: A functional dissociation? *Journal of Cognitive Neuroscience, 15*(1): 1–9.

Frankland, P. W., Bontempi, B., Talton, L. E., Kaczmarek, L., & Silva, A. J. (2004). The involvement of the anterior cingulate cortex in remote contextual fear memory. *Science, 304*(5672): 881–883.

Freeman, W. H. (2000/2002). Protein synthesis, animation. http://www. biostudio.com/demo_freeman_protein_synthesis.htm

Freud, S. (1895). Project for a scientific psychology. *Standard Edition, 1*: 295–397. London, Hogarth Press, 1966.

Freud, S. (1914–1916). The Unconscious. *S.E.,* 14:166–215.

Freud, S. (1918) From the history of an infantile neurosis. *S.E.,* 17: 3–122.

Freud, S. (1940). An Outline of Psycho-Analysis. *S.E.,* 23: 139–208.

Freud, S. (1973). *Abstracts of the Standard Edition of the Complete Psychological Works of Sigmund Freud.* Carrie Lee Rothgeb (Ed.), NY:Jason Aronson.

Frick, R. B. (1982). The ego and the vestibulocerebellar system. *Psa. Q., 51*: 93–122.

Fuster, J. M. (1989). *The Prefrontal Cortex.* New York: Raven.

Ganguly-Fitzgerald, I., Donlea, J., & Shaw, P. J. (2006). Waking experience affects sleep needed in drosophila. *Science, 313*: 1775–1781.

Geary, D. C. (2004). *The Origin of Mind: Evolution of Brain, Cognition, and General Intelligence.* Washington, DC: American Psychological Association.

Gedo, J. E. (1991a). The biology of mind, Foreward to *Mapping the Mind,* by Fred M. Levin. Hillsdale, NJ: The Analytic Press.

Gedo, J. E. (1991b). *The Biology of Clinical Encounters.* Hillsdale, NJ: The Analytic Press.

Gedo, J. E. (1996a). Epigenesis, regression, and the problem of consciousness. *The Annual of Psychoanalysis, 24,* 93–102, Hillsdale, NJ: The Analytic Press.

Gedo, J. E. (1996b). *The Languages of Psychoanalysis.* Hillsdale, NJ: The Analytic Press.

Gedo, J. E. (1997). Reflections on metapsychology, theoretical coherence, hermeneutics, and biology. *Journal of the American Psychoanalytic Association, 45*(3), 779–807.

Gedo, J. E. (1999). *The Evolution of Psychoanalysis: Contemporary Theory and Practice.* New York: Other Press.

Gedo, J. E., & Goldberg, A. (1973). *Models of the Mind.* Chicago: University of Chicago Press.

George, M. S., Ketter, T. A., Parekh, P. I., Rosinsky, N., Ring, H. A., Pazzaglia, P. J., Marangell, L. B., Callahan, A. M., & Post, R. M. (1997). Blunted left cingulate activation in mood disorder subjects during a response interference task (the Stroop). *Journal of Neuropsychiatry, 9:* 55–63.

Geschwind, D. H. (1999). Focusing attention on cognitive impairment in the various spinocerebellar ataxia. *Arch. Neurol., 56:* 20–22.

Ghosh, A. (2002). Learning more about NMDA receptor regulation. *Science, 295:* 449–451.

Giampieri-Deutsch, P. (2004). *Dialogue in Science: Anglo-American Perspectives.* Stuttgart, Germany: Kohlhammer Press.

Goldberg, A. (2002). American pragmatism and American psychoanalysis. *Psa. Q., LXXI:* 235–250.

Goldman-Rakic, P. S. (1993). Working memory and the mind. In: *Mind and Brain: Readings from Scientific American Magazine.* (pp. 66–77). New York: W. H. Freeman.

Gordon, N.S., Panksepp, J., Dennis, M., & McSweeny, J. (2005). The instinctual basis of human affect: affective and fMRI imaging of laughter and crying. *Neuro-Psychoanalysis, 7*(2): 215–217.

Gould, E., Reeves, A. J., Graziano, M. S., & Gross, C. G. (1999). Neurogenesis in the neocortex of adult primates. *Science, 286:* 548–552.

Gowen, E., & Miall, R. C. (2005). Behavioral aspects of cerebellar function in adults with Asperger syndrome. *The Cerebellum*, 4: 1–11.

Gorman, C. (2004). Why we sleep. *Time* (2004, December 20), pp. 46–56.

Green, A. (1999). Consilience and Rigour: Commentary on Target Articles. *Neuro-Psychoanalysis* 1(1): 40–44.

Greenberg, R. (1999). Book Review: *The Neuropsychology of Dreams: A Clinical-Anatomical Study* by Mark Solms, *Neuro-Psychoanalysis*, 1(1): 128–130.

Greenberg, R. (2003). Where is the forest? Where is the dream? In: E. F. Pace-Schott, M. Solms, M. Blagrove, & S. Harnad (Eds.), *Sleep and Dreaming: Scientific Advances and Reconsiderations*. (pp. 154–156). Cambridge, UK: Cambridge University Press. [The republication and updating of the special issue of the journal *Behavioral and Brain Sciences*, December, 2000.]

Greenberg, R. (2005). Old wine (most of it) in new bottles: Where are dreams and what is the memory? *Behavioral and Brain Sciences*, 28: 72–7 2–73.

Greenberg, R., & Pearlman, C. (1974). Cutting the REM nerve: An approach to the adaptive function of REM sleep. *Perspectives in Biology and Medicine*, 17: 513–552.

Hammond, S. M., Bernstein, E., Beach, D., & Hannon, G. J. (2000). An RNA directed nuclease mediates post-transcriptional gene silencing in Drosophila cells. *Nature*, 404: 293–296.

Harnad, S. (Ed.) (2003). *Sleep and Dreaming: Scientific Advances and Reconsiderations*. Cambridge, UK: Cambridge University Press. [The republication and updating of the special issue of the journal *Behavioral and Brain Sciences*, December, 2000.]

Hartmann, H. (1939). Ego psychology and the problem of adaptation. In: D. Rapaport (Ed.), *Organization and Pathology of Thought: Selected Sources* (pp. 362–396). New York: Columbia University Press, 1951.

Hau, S., Russ, M.O., Leuzinger-Bohleber, M., & Solms, M. (2004). Characterization of brain activity during sleep and dreaming. Presented at the 43rd Congress of the IPA in New Orleans, 13 March, 2004.

Hellmuth, L. (2001). Glia tell neurons to build synapses. *Science*, 291: 569–570.

Herrick, C. J. (1948). *The Brain of the Tiger Salamander*. Chicago: University of Chicago Press.

Hobson, J. A. (1999). The new neuropsychology of sleep: implications for psychoanalysis. *Neuro-Psychoanalysis*, 1(2): 157–183.

Hobson, J. Å. (2004). Counterpoint: Freud returns? Like a bad dream. *Scientific American*, 290(5): 89.

Hobson, J. A., & McCarley, R. W. (1977). The brain as a dream state generator: An activation-synthesis hypothesis of the dream process. *American Journal of Psychiatry, 134*: 1335–1348.

Hobson, J. A., Pace-Schott, E. F., & Stickgold, R. (2000). Reprinted In: E. F. Pace-Schott, M. Solms, M. Blagrove, & S. Harnad (Eds.), *Sleep and Dreaming: Scientific Advances and Reconsiderations*. (pp. 1–50). Cambridge, UK: Cambridge University Press. 2003.

Hodgkin, A. L., Huxley, A. F., & Katz, B. (1952). A quantitative description of membrane current and its application to conduction and excitation in nerve. *Journal of Physiology, 117*: 500–544.

Hyman, S. E. (2005). Addiction: A disease of learning and memory, *American Journal of Psychiatry, 162*(8): 1414–1422.

Ibelgauft, H., (1999), Cytokines Online Pathfinder Encyclopedia, http://www.copewithcytokines.de

Ikemoto, S., & Panksepp, J. (1999). The role of nucleus acumbens DA in motivated behavior: a unifying interpretation with special reference to reward-seeking. *Brain Research Reviews, 25*: 261–274.

Ito, M. (1981). *Blueprints of the Brain*. Tokyo: Shizen.

Ito, M. (1984a). *The Cerebellum and Neural Control*. NY: Raven Press.

Ito, M. (1984b). Cerebellar plasticity and motor learning. *Exp. Brain Res., 9*: 165–169.

Ito, M. (1998). Consciousness from the viewpoint of the structural-functional relationships of the brain. *International Journal of Psychology, 33*(3): 191–197.

Ito, M. (2001). Cerebellar long-term depression: characterization, signal transduction, and functional roles. *Physiological Reviews, 81*(3): 1143–1195.

Ito, M. (2002). Historical review of the significance of the cerebellum and the role of Purkinje cells in motor learning. *Annals of the NY Academy of Science, 978*: 273–288.

Izquierdo, I., & Cammarota, M. (2004). Zif [268] and the survival of memory. *Science*, 304: 829–830.

Jacob, P., & Jeannerod, M. (2005). The motor theory of social cognition: a critique. *Trends in Cognitive Sciences, 9*: 21–25.

Jacobson, L. K., Giedd, J. N., Berquin, P. C., Krain, A. L., Hamburger, S. D., Kumra, S., & Rapoport, J. L. (1997). *American Journal of Psychiatry, 154*: 1663–1669.

James, A. C., James, S., Smith, D. M., & Jovaloyes, A. (2004). Cerebellar, prefrontal cortex, and thalamic volumes two time points in adolescent-onset schizophrenia. *American Journal of Psychiatry, 161*: 1023–1029.

James, W. (1890). *The Principles of Psychology*. Vol. I. NY: Dover, 1950.

Jeannerod, M. (1985). *The Brain Machine*. Translated by D. Urion. Cambridge, MA: Harvard University Press.

Jiménez, J. P. (2006). After pluralism: Towards a new integrated paradigm. *International Journal of Psychoanalysis, 87*(6): 1487–1508.

Johnston, D. (1997). A missing link? LTP and learning. *Science, 278*: 401–402.

Khan, A. A., Bose, C., Yam, L. S., Soloski, M. J., & Rupp, F. (2001). Physiological regulation of the immunological synapse by agrin. *Science, 292*:5522: 1681–1686.

Kandel, E. (1983). From metapsychology to molecular biology: Explorations into the nature of anxiety. *American Journal of Psychiatry, 140*: 1277–1293.

Kandel, E. (1998). A new intellectual framework for psychiatry. *American Journal of Psychiatry, 155*: 457–469.

Kandel, E. (1999). Biology and the future of psychoanalysis: A new intellectual framework for psychiatry revisited. *American Journal of Psychiatry, 156*: 505–524.

Kandel, E. (2006). Interview: Biology of Mind. *Newsweek*, p. 47.

Kaplan-Solms, K., & Solms, M. (2000). *Clinical Studies in Neuro-Psychoanalysis: An Introduction to a Depth Neuropsychology*. London: Karnac Books.

Klein, G. (1972). The vital pleasures. *Psychoanalysis and Contemporary Science, 1*: 181–205.

Kohon, G. (1999). *The Dead Mother: The Work of Andre Green*. NY: Routledge.

Kolb, B., & Winshaw, I. Q. (1980). The frontal lobes. In: B. Kolb & I. Q. Winshaw (Eds.), *Fundamentals of Human Neurophysiology* (pp. 277–307). San Francisco: W. H. Freeman.

Kosslyn, S. M. (1994). *Image and Brain*. Cambridge, MA: MIT Press.

Langer, S. (1942). *Philosophy in a New Key: A Study in the Symbolism of Reason, Rite, and Art*. Cambridge: Harvard University Press.

Langer, S. (1953). *Feeling and Form*. New York: Charles Scribner's Sons.

Langer, S. (1967). *Mind: An Essay on Human Feeling. Vol. 1*. Baltimore: The Johns Hopkins University Press.

Langer, S. (1972). *Mind: An Essay on Human Feeling, Vol. 2*. Baltimore: The Johns Hopkins University Press.

Langer, S. (1982). *Mind: An Essay on Human Feeling, Vol 3*. Baltimore: The Johns Hopkins University Press.

Langer, S. (1988). *Mind: An Essay on Human Feeling*. Abridged by G. Van Den Heuvel. Baltimore: The Johns Hopkins University Press.

Le, H.T., Pardo, J. V., & Hu, X. (1998). 4 T-fMRI study of non-spatial shifting of selective attention: cerebellar and parietal contributions. *Journal of Neurophysiology, 79*: 1535–1548.

LeDoux, J. (1994). Emotion, memory, and brain. *Scientific American 270*: 32–39.

LeDoux, J. (1995). Emotions: Clues from the brain. *Annual Review of Psychology 46*: 209–235.

LeDoux, J. (1996). *The Emotional Brain: The Mysterious Underpinnings of Emotional Life*. New York: Simon and Schuster.

LeDoux, J. (1999). Psychoanalytic theory: Clues from the brain. *Neuro-Psychoanalysis, 1*(1): 44–49.

Lee, D. N. (1998). Guiding movement by coupling taus. *Ecological Psychology, 10*: 221–250.

Lee, J. L., Everitt, B. J., & Thomas, K. L. (2004). Independent cellular processes for hippocampal memory consolidation and reconsolidation. *Science, 304*(5672): 829–830.

Lena, I., Parrot, S., Deschaux, O., Muffat, S., Sauvinet, V., Renaud, B., Suaud-Chagny, M. F., & Gottesmann, C. (2005). Variations in the extracellular levels of dopamine, noradrenaline, glutamate, and aspartate across the sleep-wake cycle in the medial prefrontal cortex and nucleus acumbens of freely moving rats. *Journal of Neuroscience Research, 81*: 891–899.

Leroi, I., O'Hearn, E., Marsh, L., Lyketsos, C. G., Rosenblatt, A., Ross, C. A., Brandt, J., & Margolis, R. L. (2002). Psychopathology in patients with degernerative cerebellar diseases: A comparison with Huntington's Disease. *American Journal of Psychiatry, 159*: 1306–1314.

Levin, F. M. (1962). The effect of epinephrine and 3'5'AMP on the perfused rabbit liver. *The Physiologist, 5*: 175.

Levin, F. M. (1980). Metaphor, affect, and arousal: How interpretations might work. *The Annual of Psychoanalysis, 8*: 231–248.

Levin, F. M. (1988). Introduction: In: Max Stern, *Repetition and Trauma* (pp. 1–38). Hillsdale, NJ: The Analytic Press.

Levin, F. M. (1991). *Mapping the Mind: The Intersection of Psychoanalysis and Neuroscience*. Hillsdale, NJ: T.A.P. [New York and London: Karnac Books, 2003.]

Levin, F. M. (1995), Psychoanalysis and knowledge, Part 1: The problem of representation and alternative approaches to learning. *The Annual of Psychoanalysis, 23*: 95–114. Hillsdale, NJ: The Analytic Press.

Levin, F. M. (1997). Integrating some mind and brain views of transference: the phenomena. *Journal of the American Psychoanalytic Association, 45*: 1121–1151.

Levin, F. M. (2002a). The Neuroimmune network and its relevance to psychoanalysis. *Psychoanalytic Quarterly, LXXI*: 617–627.

Levin, F. M. (2002b). Invited lecture on: Cytokines, the cerebellum and clinical psychoanalysis: How mind and brain cascades coincide, presented September 3, 2002 at RIKEN Frontier Institute Brain Science Laboratory of Dr. Masao Ito, Wako, Japan.

Levin, F. M. (2002c). Review of Horst Ibelgauft's webpage on Cytokines, *Psa. Q.*. CT. *71*(3): 617–627.

Levin, F. M. (2003). *Psyche and Brain: The Biology of Talking Cures.* Madison, CT: I.U.P.

Levin, F. M. (2004a). Commentary on "Freud's theory of mind and functional imaging experiments" [Review of a paper by Shulman and Reiser], *Neuro-Psychoanalysis,* pp. 143–144.

Levin, F. M. (2004b). Long-term potentiation (LTP), long-term depression (LTD), and the creation of new long-term memories (LTM), on the basis of emotional demand: the critical role of cytokines (CK). *Samiksa: Journal of the Indian Psychoanalytical Society, 57*: 13–24.

Levin, F. M. (2004c). On dream actors in the theatre of memory: Their role in the psychoanalytic process. *International Journal of Psychoanalysis, 85*: 1275–1276.

Levin, F. M. (2004d). Comments on a paper by Mauro Mancia. Letter to the Editor of *International Journal of Psychoanalysis, 84*: 945–952.

Levin, F. M. (2005a). Chapter IX: Cytokines (CK) and long-term memory (LTM): An interdisciplinary look at how psychoanalysis might activate learning via its effects on emotional attention. In: P. Giampieri-Deutsch (Ed.), *Psychoanalysis as an Empirical Interdisciplinary Science: Collected Papers on Contemporary Psychoanalytic Research* (pp. 211–238). Vienna, Austria: Austrian Academy of Sciences.

Levin, F. M. (2005b). An introduction to Neuro-Psychoanalysis, presented in Santiago Chile, to the National Meeting of the Chilean Psychoanalytical Association, January 7, 2005.

Levin, F. M. (2006). Book Review: J. Corrigal, & H. Wilkinson (Eds.), *Revolutionary Connections: Psychotherapy and Neuroscience.* In: *Neuro-Psychoanalysis, 7*(1): 107–111. London and New York: Karnac Books.

Levin, F. M. (2005c). Ineracciones mente-cerebro: una perspectiva neuro-psicoanalitica de la atension emocional, citiquinas y nuevas memorias de largo plazo, *Rev. Chil. Psicoanal., 22*(1): 41–52 [Spanish].

Levin, F. M., Trevarthen, C., Colibazzi, T., Ihanus, J., Talvitie, V., Carney, J., Panksepp, J., & Watt, D. F. (2005d). Sleep and Dreaming. Paper presented at the Sixth International Neuro-Psychoanalysis Conference, Rio De Janeiro, Brazil (27 July). [A brief version of Chapters 1 and 2 of this book.]

Levin, F. M., Gedo, J. E., Ito, M., & Trevarthen, C., (2003a). Chapter 9: In: *Psyche and Brain: The Biology of Talking Cures.* Conscious and unconscious systems—Part I, pp.147–164. Madison, CT: I.U.P.

Levin, F. M., Gedo, J. E., Ito, M., & Trevarthen, C. (2003b). Chapter 10: The Conundrum of conscious-unconscious relations: Part 2—The tagging of memory, the dynamic unconscious, and the executive control network (ECN). In: *Psyche and Brain: The Biology of Talking Cures.* Madison, CT: International Universities Press.

Levin, F. M., and Kent, E. W. (1994a). Psychoanalysis and knowledge: the relationship between similarity judgment, memory priming, and psychoanalytic transference. Presented to The American Psychoanalytic Association, Philadelphia, PA. May 19, 1994.

Levin, F. M., & Kent, E. W. (1994b). The isomorphism of similarity, priming, and transference, presented to Psyche '94, International Meeting on Mind and Brain, Osaka University Medical School, Osaka, Japan, Oct. 6–7, 1994.

Levin, F. M., & Vuckovich, D. M. (1983). Psychoanalysis and the two cerebral hemispheres. *The Annual of Psychoanalysis,* 11:171–198. NY: International Universities Press.

Levin, F. M., & Vuckovich, D. M. (1987). Brain plasticity, learning and psychoanalysis. *Annual of Psychoanalysis, 15:* 19–96.

Levy, J., & Trevarthen, C. (1976). Metacontrol of hemispheric function in human split brain patients. *Journal of Experimental Psychology: Human Perception and Performance, 2:* 299–312.

Li, L., Thomas, R. M., Suzuki, H., Brabander, M. K. De, Wang, X. H., & Harran, P. G., (2004). A small molecule Smac mimic potentiates TRAIL- and TNFalpha-mediated cell death. *Science, 305:* 1471–1474.

Lien, W.-H., Klezovitch, O., Fernandez, T. E., Delrow, J., & Vasioukhin, V. (2006). AlphqE-Catenin controls cerebral cortical size by regulating the hedgehog signaling pathway. *Science, 311:* 1609–1612.

Linden, D. J., & Routtenberg, A. (1989). The role of protein kinase C in long-term potentiation: a testable model. *Brain Research Reviews, 14:* 279–296.

Lisman, J. E., & Fallon, J. R. (1999). What maintains memories? *Science, 283:* 339–340.

Liu, J., Carmell, M.A., Rivas, F.V., Marsden, C. G., Thomson, J. M., Song, J.-J., Hammond, S.M., Joshua-Tor, L., & Hannon, G. J. (2004). Argonaut2 is the catalytic engine of mammalian RNAi. *Science, 305:* 1437–1441.

Lou, H., Kim, S. K., Zaitsev, E., Sneil, C. R., Lu, B., & Loh, Y. P. (2005). Sorting and activity-dependent secretion of BÎNF require interaction of a specific motif with the sorting receptor carboxypeptidase E. *Neuron, 45*: 245–255.

Maier, S. F., & Watkins, L. R. (1998). Cytokines for Psychologists: Implications of bidirectional immune-to-brain communication for understanding behavior, mood, and cognition. *Psychological Review,105*(1): 83–107. American Psychological Association.

Malenka, R. C., & Nicoll, R. A. (1999). Long-term potentiation—A decade of progress? *Science, 285*: 1870–1874.

Mancia, M. (2003). Dream actors in the theatre of memory: Their role in the psychoanalytic process. *International Journal of Psychoanalysis, 84*: 945–952.

Margolis, R. L. (2001). Editorial: Cerebellum and psychiatry. *International Review of Psychiatry, 13*: 229–231.

Martinez-Conde, S., & Macknik, S. L. (2007). Windows on the mind, *Scientific American* [August]: 56–63.

Marx, J. (2005). Molecular biology: P-bodies mark the spot for controlling protein production. *Science, 310*: 764–765.

Mathew, D., Ataman, B., Chen, J., Zhung, Y., Cumberledge, S., & Budnik, V. (2005). Wingless signaling at synapses is through cleavage and nuclear transport of receptor dfrizzled2, *Science, 310*: 1344–1347.

Mauch, D.H., Nägler, K., Schumacher, S., Göritz, C., Müller, E.-C., Otto, A., & Pfrieger, F. W. (2001). CNS synaptogenesis promoted by Glia-derived cholesterol. *Science, 294*: 1354–1357.

Mayberg, H. S., Liotti, M., Brannan, S. K., McGinnis, S., Mahurin, R. K., Jerabek, P. A., Silva, J. A., Tekell, J. L., Martin, C. C., Lancaster, J. L., & Fox, P. T. (1999). Reciprocal limbic-cortical function and negative mood: Converging PET findings in depression and normal sadness. *American Journal of Psychiatry, 156*: 675–682.

Mesulam, M.-M. (2000). *Principles of Behavioral and Cognitive Neurology.* (2nd edn) New York: Oxford University Press.

Mesulam, M. M., Nobre, A. C., Kim, Y. H., Parrish, T. B., & Gitelman, D. R. (2001), Heterogeneity of cingulate contributions to spatial attention. *Neuroimage, 13*: 1065–1072.

Milekic, M. H., & Alberini, C. M. (2002). Temporarily graded requirement for protein synthesis following memory reactivation. *Neuron, 36*(3): 521–525.

Miller, G. (2004). News: Behavioral neuroscience uncaged. *Science, 306*: 432–434.

Minamimoto, T., Hori, Y., & Kimura, M. (2005). Complementary process to response bias in the Centromedian nucleus of the thalamus. *Science, 308*: 1798–1801.

Mishkin, M., & Appenzeller, T. (1987). The anatomy of memory. *Sci. Am., 256*: 80–86.

Modell, A. (1993). *The Private Self.* Cambridge, MA: Harvard University Press.

Moore, B. E., & Fine, B. D. (Eds.) (1968).. *A Glossary of Psychoanalytic Terms and Concepts.* (2nd. edn). New York: The American Psychoanalytic Association.

Morgado, I. (2005). [The psychobiology of learning and memory: fundamentals and recent advances]. *Rev. Neurol., 40*(5): 289–297) [In Spanish].

Murakami, J. W., Courchesne, E., Press, G. A., Yeung-Chourchesne, R., & Hesselink, J. R. (1989). Reduced cerebellar hemisphere size and its relationship to vermal hypoplasia in autism. *Archives of Neurology, 46*(6): 689–694.

Nader, K., Schafe, G. E., & LeDoux, J. E., (2000). The labile nature of consolidation theory. *Nat. Rev. Neurosci., 1*(3): 216–219.

Newman, J., & Baars, B. J. (1993). A Neural Attentional Model for Access to Consciousness: A Global Workspace Perspective. *Concepts in Neuroscience, 4*(2): 255ñ290.

Najib, A., Lorberbaum, J. P., Kose, S., Bohning, D. E., & George, M. S. (2004). Regional brain activity in women grieving a romantic relationship breakup. *American Journal of Psychiatry, 161*: 2245–2256.

Nakagawa, T., & Sheng, M. (2000). A stargazer foretells the way to the synapse, *Science, 290*: 2270–2271.

Okugawa, G., Sedvall, G. C., & Agartz, I. (2003). Smaller cerebellar vermis but not hemisphere volumes in patients with chronic schizophrenia. *American Journal of Psychiatry, 160*: 1614–1617.

Olds, D. (1992). Consciousness: A brain-centered informational approach. *Psychoanalytic Inquiry, 12*(3): 419–444.

Olds, D. (1994). Connectionism and psychoanalysis. *Journal of American Psychoanalytic Association, 42*: 581–612.

Olds, D. (2006). Interdisciplinary studies and our [psychoanalytic] practice. *J. Amer. Psa. Assoc., 54*(3): 857–876.

Opatow, B. (1999). On the scientific standing of psychoanalysis. *JAPA, 47*(4): 1107–1124.

Pace-Schott, E. F., & Hobson, A. (2000). The Neurobiology of Sleep: Genetics, Cellular Physiology, and Subcortical Networks. *Nature Reviews: Neuroscience, 3*: 591–603, 2002.

Pace-Schott, E. F., Solms, M., Blagrove, M., & Harnad, S. (Eds.) (2003), *Sleep and Dreaming: Scientific Advances and Reconsiderations*. Cambridge, UK: Cambridge University Press.

Pally, R. (2005). Chapter VIII. Emotion and the role of the body in mental life. In: Patrizia Giampieri-Deutsch (Ed.), *Psychoanalysis as an Empirical, Interdisciplinary Science*. (pp. 179–209). Vienna, Austria: The Austrian Academy of Sciences.

Pang, P. T., Teng, H. K., Zaitsev, E., Woo, N. T., Sakata, K., Zhen, S., Teng, K. K., Yung, W.-H., Hempstead, B. L., & Lu, B. (2004). Cleavage of proBDNF by tPa/plasmin is essential for long-term hippocampal plasticity. *Science, 306*(5695): 487–491.

Panksepp, J. (1985). Mood changes. In: P. Vinken, G. Bruyn, & H. Klawans (Eds.), *Handbook of Clinical Neurology* (45th edn) Elsevier.

Panksepp, J. (1998a). *Affective Neuroscience: The Foundations of Human and Animal Emotions*. New York and Oxford: Oxford University Press.

Panksepp, J. (1998b). Anticipation of play elicits high-frequency ultrasonic vocalizations in young rats. *J. Comp. Psychology, 112*: 65–73.

Panksepp, J. (1998c). Chapter 10. Nature Red in Tooth and Claw: The Neurobiological sources of rage and anger. In: *Affective Neuroscience: The Foundations of Human and Animal Emotions* (pp. 187–205). New York and Oxford: Oxford University Press.

Panksepp, J. (1999a). Emotions as viewed by psychoanalysis and neuroscience: an exercise in consilience. *Neuro-Psychoanalysis, 1*(1): 15–38.

Panksepp, J. (1999b). Drives, affects, id energies, and the neuroscience of emotions: Response to the commentaries. *Neuro-Psychoanalysis 1*(1): 69–89.

Panksepp, J. (2000). The neurodynamics of emotions: An evolutionary-neurodevelopmental view. In: M. D. Lewis & I. Granic (Eds.), *Emotion, Self-Organization, and Development* (pp. 236–264). New York: Cambridge University Press.

Panksepp, J. (2001). The neuro-evolutionary cusp between emotions and cognitions. *Evolution and Cognition, 7*(2): 141–163.

Panksepp, J. (2003). "The dream of reason creates monsters"… especially when we neglect the role of emotions in REM-states. In: E. F. Pace-Schott, M.Solms, M. Blagrove, & S. Harnad (Eds.), *Sleep and Dreaming: Scientific Advances and Reconsiderations* (pp. 200–202). Cambridge, UK: Cambridge University Press.

Panksepp, J. (2005a). Affective consciousness: Core emotional feelings in animals and in humans. *Consciousness and Cognition* (In Press).

Panksepp, J. (2005b). Beyond a joke: From animal laughter to human joy. *Science, 308*: 62–63.

Panksepp, J., & Burgdorf, J. (2003). "Laughing" rats and the evolutionary antecedents of human joy? *Physiology and Behavior, 79*: 533–547.

Pearlman, C. (1971). Latent learning impaired by REM sleep deprivation. *Psychosomatic Science, 25*: 135–136.

Pearlman, C. (1973). Posttrial REM sleep: A critical period for consolidation of shuttlebox avoidance. *Animal Learning and Behavior, 1*: 49–51.

Pearlman, C. (1979). REM sleep and information processing: Evidence from animal studies. *Neuroscience and Biobehavioural Reviews, 3*: 57–68.

Pearlman, C., & Becker, M. (1973). Brief posttrial REM sleep deprivation impairs discriminative learning in rats. *Physiological Psychology,1*: 373–376.

Pearlman, C., & Becker, M. (1974). REM sleep deprivation impairs barpress acquisition in rats. *Physiology and Behavior, 13*: 813–817.

Pompeiano, M., Cirelli, C., & Tononi, G. (1994). Immediate-early genes in spontaneous wakefulness and sleep: Expression of c-fos, NGFI-A mRNA, and protein J. *Sleep Research, 3*: 80–96.

Porges, S. W. (2003). The polyvagal theory: Phylogenetic contributions to social behavior. *Physiology and Behavior, 79*: 503–513.

Poulet, J. F. A., & Hedwig, B. (2006). The cellular basis of a corollary discharge. *Science, 311*(5760): 518–522.

Pratt, C. (1952). *Music and the Language of Emotion*. Washington, DC: U.S. Library of Congress and New York: International Universities Press.

Quinodoz, J.–M. (2004). On chaotic possibilities: Toward a new model of development [Letter to the Editor re. Galatzer-Levy, 2004], *I.J.Psa., 85*: 1019–1010.

Rae, C., Karmiloff-Smith, A., Lee, M. A., Dixon R. M., Grant, J., Blamire, A. M., Thompson, C. H., Styles, P., & Radda, G. K. (1998), Brain biochemistry in Williams syndrome: Evidence for a role of the cerebellum in cognition? *Neurology, 51*: 33–40.

Ramachandran, V., & Oberman, L. (2006). Broken Mirrors. *Scientific American, 295*(5): 38–45.

Reiser, M. (2001). Review: The dream in contemporary psychiatry, *American Journal of Psychiatry, 158*(3): 351–359.

Rescher, N. (1995). Pragmatism. In: T. Honderich (Ed.), *The Oxford Companion to Philosophy* (pp. 710–713). Oxford and New York: Oxford University Press.

Revonsuo, A. (2000). The reinterpretation of dreams: An evolutionary hypothesis of the function of dreaming. *Behavioral and Brain Sciences, 23*(6): 1–48; or reprinted In: E. F. Pace-Schott, M. Solms, M. Blagrove, &

S. Harnad (Eds.), *Sleep and Dreaming: Scientific Advances and Reconsiderations* (pp. 85–109). Cambridge, UK: Cambridge University Press.

Revonsuo, A., & Valli, K. (2000). Dreaming and consciousness: Testing the threat Simulation theory of the function of dreaming, *Psyche, 6*(8), http://psche.cs.monash.edu.au/v6/psyche-6-08-revonsuo.html

Rizzolatti, G., Fogassi, L., & Gallese, V. (2006). Mirrors of the mind. *Scientific American, 295*(5): 30–37.

Riva, M. A., Molteni, R., Bedogni, F., Racagni, G., & Fumagalli, F. (2005). Emerging role of the FGF system in psychiatric disorders. *Trends in Neurosciences, 26*: 228–231.

Rogoff, B., Paradise, R., Mejia-Arauz, R., Correas-Chavez, M., & Angelillo, C. (2003). Firsthand learning by intent participation. *Annual Review of Psychology, 54*: 175–303.

Roland, E. J. (1981). Somatotopical tuning of post-central gyrus during focal attention in man. A regional cerebral blood flow study. *Journal of Neurophysiology, 46*: 744–754.

Roland, E.J., & Friberg, L. (1985). Localization of cortical area activated by thinking. *Journal of Neurophysiology, 53*: 1219–1243.

Ross, D. A., & Martin, A. (2006). Book Review: The Origin of the Mind: Evolution of Brain, Cognition, and General Intelligence, by David C. Geary, *American Journal of Psychiatry, 163*(9): 1652–1653.

Rubia, K., Smith, A. B., Brammer, M. J., Toone, B., & Taylor, E. (2005). Abnormal brain activation during drug inhibition and error detection in medication-naïve adolescents with ADHD. *American Journal of Psychiatry, 162*(6): 1067–1075.

Rubinstein, B. B. (1997). *Psychoanalysis and the Philosophy of Science.* R. Holt (Ed.), *Psychological Issues Monograph, 62/63,* Madison, CT: International

Universities Press.

Saskia, J. M. C., Palmen, S., van Engeland, H., Hof, P. R., & Schmitz, C. (2004). Neuropathological findings in autism. *Brain: A Journal of Neurology, 127*(12): 2572–2583.

Schacter, D. L., & Buckner, R. L. (1998). Priming and the brain. *Neuron, 20*: 1–20, Cell Press.

Schoffelen, J.-M., Oostenveld, R., & Fries, P. (2005). Neuronal coherence as a mechanism of effective corticospinal interaction. *Science, 308*: 111–113.

Schmahmann J. D. (1996). From movement to thought: anatomic substrates of the cerebellar contribution to cognitive processing. *Hum Brain Mapp, 4*: 174–198.

Schmahmann, J. D. (2004). Disorders of the cerebellum: ataxia, dysmetria of thought, and the cerebellar cognitive affective syndrome. *J. Neuropsychiatry Clin. Neurosci., 16*: 367–378.

Schore, A. N. (1999). Commentary on target articles. *Neuro-Psychoanalysis 1*(1): 49–55.

Schott, E. F., Solms, M., Blagrove, M., & Harnad, S. (Eds.) (2003). *Sleep and Dreaming: Scientific Advances and Reconsiderations.* Cambridge UK: Cambridge University Press.

Shevrin, H. (1999). Commentary on target articles. *Neuro-Psychoanalysis, 1*(1): 55–60.

Shevrin, H., Bond, J. A., Brakel, L. A. W., Hertel, R. K., & Williams, W. J. (1996). *Conscious and Unconscious Processes: Psychodynamic, Cognitive, and Neurophysiological Convergences.* New York and London: The Guildford Press.

Shevrin, H., & Eiser, A. S. (2003). Continued vitality of the Freudian theory of dreaming. In: E. F. Pace-Schott, M. Solms, M. Blagrove, & S. Harnad (Eds.), *Sleep and Dreaming: Scientific Advances and Reconsiderations.* Cambridge, UK: Cambridge University Press, 2003. [The republication and updating of the special issue of the journal *Behavioral and Brain Sciences,* December, 2000.]

Shi, S.-H. (2001). AMPA receptor dynamics and synaptic plasticity. *Science, 294*: 1851–1852.

Shimizu, E., Tang, Y.-P., Rampon, C., & Tsien, J. Z. (2000). NMDA receptor-dependent synaptic reinforcement as a crucial process for memory consolidation. *Science, 290*: 1170–1173.

Simmel, B. (2004). Review of Gregorio Kohon's book, *The Dead Mother: The Review of André Green,* Website of the American Psychological Association, Division 39, file:///Users/fred/Desktop/GREENDivision%20of%20Psychoanalysis%20-%20APA.webarchive.

Simon, T. J., Bish, J. P., Bearden, C. E., Ding, L., Ferrante, S., Nguyen, V., Gee, J. C., McDonald-McGinn, D. M., Zackal, E. H., & Emanuel, B. S. (2005). A multilevel analysis of cognitive dysfunction and psychopathology associated with chromosome 22q11.2 deletion syndrome in children. *Dev. Psychopathol., 17*: 753–784.

Snider, S. R. (1982). Cerebellar pathology in schizophrenia—cause or consequence? *Neurosci. Behav. Rev, 6*: 47–53.

Sohl, G., Maxeiner, S., & Willecke, K. (2005). Expression and functions of neuronal gap junctions. *Nat. Rev. Neurosci., 6*(3): 191–200. PMID: #15738956#

Solms, M., (1997). *The Neuropsychology of Dreams.* Hillsdale, NJ: Lawrence Erlbaum Associates.

Solms, M. (1999). The new neuropsychology of sleep: commentary by Mark Solms (London), *Neuro-Psychoanalysis*, 1(2): 183–195.

Solms, M. (2000). A psychoanalytic perspective on confabulation. *Neuro-Psychoanalysis*, 2: 133–138.

Solms, M. (2003a). Target Chapter 2: Dreaming and REM sleep are controlled by different brain mechanisms.In: E. F. Pace-Schott, M. Solms, M. Blagrove, & S. Harnad (Eds.), *Sleep and Dreaming: Scientific Advances and Reconsiderations*. Cambridge UK: Cambridge University Press, 2003. Cambridge, UK. [The republication and updating of the special issue of the journal *Behavioral and Brain Sciences*, December, 2000.]

Solms, M. (2003b). The mechanism of the REM state is more than a sum of its parts. In: E. F. Pace-Schott, M. Solms, M. Blagrove, & S. Harnad (Eds.), *Sleep and Dreaming: Scientific Advances and Reconsiderations* (pp. 220–221). Cambridge, UK: Cambridge University Press, 2003.

Solms, M. (2003c). Authors responses: Forebrain mechanisms of dreaming are activated from a variety of sources. In: E. F. Pace-Schott, M. Solms, M. Blagrove, & S. Harnad (Eds.), *Sleep and Dreaming: Scientific Advances and Reconsiderations* (pp. 247–252). Cambridge, UK: Cambridge University Press, 2003. [The republication and updating of the special issue of the journal *Behavioral and Brain Sciences*, December, 2000.]

Solms, M. (2003c). Authors responses: Forebrain mechanisms of dreaming are activated from a variety of sources. (pp. 247–252). In: M. Pace-Solms (2004). Neuroscience: Freud returns. *Scientific American*, 290(5): 82–89.

Solms, M., (2004). Neuroscience: Freud returns. *Scientific American*, 290(5): 82–89.

Solms, M., & Nersessian, E. (1999). Freud's theory of affect: Questions for neuroscience. *Neuro-psychoanalysis*. 1(1): 5–14.

Solms, M., & Turnbull, O. (2002). *The Brain and the Inner World: An Introduction to the Neuroscience of Subjective Experience*. New York: Other Press.

Song, J.-J., Smith, S.K., Hannon, G.J., & Joshua-Tor, L. (2004). Crystal structure of Argonaute and its implications for RISC Slicer activity. *Science*, 305(5689): 1434–1437.

Sontheimer, E.J., & Carthew, R. W. (2005). Molecular biology: Argonaute journeys into the heart of RISC. *Science*, 305: 1409–1410.

Squire, L. (1998). Memory and brain systems.(chap. 4). In: S. Rose (Ed.), *From Brains to Consciousness?: Essays on the New Sciences of the Mind* (pp. 53–72). Princeton, NJ: Princeton University Press.

Stahl, S. M. (2000). Molecular neurobiology for practicing psychiatrists, Part 5: How a leucine zipper can turn on genes—Immediate-Early [Early response] Genes activate late-gene expression in the brain. *J. Clin. Psychiat.*, *61*(1): 7–8.

Stein, A. (2004). Music and trauma in Polansky's *The Pianist* (2002). *International Journal of Psychoanaysis*, *85*: 755–765.

Stern, D. (2004). *The Present Moment in Psychotherapy and Everyday Life*. New York: W. W. Norton.

Stern, M. (1988). *Repetition and Trauma: Toward a Teleonomic Theory of Psychoanalysis*. (Ed.) L. B. Stern. Hillsdale, NJ: The Analytic Press.

Stickgold, R. J. (2004). Bedtime reading—Review of *The Mind at Night: The New Science of How and Why We Dream*, by Andrea Rock (Basic Books, 2004). *Nature Neuroscience*, *7*(11): 1165.

Stickgold, R. J., Whidbee, D., Schimer, B., Patel, V., & Hobson, J. A. (2000). Visual discrimination task improvement: A multi-step process occurring during sleep. *Journal of Cognitive Neuroscience*, *12*(2): 246–254.

Stickgold, R. J., Scott, L. C., Rittenhouse, C., & Hobson, J. A. (1999). Sleep-induced changes in associative memory. *Journal of Cognitive Neuroscience*, *11*(2): 182–193.

Suzuki, A., Josselyn, S.A., Frankland, P. W., Masushige, S., Silva, A. J., & Kida, S. (2004). Memory reconsolidation and extinction have distinct temporal and biochemical signatures. *Journal of Neuroscience*, *24*(20): 4787–4795.

Szpilman, W. ([1946] 1999). *The Pianist; The Extraordinary Story of One Man's Survival in Warsaw, 1939–1945*. Translated by A. Bell. New York: Picador/St. Martin's Press.

Takasu, M. A., Dalva, M. B., Zigmond, R. E., & Greenberg, M. E. (2002). Modulation of NMDA receptor-dependent calcium influx and gene expression through EphB receptors. *Science*, *295*: 491–495.

Talvitie, V. (2003). Repressed contents reconsidered: Repressed contents and Dennett's intentional stance approach. *Theoria et. Historia Scientiarum*, *2*: 19–30.

Talvitie, V. (2006). The Freudian Unconscious in the Context of the Cognitive Orientation. [Ph.D. thesis in Psychology], The University of Helsinki. vesa.Talvitie@helsinki.fi.

Talvitie, V., & Ihanus, J. (2003). On the nature of repressed contents: A working through of John Searle's critique. *NP*, *5*: 133–142.

Talvitie, V., & Ihanus, J. (2002). The repressed and implicit knowledge. *International Journal of Psychoanalysis*, *83*: 1311–1324.

Tononi, G., & Cirelli, C. (2001). Modulation of brain gene expression during sleep and wakefulness: a review of recent findings. *Neuropsychopharmacology*, *25* (Supplement, 5): S28–35.

Thorndike, E. L. (1913). *The Psychology of Learning*. NY: Teachers College Press.

Tomkins, S. S. (1962–1992). *Affect, Imagery, Consciousness*. NY: Springer. [Four volumes: Vol. 1: *The Positive Affects*. (1962). Vol. 2: *The Negative Affects*. (1963). Vol. 3: *The Negative Affects—Anger and Fear*. (1991). Vol. 4: *Cognition. (1992).*]

Tomkins, S. S., Smith, B., & Demos, E. V. (Eds.) (1995). *Exploring Affect: The Selected Writings of Silvan S. Tomkins: Studies in Emotion and Social Interaction*. London and New York: Cambridge University Press.

Tononi, G., & Cirelli, C. (2003). Sleep and synaptic homeostasis: a hypothesis. *Brain Research Bulletin*, *62*: 143–150.

Townsend, J., Courchesne, E., & Egaas, B. (1996). Slowed orienting of covert visual-spatial attention in autism: specific deficits associated with cerebellar and parietal abnormality. *Dev. Psychopathol., 8*: 563–584.

Trevarthen, C. (1986). Brain science and the human spirit. *Zygon: Journal of Religion and Science*, *21*(2): 161–200.

Trevarthen, C. (2003). Chapter Two, Neuroscience and intrinsic psychodynamics: current knowledge and potential for therapy. In: J. Corrigal & H. Wilkinson (Eds.), *Revolutionary Connections: Psychotherapy and Neuroscience* (pp. 53–78). London and New York: Karnac Books.

Urade, Y., Kitahama, K., Ohishi, H., Haneko, T., Mizuno, N., & Hayashi, O. (1993). Dominant expression of mRNA for prostaglandin D synthase in leptomeninges, choroid plexus, and oligodendrocytes of the adult rat brain. *Proc. Natl. Acad. Sci. USA, 90*: 9070–9074.

Varambally, S., Venkatasubramanian, G., Thirhalli, J., Janakirmaiah, N., & Gangadhar, B. N. (2006). Cerebellar and other neurological soft signs in antipsychotic-naïve schizophrenia. *Acta Psychiatrica Scandinavia* (Online Early), Vol. 0, Issue 0.

Venkatasubramanian, G., Gangadhar, B. N., Jayakumar, P. N., Janakiramiaiah, N., & Keshavan, M. S. (2003). Striato-cerebellar abnormalities in never-treated schizophrenia: Evidence for neurodevelopmental etiopathogenesis. *German Journal of Psychiatry, 6*: 1–7.

Vianna, M. R., Igaz, L. M., Coitinho, A. S., Medina, J. H., & Izquierdo, I. (2003). Memory extinction requires gene expression in rat hippocampus. *Neurobiol. Learn. Mem., 79*: 199–203.

Walensky, L. D., Kung, A. L., Escher, I., Malia, T. J., Barbuto, S., Wright, R. D., Wagner, G., Verdine, G. L., & Korsmeyer, S. J. (2004). Activation of apoptosis in vivo by a hydrocarbon-stapled BH3 helix, *Science*, 305(5689): 1466–1470.

Volgel, M. (2005). Images in Neuroscience: The Cerebellum. *American Journal of Psychiatry, 162*: 7.

Volkow, N. D., Gur, R. C., Wang, G.-J., Fowler, J. S., Moberg, P. J., Ding, Y.-S., Hitzemann, R., Smith, G., & Logan, J. (1998). Association between decline in brain dopamine activity with age and cognitive and motor impairment in healthy individuals. *American Journal of Psychiatry, 155*: 344–349.

Walensky, L. D., Kung, A. L., Escher, I., Malia, T. J., Barbuto, S., Wright, R. D., Wagner, R. D., Wagner, G., Verdine, G. L., & Korsmeyer, S. J. (2004). Activation of apoptosis in vivo by a hydrocarbon-stapled BH3 helix. *Science, 305*(5689): 1466–1470.

Wang, X.-H., Aliyari, R., Li, W.-X., Li, H.-W., Kim, K., Carthew, R. W., Atkinson, P., & Ding, S.-W. (2006). RNA interference directs innate immunity against viruses in adult drosophila. *Science, 312*: 452–454.

Walker, M. P. (2005). A refined model of sleep and the time course of memory formation. *Behavioral and Brain Sciences, 28*: 51–104.

Watt, D. F. (2003). Chapter Three: Psychotherapy in the age of neuro-science: Bridges to affective neuroscience. In: J. Corrigall & H. Wilkins (Eds.), *Revolutionary Connections: Psychotherapy and Neuroscience* (pp. 79–115). London and New York: Karnac Books.

Weinberger, J., & Weiss, J. (1997). Chapter 2, The psychoanalytic versus cognitive conception of the unconscious. In: D. J. Stein (Ed.), *Cognitive Science and the Unconscious* (pp. 23–54). Washington, D.C. and London: American Psychoanalytic Press.

Westen, D. (1999). The scientific status of unconscious processes: Is Freud really dead? *JAPA, 47*(4): 1061–1106.

Wikipedia (2006). http://en.wikipedia.org/wiki/Limbic_system

Wilson, R. I., & Nicoll, R. A. (2002). Endocannabinoid signaling in the brain. *Science, 296*: 678–682.

Yorke, C. (1999). Affects, psychoanalysis, and neuroscience. *Neuro-Psychoanalysis 1*(1): 60–69.

Yu, C. K-C. (2001). Neuroanatomical correlates of dreaming: the supra-marginal gyrus controversy (dreamwork). *Neuro-Psychoanalysis, 3*(1): 47–59.

Zacharias, D. A., Violin, J. D., Newton, A. C., & Tsien, R. Y. (2002). Partitioning of lipid-modified monomeric GFPs into membrane microdomains of live cells. *Science, 296*: 913–916.

Zaraiskaya, I., Alexandrova, E., Efimova, O., Lazutkin, A., & Anokhin, K. (2004). Developmental dynamics of learning-induced c-fos and Zif/268 expression in the mouse brain. Poster 138—Sunday 11/07/2004, Hall I, Session 044, Development of Behavior, Abstract A044.19, published in *FENS Forum Abstracts*, vol. 2, 2004, Ref. FENS Abstract., vol. 2, A044.19, 2004.

INDEX